"We Will Be Satisfied With Nothing Less"

"We Will Be Satisfied With Nothing Less"

The African American Struggle for Equal Rights in the North during Reconstruction

Hugh Davis

Cornell University Press
Ithaca and London

Copyright © 2011 by Cornell University

All rights reserved. Except for brief quotations in a review, this book, or parts thereof, must not be reproduced in any form without permission in writing from the publisher. For information, address Cornell University Press, Sage House, 512 East State Street, Ithaca, New York 14850.

First published 2011 by Cornell University Press
Printed in the United States of America

Library of Congress Cataloging-in-Publication Data

Davis, Hugh, 1941–
  We will be satisfied with nothing less : the African American struggle for equal rights in the North during Reconstruction / Hugh Davis.
       p. cm.
  Includes bibliographical references and index.
  ISBN 978-0-8014-5009-9 (cloth : alk. paper)
    1. African Americans—History—1863–1877. 2. African Americans—Civil rights—History—19th century. 3. Equality before the law—United States—History—19th century. 4. Reconstruction (U.S. history, 1865–1877) I. Title.

  E185.2.D38   2011
  973.8—dc23   2011020008

Cornell University Press strives to use environmentally responsible suppliers and materials to the fullest extent possible in the publishing of its books. Such materials include vegetable-based, low-VOC inks and acid-free papers that are recycled, totally chlorine-free, or partly composed of nonwood fibers. For further information, visit our website at www.cornellpress.cornell.edu.

Cloth printing   10 9 8 7 6 5 4 3 2 1

For Jean

Contents

Preface	ix
Acknowledgments	xv
Prologue	1
1. Launching the Equal Rights Movement	6
2. Toward the Fifteenth Amendment	40
3. The Crusade for Equal Access to Public Schools, 1864–1870	72
4. The Equal Rights Struggle in the 1870s	97
5. The Republican Retreat from Reconstruction	133
Epilogue	149
Notes	151
Bibliography	183
Index	203

PREFACE

My decision to write this book was prompted in part by the fact that the most important general accounts of Reconstruction published since 1960 have focused almost entirely on the South. Studies by Eric Foner, John Hope Franklin, Kenneth M. Stampp, Robert Cruden, Rembert W. Patrick, Allen W. Trelease, and W. R. Brock have provided valuable insights into the broad social, economic, and political changes that occurred in southern life and how southern blacks helped to shape the contours of change during the Reconstruction era.[1] Yet these works have largely ignored the northern racial climate and especially African Americans' struggle for equal rights throughout the North. For example, Foner's *Reconstruction,* which remains the best treatment of this period, does not even mention the role of northern blacks in the crusade for full citizenship rights. Likewise, Franklin's *Reconstruction after the Civil War* and Stampp's *The Era of Reconstruction, 1865–1877,* which dominated the field of Reconstruction studies until the appearance of Foner's book in 1988, briefly note that most northern states had long maintained discriminatory laws against African

Americans but make only passing reference to northern blacks' agitation for black manhood suffrage and desegregation of the public schools following the Civil War.[2]

A few scholars have recently argued that, because the historical literature on the modern civil rights movement in the mid-twentieth century has likewise tended to focus on the southern crusade against the Jim Crow system, it fails to reflect the national scope of racial inequality or the geographical breadth of the challenges to it. In his *Sweet Land of Liberty*, Thomas Sugrue notes that most studies continue to concentrate on the epic struggle in the South and turn northward only in the mid-late 1960s, when the urban riots erupted and the black power movement emerged. Sugrue, as well as Robert O. Self and Matthew J. Countryman, in their studies of the civil rights cause in Oakland and Philadelphia, respectively, call for historical accounts that recognize the important role that northern activists played in what was truly a national movement. While acknowledging that the southern cause richly deserves attention, they insist that to concentrate so heavily on the southern movement as the paradigmatic post–World War II black struggle is a serious distortion.[3]

Much as Sugrue, Self, and Countryman have argued that the narrative of the mid-twentieth century civil rights cause needs to be reframed, I believe that historians must similarly expand the geographical reach of their studies of Reconstruction to include, in a substantive manner, northern racism and the northern black struggle to eradicate racial segregation and inequality. In her 2009 work on race and reconstruction in the Upper Midwest, Leslie A. Schwalm has articulated this conviction that the Reconstruction-era black quest for equal rights—and Reconstruction itself—was in fact national in scope. Because so little attention has been devoted to Reconstruction in the North and so much of the historical literature that has taken northern society into account has concentrated on how northern whites viewed and participated in the reconstruction of the South, Schwalm argues, the history of how black freedom and citizenship were understood and defended in the post–Civil War years is still only partially chronicled.[4]

Recent studies by Andrew Deimer and David Quigley have further clarified my understanding that the northern black equal rights movement must be placed in a broader national context.[5] While warning that one should not push the parallel between Reconstruction Philadelphia and the

South too far, Deimer calls for a reassessment of traditional North-South boundaries in Reconstruction historiography. In concluding that the retreat from Radical Republican politics in Philadelphia was largely the result of local political conflict over racial equality, he elucidates the relationship between events in the South and the North. In his *Second Founding,* a study of Reconstruction politics in New York City, Quigley addresses this issue from a slightly different angle. He maintains that the intense debate as to who would be part of the democratic process and on whose terms involved black and white men and women in both the North and South. By emphasizing the northern black contributions to the debate on interracial democracy and identifying links between events in the North and the South, my book helps to meet the need for positing a national, not just a southern, vision of what Reconstruction could accomplish and for connecting local and state agitation for equal rights to a national Reconstruction.

A fairly substantial body of work on the northern black struggle for equal rights during the Reconstruction era does indeed exist. Studies by scholars such as David A. Gerber, Ira Brown, Davison M. Douglas, Elmer R. Rusco, Emma Lou Thornbrough, Eugene H. Berwanger, Roger D. Bridges, Edward R. Price, Arthur O. White, and Marion Thompson Wright have deepened our understanding of the northern movement.[6] However, these studies have almost invariably examined the northern black quest in a particular state, territory, or community. Even the few works that transcend these geographical limits are rather restricted in scope. For example, Schwalm studies Iowa, Minnesota, and Wisconsin, while Berwanger examines only the states and territories that lay west of the Mississippi River. Likewise, though Douglas explores the school integration issue as it unfolded from New England to the West Coast, his study focuses largely on the legal dimensions after 1880, analyzes this struggle primarily from the northern white perspective, and does not investigate the suffrage issue. Moreover, Leslie H. Fishel's 1953 dissertation on "The North and the Negro, 1865–1900," which Schwalm cites as the most comprehensive survey of northern blacks and the race issue during the Reconstruction era, is dated and focuses primarily on the views of northern whites on racial discrimination in northern society.[7]

In researching this subject, I encountered several problems. One was the paucity of newspapers owned and edited by northern blacks. The limited number of northern black papers published during these years can be explained in part by the widespread poverty in black communities and the relatively small black population, which comprised only 2 percent of the northern population. Likewise, that few manuscript collections of black leaders are available can be attributed partly to the lack of interest among white archivists in collecting and preserving African American sources. Similarly, with the significant exception of the Pennsylvania State Equal Rights League, the records of black equal rights organizations either do not exist or are quite limited in scope.

Further, though northern black women attended and spoke at public meetings, collected signatures for petitions, filed lawsuits, engaged in acts of civil disobedience in defense of their children's right to an equal education, and at times espoused universal suffrage, black men, whose views on gender roles were often similar to those of white males, tended to dominate the equal rights organizations, edit the newspapers, and lobby public officials. Consequently, while I have sought to take the views and actions of African American women into account wherever possible, it has been difficult to give them the voice they deserve.

Likewise, the extent to which the black non-elites were involved in the equal rights cause is not easily discerned. Steven Hahn's *A Nation under Our Feet,* as well as documents in the series on the history of emancipation, edited by Hahn, Ira Berlin, and others, provide valuable insights into the role that freed people played in shaping their world following the end of slavery.[8] Research in similar sources pertaining to the North—such as records of public meetings and local equal rights organizations, petitions, lawsuits, voting data, and reports of acts of civil disobedience—indicate that the crusade for full citizenship rights elicited broad support within northern black communities. One must, however, be careful not to overstate the role of northern black non-elites in the movement, for the documents of black elites—including newspaper editorials, reports, memorials, and personal correspondence—are much more available and tend to provide the most weighty evidence. The elites, after all, generally had the requisite money, time, and influence to be active within, and shape the agenda of, the equal rights cause.

Despite these archival limitations, my research in a broad array of primary sources sheds new and valuable light on the northern black struggle for equal rights during the post–Civil War era. Thorough research in all of the northern black newspapers and several white newspapers, government documents, proceedings of local black meetings and state and national conventions, petitions, and correspondence in the manuscript collections of both black and white leaders deepens our understanding of the role that black women and non-elites, as well as the black male leadership, played in the movement. In addition, these sources show, more clearly than any previous study, that Reconstruction began in the North and that African Americans relentlessly pressured often-reluctant white Republicans to live up to their stated ideals. At the same time, a close examination of the historical literature on the equal rights movement as it developed in specific northern states and communities breaks new ground in illuminating broad patterns of shared experience among its members as well as the diverse realities they encountered and the arguments and tactics they employed on behalf of racial justice.

This book is organized thematically, for the most part. It concentrates on the two issues that northern blacks considered most essential: black male suffrage and equal access to the public schools. Following an examination of their struggle, which culminated in the ratification of the Fifteenth Amendment in 1870, the focus shifts to their efforts to use the vote especially for the purpose of integrating the public schools. The Republican Party's retreat from Reconstruction—and the response of northern African Americans to this development—is the central theme of the last portion of the book. However, these broad themes are explored in a partially chronological order. The narrative moves forward from the launching of the equal rights cause in 1864 to the "end" of Reconstruction in the North approximately two decades later. While the male suffrage issue was the centerpiece of the movement during the 1860s, the school issue remained a major objective throughout the period. During the 1870s, northern blacks were forced to assess their place within the Republican Party and to determine how they could most effectively employ the franchise as white Republicans inexorably retreated from their commitment to protect the rights of all citizens.

This book is divided into five chapters. The first chapter examines the factors that motivated northern African Americans to launch the equal rights movement and establish the National Equal Rights League late in the Civil War. It also investigates the broad areas of agreement among these activists as well as the issues that divided them. The Pennsylvania State Equal Rights League—one of the most active and influential of the state equal rights organizations—serves as a case study of the cause.

Chapter 2 concentrates on northern African Americans' struggle to attain manhood suffrage rights. It investigates the varied arguments and tactics they marshaled on behalf of the franchise and their complex and often problematic interaction with northern white Republicans prior to the ratification of the Fifteenth Amendment.

Chapter 3 studies the drive of northern blacks to end racial segregation within and, in some states, exclusion from, the public schools across the North during the mid- and late 1860s. It analyzes divisions within the movement over whether, and to what degree, the desegregation of public schools would serve the best interests of African Americans and explains how and why most northern blacks sought to gain equal educational opportunities.

Chapter 4 concentrates on the first half of the 1870s. It examines how, following the ratification of the Fifteenth Amendment, northern blacks sought to work within the Republican Party at the state level to gain equal access to public schools and, at the federal level, to pressure congressional Republicans to pass Charles Sumner's Civil Rights Bill—especially its school integration clause. This chapter also analyzes the impact of the northern black vote on the outcome of elections and the growing frustration of northern blacks with their treatment by white Republicans.

Chapter 5 investigates the response by northern blacks to the collapse of Reconstruction in the South and tells the story of their ongoing efforts to gain equal rights into the 1880s.

Acknowledgments

It is difficult to know where to begin in expressing my gratitude to numerous individuals and institutions that have helped bring this book to completion. Their support, advice, encouragement, and insights have sustained me in many ways in the course of researching and writing this book. I was ably and generously assisted in my research by librarians and archivists at the American Antiquarian Society, Boston Public Library, California Historical Society, California State Archives, Chicago Historical Society, Chicago Public Library, Columbia University Library, Connecticut Historical Society, Connecticut State Library, Detroit Public Library, Harvard University Library, Hayes Historical Library, Historical Society of Pennsylvania, Howard University Library, Illinois State Archives, Illinois Historical Library, Indiana Historical Society, Indiana State Library, Library of Congress, Massachusetts Historical Society, Michigan Historical Center, National Archives, New Jersey Historical Society, New Jersey State Library, New York Historical Library, New York Public Library, Oberlin College Library, Ohio Historical Center, Pennsylvania

Historical Library, Rhode Island Historical Society, Rhode Island State Library, Southern Connecticut State University Library, Syracuse University Library, Temple University Library, and Yale University Library.

I have benefited at every stage of my research and writing from the support provided by Southern Connecticut State University. A sabbatical leave, research reassigned time, and Connecticut State University research grants greatly facilitated my research. Moreover, the university's Faculty Development Fund paid for the typing of the manuscript. I am especially indebted to Carol Culmo, who skillfully typed the manuscript and managed to retain her sense of humor. I deeply appreciate this generous institutional support.

I have been very fortunate to draw on the vast knowledge and keen insights of a number of exceptional scholars. When I embarked on this project, which represented a departure from much of my scholarly work, Jim Stewart, Randall Miller, and Merton Dillon reassured me that the African American struggle for equal rights in the North during Reconstruction deserved treatment and that I could see this study through to a successful conclusion. Several friends in the profession gave generously of their time in the midst of very busy and productive lives. Rich Newman and Merton Dillon read the entire manuscript, and Jim Stewart, Peter Hinks, and Stacey Robertson read portions of it. By helping me to better understand the dynamics of the northern equal rights movement and how it relates to the broader context of national Reconstruction and nineteenth-century African American history, these scholars, as well as the readers for Cornell University Press, significantly improved this book. In the final analysis, any errors or misconceptions that remain in the finished work are mine, not theirs.

In addition, a number of other friends in the scholarly community—including Stan Harrold, Jim Giglio, John Quist, Don Zelman, Harriet Applewhite, Fred Blue, Doug Egerton, Jack McKivigan, and Dick Smith—were a constant source of encouragement and inspiration. I deeply appreciate their moral support. I would hasten to add to this group of scholars my friends in the history department at Southern Connecticut State University, who exemplify the essential connection between teaching and scholarship. No acknowledgment of those who have assisted me along the way would be complete without mentioning the academic forums that enabled me to test my ideas and receive valuable feedback. I especially benefited from the recommendations offered by commentators at a symposium sponsored by the Historical Society of Pennsylvania in Philadelphia, a session at the Organization of American Historians meeting in Memphis, and a session at the Mid-America Conference on History held at Oklahoma State University.

I am deeply indebted to the editors at Cornell University Press. They have been extremely helpful and supportive throughout the process of revising and editing the manuscript. I wish, above all, to thank Michael McGandy, whose editorial talents were instrumental in making this a more coherent and polished study. I also appreciate the expert assistance of Karen Laun, who deftly guided me through the copyediting and production phases of the process.

My children—Andrew, Jenny, Kate, and Mark—deserve special mention. You have been a constant source of love and inspiration and have enriched my life in countless ways. You are very special to me, and I am extremely proud of each one of you. I also wish to acknowledge my daughters-in-law, Carolina and Kiowa, and my son-in-law, Dan. You are wonderful people who embody the meaning of family—love, concern, and caring. I have also been blessed with three beautiful grandchildren—Ryan, Liam, and Fallon—who are a source of immense pride and joy.

I am most indebted to my wife, Jean, who once again put up with a book's intrusive presence in our lives. I cherish our shared commitment to family and friends, to each other, and to a more just and equitable society. Without your love, understanding, support, and sage advice, it is difficult to imagine how I could have written this book. You are a very special person. I feel honored to dedicate this book to you.

"We Will Be Satisfied With Nothing Less"

Prologue

The 145 delegates who assembled for the National Convention of Colored Men in Syracuse, New York, in October 1864 were motivated by a complex mix of optimism and anxiety. Now emboldened to act above all by the emancipation unfolding across the South as well as the enlistment of black troops in the Union Army, they aimed to launch an equal rights movement. In addition, the rise to power of the Republican Party held out the hope of improved race relations. Yet these men and women also faced a very uncertain future. The Lincoln administration had acted cautiously against slavery, and the national elections that lay but a month ahead might conceivably place a Democrat in the White House. If George McClellan were to defeat Abraham Lincoln, there was good reason to expect the subsequent revocation of the Emancipation Proclamation and the resurrection of the Dred Scott decision, which had ruled that, because African Americans were not citizens, they deserved no rights. To make matters worse, in order to ensure its passage, congressional Republicans had recently removed any mention of black suffrage rights from the Wade-Davis

Bill. Finally, while some black rights activists considered New York City the logical place for a national convention, painful memories of the horrifying draft riots a year earlier, which had resulted in the death of large numbers of African Americans, led the convention's organizers to choose Syracuse as the site because of its central location and the active role its residents had played in the Underground Railroad. This combination of factors convinced the delegates—most of whom were Northerners—that this was a singular moment when they must organize and agitate for the full citizenship rights that had repeatedly been denied by northern whites during the past several decades.

When the delegates arrived in Syracuse, they were once again reminded of the depths of northern white racism when local toughs shouted racist slogans and physically assaulted a few of them. But the delegates were not to be deterred. The Syracuse Convention brought together a broader spectrum of northern black activists than had any previous African American meeting. Among the delegates were Frederick Douglass, George T. Downing, Henry Highland Garnet, and other prominent figures from the antebellum northern protest movement; a younger generation of African Americans, including Octavius V. Catto, George B. Vashon, and John Mercer Langston, who would occupy positions of power and influence in the postwar equal rights cause; soldiers from both the North and South; influential women such as Frances Ellen Watkins Harper; and the editors of several northern black newspapers. Although African Americans who lived west of the Mississippi River did not send delegates, and relatively few from the Midwest were present, they were fully aware of the convention's proceedings and supported its objectives. Preparations for the convention and discussion of the major issues it would address had filled the columns of black newspapers for many weeks.

The Syracuse Convention launched the northern black struggle for equal rights. Undertaken in the face of widespread white opposition and indifference, this movement stands as the most important African American crusade for full citizenship rights prior to the modern civil rights cause of the 1950s and 1960s. In order to understand the national debate on the merits of interracial democracy during the post–Civil War years as well as the national scope of Reconstruction, it is necessary to bring northern blacks into the very center of the Reconstruction narrative as significant agents of change rather than as passive recipients of rights granted by sympathetic whites. Indeed, the equal rights cause African Americans initiated and sustained should be viewed as an early, and very important, chapter in the story of Reconstruction. At the time of the Syracuse Convention and the subsequent construction of a full-fledged northern black equal rights movement, the president and Congress had scarcely begun to develop a coherent blueprint for Reconstruction in the South, and the congressional debate on a civil rights bill lay more than a year in the future. By contrast, northern blacks were already establishing an agenda and a political strategy.

The northern black struggle for equal rights during the Reconstruction era sought to harness and direct the powerful forces unleashed by the Civil War toward the creation of a more just and equitable society. Unlike the short-lived National Council established by the 1853 Rochester Convention, the National Equal Rights League, which the Syracuse Convention created to coordinate the cause, became truly national in scope, with a network of state and local auxiliaries in every northern state from New England to the West Coast and in most of the southern states. Those who founded and guided the NERL and its numerous auxiliaries, as well as the thousands of African American men, women, and children who participated in the cause at the grassroots level, at times were divided along ideological, regional, class, cultural, and gender lines, and they often focused on repealing discriminatory laws in their own states and communities. Yet they had much in common, and they were keenly aware that they were part of a broad-based movement that extended across the country.

In the broadest sense, African Americans shared the conviction that they deserved full rights and privileges as citizens. They also generally agreed that suffrage rights for black males and equal access to public schools should be the central objectives of the movement. Virtually no African American doubted that justice, morality, and the protection of their vital interests required the attainment of the franchise. Even most black women and men who favored universal suffrage ultimately decided that, for strategic and other reasons, black manhood suffrage should take precedence over woman suffrage. There was even considerable agreement on the school issue. Whatever their misgivings about school integration, most northern blacks concluded that the reality of inferior black public schools—and the stigma whites attached to them—outweighed their concerns about the potentially negative effects of integration on black students and teachers as well as the black community's already limited control over their own public schools. Further, even though their support for blacks-only (or racially exclusive) rights organizations and Republican political clubs seemed to clash with their insistence on integration and inclusion, most northern African Americans endorsed them for very practical reasons, including the desire to minimize their dependence on white allies—whom they did not entirely trust—to act on behalf of blacks' fundamental interests.

Northern blacks' relationship with white Republicans was often problematic. However, because only the Republicans were willing to support fundamental legal rights for African Americans, most northern blacks remained loyal to the party throughout the Reconstruction era. The ratification of the Fifteenth Amendment in 1870, which the Democrats overwhelmingly opposed, was perhaps the most decisive moment in the Reconstruction-era northern black struggle for equal rights. Once black males secured political rights in the U.S. Constitution, they had an opportunity to employ the franchise as leverage to gain unfettered access to public schools and other public institutions and to carve out a meaningful place within the Republican Party. Thus, to understand the nature of northern black politics during the 1870s, it is necessary to examine their wide-ranging efforts to translate the Fifteenth Amendment into tangible political results, including their campaign to expand and clarify those rights articulated in the Fourteenth Amendment. Northern African Americans brought to this campaign a mix of pragmatism, idealism, tenacity, and creativity. An important facet of this endeavor was their effort between 1870 and 1875, in concert with southern blacks, to pressure white Republicans in Congress to pass Charles Sumner's Civil Rights Bill, which called for a ban on segregation in many areas of the public sphere, especially the nation's public schools. In addition, throughout the 1870s they continued their multifaceted assault—which they had begun in earnest in the mid-1860s—on northern state and local laws that mandated the segregation of African Americans within, or exclusion from, public schools.

Northern African Americans were neither naive about how they could best protect their political interests and advance their rights nor rendered passive by their dependence on white Republicans for the achievement of their objectives. The evidence indicates that their experience as an oppressed and despised minority shaped a realistic appraisal of the northern political landscape. Most of them fully realized that, because the vast majority of Democrats were their sworn enemy, there was no viable alternative to working with white Republicans. Notwithstanding this stark reality—and their gratitude for Republican-sponsored abolition and civil rights—during the 1870s they were often outspoken in their criticism of white Republicans for failing to act on their stated principles and for taking the black vote for granted. They showed themselves to be politically astute, employing a balance-of-power strategy in elections that were closely contested by voting for independent candidates instead of those Republicans they believed had betrayed their trust or occasionally even by defecting to the Democratic ranks. In pursuing their vision of equal rights for all citizens, these activists presented cogent arguments, creatively and flexibly employed a variety of tactics, and mobilized and energized large numbers of northern blacks. That the impact of the black vote during the 1870s fell short of their hopes owed far less to a faulty political strategy or a deficient grasp of political realities than to their relatively small numbers and, above all, the persistence of white racial prejudice.

1

LAUNCHING THE EQUAL RIGHTS MOVEMENT

A half-century after the American Revolution, slavery had nearly disappeared in the North. Yet legal freedom seldom translated into fundamental rights and opportunities for northern blacks. Comprising only a small fraction of the northern population, they confronted pervasive and deep-seated racial prejudice among whites, who tended to favor colonization, expulsion, or segregation for African Americans. While the patterns of segregation and discrimination were varied and uneven, northern blacks were generally relegated to low-paying menial jobs; denied political rights; segregated in or altogether excluded from public schools, public transportation, and public accommodations; and frequently subjected to verbal abuse and physical intimidation.[1] Driven by the conviction that, as American citizens, they deserved respect, inclusion, and legal equality, northern blacks vigorously protested the laws and customs that oppressed them during the antebellum era and into the Civil War.

They formed organizations, held state and regional conventions, filed lawsuits, and petitioned state legislatures in a wide-ranging assault on discrimination and prejudice. One of the earliest and most important of these institutions was the National Negro Convention Movement, which was launched in 1830. During the next five years, and again in the 1840s, these conventions served as a forum for northern African American leaders to debate ideas, share a common race identity, and develop measures to combat discrimination.[2] In their quest for equal rights, blacks also received crucial support from white abolitionists. They had much in common, including their evangelical religion and democratic ideals and the conviction that slavery was sinful and must be abolished immediately. As allies in the crusade against colonization, slavery, and the doctrine of racial inferiority, black and white immediatists tested the limits of interracial collaboration.[3]

Collaborating with White Abolitionists during the Pre–Civil War Era

Northern African Americans' relationship with white abolitionists was inherently problematic. Their perspectives on slavery differed substantially: for white immediatists, the destruction of slavery was a matter of restoring America's moral vision; for blacks, it was much more personal, given that, in many instances, members of their families were still held in bondage.[4] Moreover, white abolitionists had never been forced to endure caste oppression based on their skin color. Equally important, because many abolitionists believed that African Americans needed their benevolent guidance in order to be elevated, white abolitionists at times appeared paternalistic and overbearing. Worse still, an unconscious sense of white superiority sometimes surfaced.[5]

The Colored American, a black newspaper published in New York City, expressed the growing discontent among blacks when it asserted in 1839 that "as long as we will bow to their opinion, and acknowledge that their word is counsel, so long they will outwardly treat us as men, while in their hearts they still hold us as slaves." In fact, northern blacks were substantially underrepresented in leadership positions in antislavery societies, and many white abolitionists emphasized the defense of white civil liberties, while a growing number of Garrisonians—a heterogeneous group of radical abolitionists aligned with William Lloyd Garrison—came to focus increasingly on women's rights, religious perfectionism, nonresistance, and disunionism more than agitation against racial discrimination. As their white allies grew more reluctant to defy prevailing racial customs—especially in the wake of antiabolitionist riots in the mid-1830s that, indeed, particularly targeted African Americans—northern blacks began to reassess their role in the antislavery movement and, above all, to question the white abolitionists' prerogative to speak for them.[6] The mounting friction between black and white abolitionists was exacerbated in the 1840s by a number of highly publicized disagreements, including the Garrisonians' sharp criticism of Henry Highland Garnet for arguing that slaves were justified in using violence to gain their freedom and Frederick Douglass's break with Garrison over the merits of political action and the nature of the Constitution.[7]

Although they were frustrated, and at times angered, by their white allies' paternalism, prejudice, and priorities, many black leaders were reluctant to abandon their interracial collaboration. During the 1830s, the American Moral Reform Society spurned distinctions based on color; likewise, William Cooper Nell and other black activists in Boston condemned separatism and labored alongside antislavery whites in numerous organizations directed toward self-improvement. Moreover, while Frederick Douglass considered separate black institutions necessary in some instances, he nevertheless insisted that, in the final analysis, they were merely temporary expedients. By claiming such cultural values as uplift, respectability, republicanism, individual success, and civilization as their own and by insisting that they were Americans by birth and action, Douglass and other like-minded African American leaders underscored their American identity and hoped to be accepted as full-fledged citizens by persuading whites to live up to their stated ideals.[8]

Nevertheless, as blacks collaborated with whites and wrestled with the question of how they could best achieve their objectives of equal rights, respectful treatment, and opportunity in a white-dominated society, a strong undercurrent of race pride and consciousness developed. Many African Americans concluded that they must take the initiative in shaping the tactics, strategy, and ideology of the movement for rights and freedom. This sentiment was clearly reflected in a black conference's proclamation of 1854: "Our relations to the Anti-Slavery movement must be and are changed. Instead of depending upon it we must lead it."[9]

During the 1840s, a new generation of black leaders, such as Frederick Douglass, Henry Highland Garnet, George B. Vashon, and Martin Delany, urged the black community to act in concert to define the terms of their future as Americans. These young men brought fresh leadership and organizational skills to the cause of racial justice. Their broad-ranging assault on the pervasive prejudice and discrimination in the North, however, was largely thwarted by hostile white public opinion.[10] For example, black males were disfranchised in Pennsylvania in the late 1830s, referenda on black male suffrage were defeated in New York and Connecticut in the 1840s and again in New York on the eve of the Civil War, black children in most northern states continued to be segregated within public schools or excluded from them altogether, and restrictive "Black Laws" were enacted in several northern states in the 1840s and 1850s.[11]

These setbacks did not deter northern blacks from continuing their agitation for equal rights during the 1850s. They were motivated by their firm conviction that they deserved full citizenship rights and buoyed by the fact that in some parts of the North they indeed enjoyed specific rights, such as access to public accommodations in Cleveland, male suffrage rights in all of New England except Connecticut, and, starting in 1855, admission to racially integrated public schools throughout Massachusetts. Besides this, free blacks could count on the fundamental rights of speech, press, assembly, and petition in most northern states and could use these rights to demand legal equality.[12]

The 1850s, however, also witnessed a deepening sense of despair and alienation among northern blacks. The decade began with the passage of the Compromise of 1850, which sought to preserve the political balance between the sections and to bury the disputes over slavery. While Congress's decision to admit California as a free state and to prohibit the slave trade in the District of Columbia represented concessions to the North, a draconian new Fugitive Slave Law, which placed all northern African Americans in jeopardy of being claimed as escaped slaves, seized, and sent into slavery, was intended to appease the South. At least until 1854, many northern and southern politicians, shaken by threats of civil war, desperately sought to avoid debate on the slavery question. Yet growing anti-southern sentiment in the North, fueled in part by anger against the Fugitive Slave Law, prompted southern leaders to pressure President Franklin Pierce and congressional Democrats to open the western territories to slavery. This culminated in the passage of the Kansas-Nebraska Act in 1854, which, by permitting settlers to decide whether slavery would be legal, made it possible for the institution to expand into areas previously declared free by the Missouri Compromise in 1820. This law upset a tenuous political equilibrium, undermined an already weakened two-party system by destroying the Whig Party, and produced the Republican Party, which opposed the expansion of slavery into the western territories.[13]

Growing northern fears of a slave power conspiracy were intensified by the U.S. Supreme Court's decision in *Dred Scott v. Sanford* in 1857. Written by Chief Justice Roger B. Taney, this ruling declared the Missouri Compromise unconstitutional on the grounds that Congress had no authority to legislate the limits of slavery's expansion. For northern African Americans, the most threatening aspect of the Court's decision was its gratuitous statement that blacks possessed no rights before the law that whites were obliged to respect. Thus, the *Dred Scott* decision enshrined white supremacy in American law.[14]

Both the Fugitive Slave Law and the *Dred Scott* decision seriously weakened whatever residual faith had existed among northern blacks that they could persuade whites to accept them into the mainstream of American society. African Americans responded to the Fugitive Slave Law by engaging in acts of civil disobedience and, occasionally, violent resistance; creating state organizations to combat this and other oppressive laws; and, most important, supporting emigration.[15]

During the early 1850s, Martin Delany, a Pittsburgh physician and writer, and other proponents of emigration to Africa went beyond the call for racial solidarity and autonomy by insisting that separate black organizations would not be effective unless they established a black nationality outside of the United States. Later in the decade, Garnet and other founders of the African Civilization Society urged a more selective emigration for the purposes of Christianizing Africa and developing its economic potential.[16] Many northern black leaders rejected Delany's arguments and considered the African Civilization Society a white plot to exile free blacks. Nevertheless, as the dismal prospects of black advancement in a white-dominated society became increasingly apparent, more and more African Americans came to view the emigrationist strategy in a more favorable—yet often ambivalent—light. By the late 1850s, most black activists in fact had moved inexorably toward emigration as their sense of alienation deepened and their desire for self-determination intensified. Even Frederick Douglass, who had long opposed exclusively black organizations, considered visiting Haiti on the eve of the Civil War to survey the prospects for black emigration.[17] One month before the Civil War, Robert Hamilton, the editor of the *Weekly Anglo-African,* a black newspaper in New York City, expressed his feeling of despair when he labeled as "folly" the hope that racial discrimination would eventually disappear in the United States. "The equality for which we have been taught to sigh," he wrote, "is not attainable here."[18]

The Significance of the Emancipation Proclamation

Given such deep-seated pessimism, it is not surprising that, when the Civil War began, northern blacks held out little hope that the conflict would improve race relations. When the northern states refused the services of African Americans who sought to enlist in the Union Army, the African Methodist Episcopal Church spoke for many African Americans when it declared that the war was not about rights or inclusion for blacks but, rather, a contest between rival white political forces on the status of slavery in the territories. For blacks to attempt to enlist in the army, the *Christian Recorder,* the church's official organ, asserted a week into the war, would be to "abandon self-respect and invite insult."[19]

Yet many African Americans also realized that they must be concerned about the outcome of the war, for a Confederate victory would, at the very least, strengthen the hand of the racist Democratic party. The *Weekly Anglo-African,* which became known in some northern black circles as the black soldier's paper, predicted an even more ominous consequence of a northern defeat. "The South must be subjugated," it pointedly warned, "or we shall be enslaved." The paper thus urged African Americans to organize military companies and to drill and to exhibit their patriotism by sending clothes and other supplies to the Union soldiers.[20]

When President Abraham Lincoln set forth the Emancipation Proclamation in late 1862, many northern blacks were ambivalent about its long-term significance. Because the president had been slow to act against slavery during the first eighteen months of the war, they understandably expressed suspicion regarding the motives that underlay its promulgation. For example, Frederick Douglass claimed that the Emancipation Proclamation probably reflected more a hatred of slaveholders than a concern for the welfare of slaves or free blacks, while Robert Hamilton labeled it "simply a war measure" and therefore "*per se* no more humanitarian than a hundred pounder rifled cannon." Yet, having expressed their doubts, both Douglass and Hamilton—perhaps to convince themselves and buoy the spirits of other blacks—termed the proclamation "the greatest event in our nation's history" and "a great and glorious" document.[21]

Perhaps the most immediate effect of the proclamation on northern blacks was that it provided a basis for their growing optimism that the war might well portend a brighter future for all African Americans. Indeed, by late 1862 the prolonged and often acrimonious debate over how to achieve equal rights—or even whether that struggle was realistic—had begun to diminish in intensity. As the war raged on and slaves escaped to the Union lines in ever larger numbers, Delany, Garnet, and their supporters came to focus more on the war's potential for ending slavery and less on emigration. The American Civilization Society shifted its attention from Africa to the South at the same time that the African and Haitian emigration efforts collapsed. These developments paved the way for a gradual reconciliation between the emigrationists and their most vocal critics. This reconciliation was manifested most clearly in late 1862, when Garnet agreed to share the platform at Cooper Institute in New York City with such old nemeses as George Thomas Downing, a wealthy Rhode Island restaurant owner and civil rights activist, and Charles Bennett Ray, a New York journalist, educator, and minister. At this time, they were able to set aside their animosity in the name of furthering the larger cause. In his speech to a large and enthusiastic audience, Garnet stated emphatically that a Union victory and the destruction of slavery must be the foremost objectives of African Americans.[22]

Their growing optimism was rooted above all in the conviction that the enlistment of black males in the Union Army, which the Emancipation Proclamation provided for, would help to usher in an era of racial justice. If these soldiers performed well, the *Weekly Anglo-African* editorialized, it "will give us a certain force which we have hitherto lacked in our struggle for equality." By early 1863, various northern black leaders were actively engaged in recruiting African Americans for military service. For example, the Social, Civic, and Statistical Association of the Colored People of Pennsylvania, founded by William Still, a wealthy businessman, veteran abolitionist, and prominent figure in the Underground Railroad, and other Philadelphia black leaders in the late 1850s urged young blacks to enlist in the 54th Massachusetts Regiment, as did a mass meeting in New York City attended by Garnet, Douglass, Downing, and other leaders. In addition, the Black Committee, consisting of influential activists such as Garnet, Downing, and Delany, sought to coordinate recruiting on a national scale. At the same time, various African Americans warned leading Republicans that the party must unequivocally endorse these recruiting efforts. The *Weekly Anglo-African* reflected the sense of urgency among those involved in the recruitment campaign when it urged immediate action in mobilizing a black regiment in every large northern city.[23]

These recruiting efforts, however, soon experienced serious problems. Most Democrats vigorously opposed the enlistment of black troops, and the deadly draft riots in New York City and other northeastern cities in 1863 tempered the hopes of many blacks that the presence of African Americans in the army presaged a brighter future. In addition, because the pool of potential northern black recruits was relatively small, governors were forced to send Downing, Garnet, and other northern blacks into the South to recruit African Americans.[24]

Yet it was the systematic discrimination experienced by blacks in the military that most seriously impeded the work of the Black Committee and even led some recruiters to suspend their labor. African Americans felt a profound sense of betrayal, for discrimination by Union officials challenged their rights as citizens at a time when they assumed military service would affirm racial equality. It therefore intensified their awareness that black soldiers would be forced to fight two wars: one against the South and the other against northern discrimination. Downing and other black activists continued to pressure congressional Republicans to provide equal protection and benefits for all soldiers regardless of color. At the same time, black soldiers, who saw this issue as a symbol of the larger struggle for racial justice, vigorously protested the government's policy. As one Ohio soldier angrily declared, "Give me my rights, the rights that this Government owes me, the rights that the white man has. I would be willing to fight three years for the Government without one cent of the mighty dollar.... Now I am fighting for the rights of white men." Indeed, even if black soldiers had been provided equal benefits, some were unwilling to serve under a wholly white officer corps.[25]

The editor of the *Weekly Anglo-African* forcefully and eloquently articulated the tension that existed between northern blacks' anger at the government's blatant discrimination and their realization that they must not turn their backs on the war. Citing the "relentless proscription and outrage" that African Americans were subjected to in many northern cities as well as the white Union troops' "positively horrible" treatment of southern blacks, Robert Hamilton predicted in early 1863 that African Americans might well choose not to enlist. Yet in the very same editorial, he concluded that, if African Americans were not found with rifles on their shoulders at the end of the war, a century might pass before another opportunity arose to claim their fundamental rights.[26]

This tension goes far to explain why northern blacks remained skeptical of the Republican Party's commitment to racial justice. In 1863 and 1864, many even questioned how much emancipation would improve their lives. Even though Republicans now controlled the federal government and a growing number of northern state governments, blacks continued to experience widespread discrimination. Thus, they tended to look at equality before the law, economic self-sufficiency, and especially suffrage rights as more likely than emancipation to secure equality. In declaring that emancipation without enfranchisement would be "a partial emancipation unworthy of the name," the editor of the *Weekly Anglo-African* underscored the conviction that only the franchise would make northern blacks truly free.[27]

Yet there was some cause for optimism that African Americans could trust the Republican Party to act on behalf of their interests. With emancipation unfolding across the South and the number of black troops (and casualties) mounting steadily, it became increasingly possible to imagine improved race relations at the end of the war. Likewise, declarations by federal officials such as Attorney General Edward Bates, who eviscerated the *Dred Scott* decision as it applied to African Americans by affirming that every free person born in the United States was "prima facie a citizen," encouraged growing numbers of northern blacks to embrace a more hopeful vision of the future.[28]

This optimism led northern blacks to launch a sustained assault on racial discrimination in 1863 and 1864. One issue that blacks addressed was the right to testify against whites in court. In California, laws passed in the early 1850s barring such testimony were interpreted by some whites as license to abuse blacks without fear of penalty. Unsuccessful in challenging these laws during the 1850s, black Californians pressed their case with renewed energy during the war. With strong support from Unionist legislators, the California legislature, motivated by both humanitarian impulses and antipathy toward pro-southern forces in the state, repealed the testimony laws in 1863.[29]

San Francisco blacks then used their newly-won right of testimony to challenge the ban against African Americans using one of the major omnibus lines in the city. In 1864, two blacks sued the railroad and won in both the local and district courts; the decision by the Twelfth District Court, which banned the railroad from discriminating against riders on the basis of race, was particularly significant. Although ejections of African Americans from railroad cars continued for two years, this and other court decisions sharply decreased such discrimination by mid-1864.[30]

Similar protests against segregation in, and expulsion from, public transportation occurred in Boston, New York, Cincinnati, Chicago, and other northern cities. In response to being confined to cars that were of inferior quality or being forced to stand in open areas exposed to inclement weather, black men and especially women frequently filed lawsuits against those who physically removed them from whites-only cars (or authorized employees to do so). One of the most successful legal challenges occurred in New York in 1864, after a war widow who sat in a whites-only car was forcibly ejected by a police officer. Her victory in court effectively ended Jim Crow in the city's transit system—at least on paper. By 1864, Cincinnati also permitted blacks to ride on all of the city's cars, and lawsuits by black women and men would soon end separate cars in Boston. Black women played an important role in other facets of the equal rights cause. In fact, African American women in both the North and the South were more likely than men to challenge segregation and discrimination in urban transit systems, for public transportation was particularly important to them for access to their jobs, churches, and shops. In resorting to acts of civil disobedience and legal action, these women confronted public officials, transit workers and their employers, the white public, and the courts. Consequently, they were subjected to insults, humiliation, and, at times, physical assaults that resulted in serious injury. Even some black men criticized women who resorted to legal action. Nevertheless, the protests by black women achieved a measure of success in a few northern cities.[31]

By 1864, northern blacks had also launched assaults on various states' Black Laws, which generally forbade black testimony in courts, prohibited African Americans from entering a state, denied voting rights, and the like. The most sustained and organized repeal campaign occurred in Illinois, where blacks, led by John Jones, a prominent Chicago businessman and civil rights activist who had been vigorously calling for repeal since the late 1840s, mobilized to pressure the legislature to act in 1863 and 1864. In an 1864 pamphlet Jones acknowledged that some of the discriminatory laws were not well enforced. But he argued emphatically that the restrictions they imposed on blacks were a "living, active reality" and that African Americans were citizens who deserved equal rights. Blacks from across the state presented petitions to the legislature and the governor in 1864, and the Repeal Association of Illinois sent Jones to Springfield to lobby for repeal. Although most Illinois Republicans did not support male suffrage rights or equal access to the public schools for blacks at this time, African Americans' protest finally succeeded in pressuring the legislature to repeal most of the Black Laws in early 1865.[32]

The promulgation of the Emancipation Proclamation and especially the enlistment of black troops also reinvigorated the drive for black male suffrage rights. Without exception, northern blacks' demands for voting rights had been rebuffed during the antebellum era. But by 1863, African Americans in New Jersey, Michigan, Kansas, Pennsylvania, Connecticut, and a number of other northern states had begun in earnest to petition their legislatures to strike the word *white* from the state constitutions and, in New York, to end the property requirement imposed on blacks. Although the suffrage movement made no headway during the Civil War, a Kansas black convention held in 1863 expressed the growing conviction among northern African Americans that the war, as well as changing racial attitudes among Republicans, would eventually enable their cause to prevail. "In the progress of the war, destructive of so many prejudices and fruitful of so many new ideas," the delegates proclaimed, "it will doubtless be discovered that it is as necessary to make the black man a voter, as it was to make him a soldier. He was made a soldier to RESTORE the Union. He must be made a voter to preserve it."[33]

Robert Purvis's odyssey from despair to hope in the course of a few years graphically illustrates the distance that many northern blacks had covered since the dark days of the 1850s. In the late 1850s Purvis, a wealthy

Philadelphia businessman and Garrisonian abolitionist, had bitterly condemned the United States for practicing "the basest despotism" and even hinted that some sort of revolutionary action by blacks might be appropriate and necessary. However, at the May 1864 annual meeting of the American Anti-Slavery Society, he enthusiastically declared that the future held great promise for the long-thwarted black struggle for rights and dignity. "The old things are passing away," Purvis exulted, "all things are becoming new.... The damnable doctrine of the detestable Taney is no longer the doctrine of the country." Later that year, John Rock, a Boston lawyer, abolitionist, physician, and dentist who would soon become the first African American to be admitted to practice before the U.S. Supreme Court, echoed Purvis's sense that a new era was dawning when he said: "Every day seems almost to be an era in the history of our country. We have at last reached the dividing line."[34]

The Syracuse Convention

Not far beneath the surface lay a sense of foreboding that the war might end before slavery was completely destroyed. The most frightening scenario was that, if the Democrats won the White House and gained control of Congress in the 1864 election, they would repeal the Emancipation Proclamation and resurrect the *Dred Scott* ruling that African Americans were not citizens and therefore deserved no legal rights. These fears were exacerbated by the Republicans' relative silence in 1864 on the proposed constitutional amendment that would abolish slavery throughout the United States, leading some blacks to suspect that the party might abandon its commitment to emancipation at the first sign of peace with the Confederacy.[35]

This complex mix of optimism and anxiety was instrumental in moving some northern blacks to call for a convention in 1864 for the purpose of creating a national rights organization. It is not entirely clear who initiated this idea, but it quite likely was Henry Highland Garnet, now a minister in the District of Columbia. By the spring of 1864, other northern blacks were expressing a similar interest. These included a group in Boston, who held a mass meeting to urge such a convention. Some African Americans, including Rock and John Mercer Langston, a young Ohio lawyer and Oberlin graduate, questioned whether blacks were prepared to take this bold step. Above all, they were concerned that Garnet might use the meeting to push his old emigration agenda. Nevertheless, Rock confided to George Downing and Charles Lenox Remond, a longtime agent for the American Anti-Slavery Society who was active in recruiting black soldiers, that he hoped the convention would produce more good than not. But Rock's desire for consultation among northern black leaders before the announcement of the gathering was rendered moot when Garnet publicly proposed in July that such a national meeting be held in New York City. Informing Garnet that the Boston group had already taken preliminary steps to hold a convention in their city, Rock suggested Boston as a better location than New York City, which Garnet preferred.[36]

While Rock and his colleagues hoped to "harmonize entirely" with Garnet so as to appear as united as possible, Langston and others so distrusted Garnet's motives that they were unwilling to support his call.[37] And even though the Boston group agreed with Garnet on the business to be brought before the convention and accepted his offer to prepare an address to the public, they categorically rejected New York as the site for the meeting. Their concern that a "rowdy Negro-hating spirit" in that city could recreate the horrendous acts committed by the draft rioters a year earlier was shared by the editor of the *Weekly Anglo-African,* who suggested Cleveland as a means of accommodating western blacks. Ultimately, Syracuse was the compromise choice because it was more centrally located than Boston or Cleveland; furthermore, because of its history of Underground Railroad activity, it was deemed safer than New York.[38]

The organizers chose October 4–7 as the dates for the convention and sent notices to black leaders throughout the North and those parts of the South that were under Union control. The principle of proportional representation appears to have been only loosely applied in determining representation at the convention: Pennsylvania, which had the largest black population of any northern state, had only thirty-six delegates, while New York had fifty. Likewise, Ohio, with the second-largest black population among the northern states, sent only a handful of delegates. Geographical proximity to Syracuse ultimately was the decisive factor, for most of the delegates were from the Northeast; conversely, there were no delegates from northern states west of the Mississippi River, and relatively few delegates came from the eight southern states that were represented. Yet the organizers were rather specific in determining how many delegates were allotted to a given city. For example, in Trenton, New Jersey, and Philadelphia, meetings were called to select delegates. At each meeting a committee was then appointed to choose delegates, and another group of men and women was given the task of raising money in the black churches to defray the expenses of the delegates. The participants at these meetings then pledged to inform the black community of the upcoming convention.[39]

The delegates, as well as approximately two thousand black and white spectators, came to Syracuse in early October from as far away as Louisiana and Illinois. They streamed into the city by train and canal boat. Many of the black delegates appear to have stayed with families in the city's African American community. Newspaper reports indicate that a sense of excitement and expectation permeated the air. But there was also concern that racist whites would attempt to disrupt the convention; shortly after the delegates arrived in the city, local toughs indeed sought to intimidate them by chanting "Here comes the niggers, here comes the moaks, they can't have any convention here" and by assaulting Garnet and two other African Americans. Rock and Downing elicited promises from city officials to protect the convention's delegates and spectators, and most delegates were determined to stay the course, no matter the obstacles that confronted them. The *Weekly Anglo-African* reflected this determination to persevere in the face of adversity when it asserted that it was necessary to "manfully take up the trumpet" and vocally demand their rights rather than merely to present appeals, complaints, grievances, and wrongs.[40]

The 145 delegates to the National Convention of Colored Men who assembled on October 4 represented a broader spectrum of the northern black leadership than any previous meeting, with the possible exception of the 1853 Rochester Convention. They included Douglass, Downing, Garnet, and many other leaders of the antebellum protest movement. These men were joined by a number of younger, well-educated men— such as John Mercer Langston, an Ohio lawyer, and George B. Vashon, a Pittsburgh teacher and journalist—who were emerging on the national scene. In addition, a few emigrationists who had returned from abroad, northern-trained teachers working among the freed people in the South, and a number of southern blacks served as delegates. A few black soldiers from both the North and the South, as well as the editors of three black newspapers—the *Weekly Anglo-African,* the *Cincinnati Colored Citizen,* and the *Christian Recorder*—were also present. Finally, despite the convention's official title, Edmonia Highgate, who taught among the freed people, and Frances Ellen Watkins Harper, a prominent writer and lecturer, served as delegates.[41]

The delegates began their four days of meetings by electing Douglass as president of the convention and Langston as chair of the Business Committee, which set the agenda for the proceedings. They also selected Douglass, Rock, and Garnet to present the major speeches. In addition, the Rules Committee determined that all major issues would be decided by majority vote.[42]

In a number of major speeches, a series of resolutions, a Declaration of Wrongs and Rights, a petition to Congress, and an address to the public, delegates to the Syracuse Convention articulated several themes that would constitute the central rationale for and the objectives of the equal rights movement during the Reconstruction era. Douglass, who served as president of the convention, eloquently summed up the purpose of the gathering. "We are here," he declared, "to promote the freedom, progress, elevation, and perfect enfranchisement of the entire colored people of the United States...and to advance in the scale of knowledge, worth, and civilization, and claim our rights as men among men."[43]

The proceedings of the Syracuse convention provide valuable insights into the mindset of many African Americans at this critical juncture. They were, perhaps above all, keenly aware of the symbolic importance of the tens of thousands of black soldiers then fighting to save the nation and destroy slavery, and they were determined to exploit it to the fullest. The tone was set by Rock, who underscored the stark contradiction of blacks' strong patriotism and the systematic discrimination they faced. In a major speech, he pointedly reminded the assembled crowd—and white America generally—that, even though they were initially spurned and later received no guarantee of rewards for their service, black soldiers had enlisted at a time when many whites hesitated to defend the nation. "We are all loyal," he stated. "Why are we not treated as friends?" Rock and others consciously and emphatically used the theme of bravery and discipline to buttress their demand for specific rights, such as male suffrage. In its address to the public, written by Peter H. Clark, a Cincinnati educator and activist, the convention posed two trenchant rhetorical questions intended to prick the conscience of whites: "Are we good enough to use bullets, and not good enough to use ballots?... May we give our lives, but not our votes, for the good of the republic?"[44]

Yet, what is perhaps most striking about the individual and collective pronouncements at the Syracuse Convention is the delicate balancing act the delegates engaged in. At the same time that the delegates vigorously demanded suffrage and other rights as citizens, they also reminded whites that this effort would in no way infringe on whites' liberties or limit their power. Appealing to white Americans in the name of fairness, the address to the public acknowledged, "You are strong, we are weak; you are many, we are few; you are protected, we are exposed." The disclaimers the delegates embedded in the constitution of the National Equal Rights League, which the convention established, sought especially to reassure white America that blacks did not wish to create disorder or to engage in radical action. In addition, they promised that their appeals for rights would be made solely to the minds and conscience of white America or by legal means wherever necessary.[45]

The convention's Declaration of Wrongs and Rights even more graphically illustrates the delegates' desire to find some balance between chastising white America for its long history of racial injustice and hypocrisy and recognizing that the rights they sought could only be attained with the assistance of sympathetic whites. On the one hand, the document recited a litany of grievances against white America. "We have for long ages," it charged, "been deeply and cruelly wronged... we have been subdued, not by the power of ideas, but by brute force, and have been unjustly deprived not only of many of our natural rights, but debarred the privileges and advantages freely accorded to other men." Pointing to the continuation of slavery in the South and prejudice in the North, the convention associated the Democrats with slavery and reactionary ideas and the Republicans with "negatively and passively" helping to perpetuate both discrimination and slavery. The delegates even chided some white abolitionists for questioning whether blacks needed suffrage rights.[46]

On the other hand, these activists appealed—in what Vincent Harding has termed the "Great Tradition" of black protest—to the better instincts of white America. Expressing confidence in the principles that underlay the American system of government and guided its people, the delegates predicted that the "generosity and sense of honor in the great heart of this nation" would ultimately accord them full citizenship rights under the Constitution.[47]

Two additional themes that would frequently be enunciated by equal rights activists over the next decade were part of the convention's effort to strike a balance between demanding their rights as citizens and seeking the approval and acceptance of white Americans, especially Republicans. In a petition that the convention sent to Congress, the delegates underscored the manhood of the black soldiers, whose valor, sacrifice, and patriotism "validates our manhood, commands our respect, and claims the attention of the civilized world." At the same time, they passed resolutions exhorting northern blacks, and especially the southern freed people, to adopt the middle-class values that northern black leaders had long espoused. To be frugal, accumulate property, and acquire knowledge, the delegates asserted, would enable African Americans to move into the mainstream of American society and advance their rights and interests.[48]

While the Syracuse Convention's official pronouncements formed the ideological underpinning of the equal rights movement, the National Equal Rights League—its most important product—was considered the mechanism for organizing and mobilizing African Americans on behalf of the cause and pressuring white Americans to act in accordance with their stated ideals. The league's structure was, in some respects, modeled on the short-lived National Council created by the Rochester Convention in 1853. But its founders went far beyond their predecessors by establishing a three-tiered structure: a national organization that would coordinate the movement's operations and formulate broad policy positions; state auxiliaries that would be responsible for many of the day-to-day activities; and local societies that would directly connect the movement to black communities across the nation. The organization's constitution provided for a vice president from each state represented at the Syracuse Convention; recording and corresponding secretaries; a treasurer; and an executive committee, which would be responsible for hiring agents, publishing reports and appeals, and distributing funds to the state auxiliaries. In a move that signaled the emergence on the national scene of a younger generation of northern black activists, the convention elected Langston as president of the league. Douglass and Garnet were offered other posts in the new organization, but neither chose to serve in an official capacity.[49]

Conflicts at the Convention

Although a broad consensus existed among the convention's delegates that the time had come to launch a movement for equal rights, with the National Equal Rights League as its engine, during the course of the convention a series of debates—at times acrimonious—revealed deep fissures on personal, ideological, procedural, regional, and other issues. Some of the most heated disputes pitted George Downing and his followers against Henry Highland Garnet and his supporters in a replay of their battles in the 1850s.

Even the debate on the Business Committee's proposal regarding the dues that would be assessed each delegate attending the league's annual meetings had ideological and class overtones. As a minister who earned a meager salary, Garnet strongly opposed the committee's recommendation that each auxiliary pay $100 for the first delegate and $60 for each additional person, contending that it was "a great mistake" that would penalize the common people. When his attempt to substitute a fee of $10 was narrowly defeated, an amendment that established a $50 charge for the first delegate and $30 for each additional representative passed. But Garnet criticized even this compromise; in a speech he delivered a few weeks following the convention, he claimed that a supporter of the amendment had told him, "We do not want the riff-raff." In an obvious jab at those he considered elites who cared little about the plight of the black masses, his response to this alleged statement was "Ah! That is it, is it? Then it's for the milk and water codfish aristocracy." From a practical standpoint, Garnet also feared that such high dues would discourage participation in the league's activities, warning that "They cannot raise a corporal's guard for the Equal Rights League on that basis."[50]

Garnet's anger was also rooted in his personal animosity toward Downing and his allies, who were instrumental in enacting the higher fees. But the intertwining of personal and ideological factors went even deeper than this, for Downing also led the effort to block Garnet's appointment as chair of the Business Committee. In an ironic twist, Douglass, in his capacity as president of the convention, appointed Garnet—with whom he had repeatedly clashed on the emigration issue in the 1850s—as chair of this important committee. He probably did so in order to mollify Garnet, who was deeply disappointed that Douglass, not he, was chosen to preside over the convention. That election was, reported George Ruffin, a Boston activist who would become the first black municipal judge in the United States, marked by "considerable feeling," with several candidates vying for the position and mounting friction developing between the Massachusetts delegation and the large Pennsylvania contingent, which Ruffin characterized as being "in full force domineering and overbearing."[51] When the Business Committee convened, Downing and his allies bypassed Garnet and selected Langston as chair, which further offended Garnet. Following the convention, Downing made it abundantly clear that he had been determined that Garnet should not be allowed to play a prominent role at the convention. He even exulted in print that Garnet had been "defeated, mortified in his pride and ambition.... I plead guilty to the charge of having favored it."[52]

The intense feelings that surfaced during this confrontation can be traced directly to the bitter debates over emigration in the 1850s, when Downing had been the most outspoken critic of Delany, Garnet, and other proponents of the nationalist-emigrationist position. Although Garnet had come to emphasize emancipation and black recruitment more than emigration during the war, the old hostilities left a residue of distrust and resentment between the two men. Their contrasting temperaments and Downing's status as a wealthy businessman while Garnet was a poor minister certainly added fuel to the fire.[53]

Their most serious confrontation at the Syracuse Convention, however, came in response to a seemingly innocuous proposal that the African Civilization Society be added to a list of organizations to be commended for working to educate the freed people. This motion triggered an emotional debate in which Downing charged that the society was "the child of prejudice" that must atone for its "disgraceful" conduct, especially its interaction with the American Colonization Society. Given the African Civilization Society's recent work among the freed people, Downing's claim that Garnet's organization believed blacks could not be elevated in the United States was not entirely accurate or fair. Nevertheless, his accusation resonated with many delegates whose call for equal rights was based on the premise that blacks could in fact move into the mainstream of American society.[54]

Garnet acknowledged that he and Downing had engaged in many contentious confrontations prior to the war but vowed that both men would continue to labor for the advancement of African Americans. Yet, late in his career, he found his critics' demand that he explain his position on black improvement to be "exceedingly humiliating." Deeply sensitive about his independence within the movement, he especially resented Downing's charge that he was the tool of white colonizationists. Garnet ultimately chose to question Downing's character. Downing, he stated derisively in a speech following the convention, "seems to be afflicted with a mania and whenever the word African Civilization is mentioned, he becomes excited, and is covered all over with porcupine quills."[55]

Some delegates deprecated this angry exchange, because they believed that the convention was not the proper forum for settling old differences and that such strife threatened the much-needed unity within the fledgling equal rights movement. Thus, George Vashon, who would play a leading role in the cause, moved that, while the delegates had no sympathy for any colonization activities on the part of the African Civilization Society, they commended the organization for its labors on behalf of the freed people. However, Garnet rejected Vashon's proposal, which was defeated; the original motion praising the African Civilization Society and other relief organizations that sought to assist the freed people then carried.[56]

The matter of where the headquarters of the National Equal Rights League would be located also produced acrimonious debate. No consensus existed among the delegates on this matter; regional and local pride played as important a role as logistics. Philadelphia, Cincinnati, and Cleveland were the major contenders. Langston and others argued that Cleveland was centrally located and was relatively progressive on race relations, while those who supported Philadelphia noted that it had the largest black population of any northern city and was located near the Upper South. The initial vote went to Cleveland, but Rev. Elisha Weaver, editor of the *Christian Recorder,* moved to reconsider the vote, and Philadelphia was eventually chosen. Two black Ohioans who favored Cleveland were so convinced that Langston had helped to engineer a "corrupt bargain," in which he would become president of the league in exchange for the headquarters being located in Philadelphia, that they voted against him for the presidency.[57]

Some of the ideological and personal differences that fueled these disputes would occasionally resurface long after the convention had adjourned. For example, the simmering resentment between the Pennsylvania State Equal Rights League officials and members of the executive board of the National Equal Rights League—whose headquarters were located in Philadelphia—erupted into open conflict later in the decade. Moreover, Downing and Garnet remained unrepentant following the convention. Downing was proud that he had been instrumental in marginalizing his adversary, while Garnet was irate, at one point even threatening to call a new "people's convention" that would act as a counterpoint to the NERL. But it is instructive that Garnet, perhaps realizing that the movement enjoyed broad support in the black community, soon lent vocal support to the PSERL. In fact, northern blacks overwhelmingly applauded the actions of the Syracuse Convention, including the creation of a national rights organization. For example, the *Christian Recorder* viewed the convention as a harbinger of progress for African Americans, exulting, "The ball has been set in motion." In a similar vein, a meeting in Bridgeport, Connecticut, pledged to fully support all of the measures adopted by the convention. While the *Weekly Anglo-African* reminded its readers that "we have a half repentant nation to deal with, implacable and deep-seated prejudices to overcome, all the vices and sins engendered by two centuries of slavery to contend with," it nevertheless urged its readers to join the equal rights movement.[58]

The Pennsylvania State Equal Rights League

The National Equal Rights League, acting in concert with various black state organizations, began operations soon after the Syracuse Convention adjourned. Langston, who oversaw the headquarters in Philadelphia and chaired the executive board, was instrumental in making the society the first viable national black rights organization in American history. Two secretaries conducted much of the league's routine business, while Langston frequently took the message directly to the people and assisted in establishing several state auxiliaries. By mid-1865, nine state leagues had been founded—most of them in the North. Two years later there were state organizations and local auxiliaries in nearly every state in the Union. Through this expanding network of state and local auxiliaries, the national league—at least during the first few years of its existence—provided a forum for devising strategy, mobilizing the black community, and pressuring white political leaders and other officials to eradicate discriminatory laws and practices.[59]

The Pennsylvania State Equal Rights League—one of the first state auxiliaries established after the Syracuse Convention—serves as an excellent case study of the equal rights movement. Not only was it one of the most active and influential state organizations and did it represent the largest number of African Americans in any northern state, its extant records are also far more complete than those of the NERL or any of its other state auxiliaries. An examination of these records and those of other state equal rights groups provides valuable insights into the strategy, agenda, progress, and problems of the movement, especially during the second half of the 1860s.[60]

One week after the Syracuse Convention adjourned, the Philadelphia delegates to the convention established the PSERL. They elected a president and an executive board, adopted a constitution, issued a public appeal to African Americans throughout the state, and called for a statewide meeting in February 1865. Much like the founding conventions in other states, the delegates echoed many of the sentiments articulated at Syracuse. While appealing to the conscience of white Americans, they emphatically proclaimed that all men were created free and equal and that no government could legitimately limit or abrogate their fundamental rights. They also consciously sought to connect the concepts of self-improvement and manhood to the attainment of equal rights and the end of slavery.[61]

The first annual meeting of the PSERL, held in Harrisburg in February 1865, witnessed what proved to be the last vestige of a longstanding rivalry between Philadelphia and Pittsburgh blacks. The Pittsburgh delegates criticized the Philadelphians' control of the state league and complained that local auxiliaries had to deal with the NERL headquarters through the state organization's executive board. Some of the Pittsburgh delegates even doubted whether state leagues were necessary. But, unwilling to see the movement derailed at its inception, the delegates struck a balance between the two regional factions by electing two men from each group as officers: John Peck, a Pittsburgh educator, as president; George B. Vashon of Pittsburgh and Octavius V. Catto, a Philadelphia activist and teacher, as corresponding secretaries; and Jacob C. White Jr., a Philadelphia businessman and educator, as recording secretary.[62]

With this compromise in place, the PSERL's officers quickly reached out to African Americans across the state and created a statewide organizational structure. They hired Sergeant Major A. M. Green, a Union army veteran, as the league's agent. During his tenure as agent, Green visited numerous communities and raised money for the cause. Peck and his successor, William Nesbit, an Altoona lawyer who served as president of the PSERL from 1866 until the end of the 1870s, also traveled around the state, speaking before local auxiliaries and assisting in the formation of new ones. Their efforts were quite successful. By early 1866, forty-three auxiliaries had been formed in cities and towns in every part of the state. Auxiliaries in Philadelphia, Harrisburg, and other major cities had hundreds of members. Even in a small city such as Williamsport one hundred residents joined the local league. These local auxiliaries in Pennsylvania and other states, acting in conjunction with the state leagues, were in many respects the linchpins of the movement, for they circulated petitions, called public meetings, wrote letters to public officials, composed public memorials, solicited money in the churches and various social organizations, sponsored parades, and more. The NERL provided an overall framework for a national movement, especially by organizing periodic national conventions, lobbying in Washington, D.C., and holding annual meetings. But even in the years immediately following the Syracuse Convention—when the NERL was most active—it was activists at the grassroots level who were in closest touch with ordinary blacks.[63]

The black non-elites in Pennsylvania and other northern states appear to have played a more limited role in the state and local auxiliaries than did middle-class African Americans, for their work lives, general poverty, limited education, and other factors made it unlikely that they would deliver speeches, write reports and memorials, attend state conventions, or lobby state legislatures and Congress. But to claim that the northern equal rights movement's leadership seldom reached out to the black masses, thereby effectively isolating them from the cause, would be inaccurate.[64] The evidence indicates that farmers, mechanics, factory workers, porters, waiters, maids, and other non-elites supported, and were involved in, the cause in a number of capacities. These included participation in public meetings that addressed a broad range of issues, as well as in mass parades, with thousands of black onlookers, to celebrate events such as the ratification of the Fifteenth Amendment and anniversaries of the Emancipation Proclamation. In addition, black males voted in large numbers, and both men and women signed equal rights petitions that circulated in black communities. Men, women, and children also donated to the cause in their churches and engaged in acts of civil disobedience on the school and transportation issues. Finally, nearly three-quarters of all northern black males between the ages of 18 and 45 saw military service during the Civil War. These men were convinced that their service to the nation obliged them to act as citizen-soldiers on behalf of full citizenship rights.[65]

This broad base of support within the black community emboldened those who held leadership positions in the Pennsylvania State Equal Rights League and other state leagues. For example, an officer in the Conneautville, Pennsylvania, auxiliary of the PSERL confidently reported that, following his visits to nearby communities in late 1865 to consult with other local auxiliaries, "the theme of most Every man says go on that our cause es right there es only one en fifty that will not sighn" the PSERL's petition demanding suffrage rights. In a similar vein, William Nesbit, the league's president, informed the *Christian Recorder* in late 1865 that the league's prospects were "onward and upward." His optimism was further buoyed by Garnet's strong endorsement of the organization. Although Garnet had left the Syracuse Convention in a foul mood and harbored some reservations about the National Equal Rights League's leadership—especially Langston—in early 1866 he praised the PSERL's lobbying efforts as "admirable and able" and stated effusively to Nesbit, "I am with you heart and hand, and wish you Godspeed." He even informed Nesbit that he was willing to "bury every thing of the past that is unpleasant to remember, and look forward in hope for the future." Garnet's enthusiastic endorsement of the Pennsylvania league contributed to the creation of auxiliaries in Philadelphia and Harrisburg—known as "Garnet Leagues"—which had hundreds of members.[66]

The PSERL, as well as other state organizations and the National Equal Rights League, were active on a number of fronts. From their inception, they directed much of their energy toward gaining male suffrage rights and ending racial segregation in, and exclusion from, the public schools. Another target of equal rights activists in Pennsylvania was the systematic discrimination against black riders on certain urban railroads. By 1864, Philadelphia was the only major northern city, other than San Francisco, that had not desegregated some or all of its railroad lines. Since 1860, the Social, Civic, and Statistical Association of the Colored People of Pennsylvania had been unsuccessful in its battle with Jim Crow. Much like the collaborative efforts by equal rights organizations in other states, in late

1864 the PSERL joined the Social, Civic, and Statistical Association, the Colored People's Union League, and sympathetic white groups on the railroad issue. The league quickly sprang into action, hiring lawyers to challenge the railroads' right to harass African Americans, sending three hundred copies of a petition to the legislature, and dispatching a committee to Harrisburg to lobby the state legislature. Younger blacks such as Octavius Catto also sought to involve the black masses in the protest movement by scheduling a number of mass meetings. Moreover, James Lynch, editor of the *Christian Recorder*, lent a powerful voice to the cause. Citing the continuing segregation of Philadelphia's streetcars at a time when most other northern cities—under sustained pressure from African Americans—had largely ended discrimination in their public transit systems, the paper angrily charged that the city was "more unmerciful in her proscription of colored men than any other city in the Union." Other northern blacks concurred with Lynch's condemnation of the city. While Philadelphia had been one of the centers of antislavery activity prior to the Civil War, its large black population, a rapidly growing white working class, and economic ties to the South fueled racial hostility and led to the most rigid patterns of racial segregation in the urban North.[67]

Radical Republicans in the city and other parts of the state denounced racial discrimination and worked with African Americans to boycott the railroads. Radical newspapers such as the *Philadelphia Press* and politicians such as Congressmen Thaddeus Stevens and William D. Kelley and State Senator Morrow D. Lowry labored tirelessly for the cause. Their collaboration showed that a viable coalition of white Radicals and African Americans was possible. Despite this agitation, Philadelphia blacks and their white allies experienced immense frustration. All of the lawsuits by individuals—especially women—against the railroads were successful in court, but these verdicts produced no change in the streetcar companies' policies. With petitions and lawsuits proving ineffective, the PSERL and other black rights organizations, with assistance from Radical Republicans, increasingly focused on lobbying the state legislature. Lowry's desegregation bill passed by a slim margin in the Senate, but it died in the House, where a number of Republican legislators feared a backlash by voters if they supported the bill. Nevertheless, Congress's passage of the 1866 Civil Rights Act as well as the Fourteenth Amendment, which the Pennsylvania Legislature ultimately ratified, intensified the pressure on the legislature to end racial discrimination in the Philadelphia transit system. Finally, another Lowry-sponsored bill passed in both houses of the Assembly in 1867.[68]

The most formidable obstacle that the crusade against Jim Crow in transit systems and the public schools confronted during these years, apart from exclusion from the political process in Pennsylvania and many other northern states, was the pervasive racism among employers, public officials, and the white public generally. Their support for racial segregation and exclusion was clearly manifested in the political arena, where Democrats consistently opposed any attempt to modify or repeal racist policies, while many Republicans were ambivalent, cautious, and opportunistic in their stance on equal rights for African Americans.

Yet part of the problem for northern black activists lay within their own ranks as well as with the larger black community. From their inception, the PSERL and other equal rights organizations experienced numerous problems—including a persistent shortage of funds, apathy on the part of some blacks, personal feuds, class and regional differences, and ideological divisions—all of which at times adversely affected the movement. Once again, the PSERL's experience provides valuable insights into a number of problems that afflicted northern equal rights organizations during this period. One of the most serious difficulties the PSERL had to contend with was the widespread poverty among northern blacks. Systematic discrimination in the job market pushed African Americans disproportionately into low-wage jobs. Consequently, many rights organizations were unable to fund their operations adequately; in some cases they scarcely functioned at all. It was often difficult for local auxiliaries to hire lecturers because they could not afford to pay them. Likewise, especially during periods of high unemployment, local leagues could send little or no money for dues to the state organization. One local leader acknowledged that in several PSERL auxiliaries, "You have the form for what it is worth[;] the substance is a myth." In some places the lack of resources also forced local rights groups to meet in churches because they could not afford to rent meeting rooms. This at times caused problems, especially when conservative trustees and ministers balked at providing space for equal rights activists whose meetings they feared might be disruptive.[69]

State and local league officials in Pennsylvania also complained that some African Americans were simply apathetic about their rights. Their anger toward those who chose not to become involved in the movement was at times palpable. Following an unsuccessful attempt to establish an auxiliary in Wilkes-Barre, one activist bitterly remarked that too many people in the community "take no pride in this great noble act"; another local leader bemoaned that "the worst set of men" would "give there [sic] life for a ball picnic or a parade but you come to muster them together to get them to advocate their rights or furnish means for others to do it for them it is like trying to force water to run uphill." A similar complaint was expressed by a Philadelphia rights activist, who chastised those who wished to be viewed as leaders in the black community yet, when called upon to labor for the cause, were either apathetic or indifferent. He was ashamed, he concluded, that "the deprivation of our rights and privileges can be laid at our door."[70]

Yet some activists associated with the PSERL blamed generational and class bias for this indifference toward the cause. For example, during the struggle to desegregate Philadelphia's railroads, younger, more militant activists such as Octavius Catto and William D. Forten, son of James Forten, a pioneer black activist, angrily accused William Still, a wealthy black businessman, and other older middle- and upper-class black leaders of denigrating the black masses in order to elevate the rights and stature of the black elite. They particularly disliked what they saw as the elite's tendency to cultivate the good will of the white elites more than to mobilize the black community in the struggle for equal rights. Still, whose coal business was boycotted by the militants in 1867, could indeed be rather patronizing toward both the black and white working class. Yet in a vigorous defense of his record, Still noted that Catto was an upstanding member of the city's black professional class and that Forten was a member of one of the wealthiest black families in Philadelphia. He also pointed to his long history of working to advance the interests of the black community. The cultural and material gaps among African Americans certainly created different expectations regarding the achievement of respectability and success in mainstream America, and the black masses had far less opportunity or reason to depend on white allies for their advancement. However, the social classes lived and interacted with each other on many levels within the black community, and they experienced in common a pervasive racial hostility. Moreover, it is apparent that Catto and Forten were also disturbed by the attitude of older black activists such as Still and James Lynch, editor of the *Christian Recorder,* who believed that the younger generation should defer to them. In the midst of this dispute, Lynch appeared to confirm the existence of a generation gap within the movement when he scolded younger African Americans for not accepting the advice of their elders.[71]

The equal rights movement was also divided at times by a complex mix of personal animosity and ideological differences. Some of these clashes were intense and resulted in deep fissures that persisted for years. In California, a bitter feud between the two most influential African Americans in the state—Peter Anderson, editor of the *Pacific Appeal,* and Philip A. Bell, editor of the *Elevator*—lasted through much of the 1860s and 1870s. Bell, who had collaborated with Anderson in editing the *Pacific Appeal* for a brief time in the early sixties before he established a rival newspaper, was more militant and outspoken than the rather cautious and diplomatic Anderson. Their differences on political strategy were quickly transformed into a struggle for control of the equal rights cause in California, with each editor frequently questioning the commitment, integrity, and wisdom of the other. At one point Bell declared that arguing with the Anderson faction, whom he provocatively referred to as "copperheads," was useless, for "we do not cast pearls before swine." For his part, Anderson accused Bell and other "restless parties" of acting in an "unwise and impolitic" manner by attempting to divide the movement.[72]

These warring factions in California never split into separate organizations. In Michigan, however, the state equal rights league was wracked by deep divisions that led to the creation, for a time, of two competing leagues. Eight months after the Michigan Equal Rights League was founded in early 1865, a convention called by a group of dissidents declared that, since a number of officers had met without the knowledge or consent of a majority of the organization's members, the league no longer enjoyed the confidence of African Americans in the state. The "gross outrage" committed by these officers, delegates to the Detroit Convention announced, effectively terminated the Michigan League; the dissenters then proceeded to establish the Equal Rights League of Michigan. When some delegates sought to reconcile the two groups by moving to invite the offending officers to the convention, the resolution was defeated. Thus, the seats for Michigan's representatives to the first annual convention of the National Equal Rights League, held in Cleveland in September 1865, were claimed by both groups. At the NERL convention delegates implored the Michigan combatants to settle their dispute. When the delegates from the Equal Rights League of Michigan insisted that only they had the right to represent Michigan's blacks at the meeting, the convention ultimately supported their claim.[73]

The NERL itself experienced problems from its inception; some were structural and procedural in nature, while others resulted from ideological and personal differences within the movement. The national organization's difficulties were due in part to the challenge of coordinating and communicating with dozens of state leagues scattered over thousands of miles. This problem was compounded by the limited funds at its disposal, which meant that only a skeleton staff worked at the national headquarters in Philadelphia. And because the first few meetings of the executive board were cancelled due to the lack of a quorum, the NERL's first annual meeting in 1865 decided that all members of the board must live in the vicinity of Philadelphia. Langston sought to offset the organization's inability to hire a fulltime agent because of inadequate funds by traveling extensively around the country, but this created something of a leadership vacuum at headquarters. There was at least some basis for the *Weekly Anglo-African*'s lament in 1865 that the NERL was "almost an unknown institution because of its great distance from the people."[74]

The editor did not blame the national officers for this deficiency. Rather, he argued that more direct representation was needed at the NERL meetings. Two years later, the executive board voted to restructure the league by establishing six districts in the nation, each with its own superintendant. But there is no evidence that this plan to create an intermediary level in the movement's bureaucracy was ever implemented. The NERL was also hampered by differences among the state and local leaders on a variety of issues. Conflict erupted at the first national meeting in 1865 over who should pay the dues to defray the national officers' expenses. Some delegates complained that no uniform dues were charged, and a number of state leaders grumbled that they too often had to assess their auxiliaries in order to raise money. This debate was resolved in favor of assessing uniform dues, though this does not seem to have solved the NERL's financial problems. Another issue related to the accreditation of delegates to the national meetings. Langston notified the state organizations in 1866 that they must limit the number of accredited members they could send. Yet, a few months later the executive board appeared to overrule Langston when it stated that all friends of equal rights, not just representatives of the state and local auxiliaries, would be invited to attend the meetings.[75]

Langston himself was partially responsible for the conflict within the movement. His biographers have noted that while he used his considerable political skills to resolve some of the disputes that arose among its members and his oratorical skills to inspire those who attended his lectures, he was extremely sensitive to criticism from other black leaders. This brought him into conflict with several prominent equal rights activists, particularly the officers of the PSERL. One of the most serious quarrels surfaced at the third annual meeting of the National Equal Rights League, held in Washington, D.C., when representatives of the PSERL led an effort to block the election of Langston to a third term as president. In nominating William Nesbit, their president, for the position, they asserted the principle of rotation in office. But other issues lay not far beneath the surface. Although Langston ultimately received the support of a majority of the delegates, his critics questioned his leadership ability. A year later, conflict erupted again when the PSERL instructed Nesbit to ask Thaddeus Stevens to confirm a conversation in which Langston had allegedly questioned the constitutionality of congressional reconstruction legislation related to the South. Stevens clearly did not trust Langston, considering his views on Reconstruction "fiddle stick nonsense." Nesbit and other PSERL leaders shared Stevens's estimation of Langston, informing the Radical Republican leader that "we have been suspicious of the double dealing, perhaps even the secret treachery of John M. Langston, and only need your testimony to enable us to take from him a post of honor that he disgraces amongst us."[76]

Langston resigned as president of the NERL in 1868, in large part because his duties as an inspector of schools for the Freedmen's Bureau and an organizer of southern black voters occupied much of his time. He also soon would be appointed head of the law department at Howard University in Washington, D.C.[77] With his departure, the National Equal Rights League became nearly inactive for almost a year, though in 1869 it helped to coordinate a national convention on behalf of black male suffrage. Equal rights activists continued to be guided by a strong sense of common purpose. But more than ever before, the state and local auxiliaries supplied the energy and funds that sustained the cause.

In addition to the disputes between state and national equal rights leaders among the delegates to the NERL's annual meetings, some of the most intense debate on ideological issues occurred within the PSERL and other state organizations. One such debate, which can be traced far back into the antebellum era, stemmed from fundamental differences over whether all-black organizations were necessary and appropriate and how African Americans should treat each other. The first issue involved considerations of both strategy and principle: whether they would achieve more success and be truer to their principles as part of a biracial alliance or as a blacks-only movement. Throughout the existence of the Reconstruction-era equal rights organizations, racial pride and identity and a legitimate distrust of potential white allies, on the one hand, lived in tension with a deep commitment to the principle of colorblindness and the necessity of coexisting with a racist white majority. This tension surfaced again and again. Some northern blacks strenuously objected to all-black organizations. In 1867, for example, Parker Smith, a Philadelphia lawyer, severely criticized both the PSERL and the Social, Civic, and Statistical Association for being "founded upon a distinctive principle—*when the necessity of the case does not demand it.*" Their aim, he asserted, should be "homogeneity" and the achievement of equal rights for all citizens "by virtue of a common humanity." Most equal rights activists, however, believed that societies organized and managed by African Americans were necessary as instruments for protection, pride, unity, and control over their own destiny in a hostile society. The *Weekly Anglo-African* spoke for many northern blacks when it stated that, while African Americans were not prejudiced against whites and were opposed to "clannishness," their treatment by whites required them to look out for themselves by establishing their own institutions. In fact, the founders of the National Equal Rights League frequently used the word "colored" in the preamble to its constitution. Following a lengthy debate at its first annual meeting, the delegates voted to delete this word wherever it occurred in the document, and the state auxiliaries followed suit. Yet there is no record of whites joining either the national or state organizations.[78]

Racial pride and identity also lay at the heart of an often emotional debate over how blacks should relate to both whites and other African Americans. For many proponents of equal rights, this issue was grounded not only in the demand for equality under the law but also—given the almost daily insults and humiliation they suffered at the hands of whites— the deeply-felt desire to be treated with respect and dignity. The debate generally focused on black businessmen's treatment of African American customers, and it invariably generated heated rhetoric and deep divisions. The most prolonged debate on this matter occurred at the PSERL's 1865 annual meeting. Supporters of a resolution stating that any African American businessman who refused to treat black and white customers in the same manner "is guilty of the greatest dereliction of duty" forcefully reminded the delegates that the cherished goal of equal rights must include equal treatment. The depth of anger and resentment was such that one delegate declared that anyone who opposed the resolution "is not entitled to our consideration."[79]

However, several delegates—including barbers, restaurant and bath house owners, and other entrepreneurs—vigorously objected to the proposal. Black businessmen, they declared, must be free to refuse service to disreputable blacks and whites alike; further, the league had no right to regulate people's private lives. In an argument that presaged white opposition to Charles Sumner's Supplementary Civil Rights Bill in the 1870s, they also pointedly reminded the resolution's proponents that the league sought legal, not social, equality and chided them for failing to grasp the realities that confronted businessmen. Even Nesbit, who agreed with the spirit of the resolution, criticized its advocates' "high-strung notions." Following heated debate, the resolution passed. But the issue did not disappear. While the matter was not debated at the National Equal Rights League's first annual meeting later that year, Langston felt compelled to denounce discrimination against blacks by African American businessmen "as tending to degrade us in the eyes of a discerning public." In a similar vein, in 1867 the *Christian Recorder* castigated blacks who continued to "stand in the way of the elevation of their race by taking the unmanly and degraded position of catering to American prejudice."[80]

A number of leading black activists were deeply disturbed by the sharp debate on these issues. William D. Forten was particularly dismayed by what he considered black Pennsylvanians' penchant for constant infighting. "We are so unreliant, so weak, antagonistical, caviling and captious," he wrote less than a year after the PSERL was founded, "that it is almost impossible to collect our scattered spiritless forces, made doubly so from the want of systematic combinations, and direct them to any point in our enemy lines, though assured of its vulnerability." The *Christian Recorder* concurred with Forten's pessimistic observation, expressing regret that blacks seemed more divided than other groups. Even the generally optimistic Nesbit, while expressing the hope that African Americans could "come together in the spirit of true brotherhood," concluded in 1865 that the divisions among blacks were "injurious and destructive in their bearing on us."[81]

Other northern blacks, however, were more philosophical about the divisions within the ranks of the equal rights movement. The Brooklyn correspondent of the *Christian Recorder* counseled black activists to regard debate and differences of opinion as natural and, at times, positive in their effects. "Our public men," he wrote, "need to learn, that great men differ in opinion, and that these differences are the result of varied habits of thought, and education, and developments; yet these are the sources of human progress." It was unfortunate, he added, that "our otherwise strong men exhibit so much weakness in their personal feuds. They forget the great, vital interests of the nation in the struggle for self-adulation."[82]

Indeed, northern blacks had long been divided on a number of personal and ideological issues.[83] It is not surprising that such divisions existed and, in some cases, intensified as they sought to take advantage of propitious developments that generated a sense of hope as well as urgency and uncertainty. After decades of frustration and despair, they realized that the moment they had long anticipated had finally arrived. But, at the same time, they were painfully aware that their efforts might well come to naught unless their white allies embraced the concept of equal rights for all American citizens. Unfortunately, Republicans were not dependable allies. Even worse, there was the nagging fear that the door to equality before the law could well close—and then might not open again for several generations.

This volatile mix of hope and anxiety was exacerbated by the lingering effects of old battles over strategy and ideology as well as personal resentments and suspicions, which at times poisoned the atmosphere. Likewise, the indignities and humiliation that had long been part of their experience in a white-dominated, racist society created a defensiveness and insecurity that frequently manifested itself in the need to vigorously defend one's manhood and motives.

Nevertheless, while these divisions within the ranks of the equal rights movement undoubtedly weakened the cause, such disagreements were certainly not unique to northern black activists. After all, white reformers and political party members had long clashed on matters of ideology, strategy, personality, and tactics. Equally important, on an issue such as black manhood suffrage—the dominant focus of the equal rights movement during the mid- and late 1860s—northern blacks were in substantial agreement on why it was a necessary and vital objective and how to go about obtaining it.

2

Toward the Fifteenth Amendment

In a speech before the Massachusetts Anti-Slavery Society in May 1865, Frederick Douglass warned that if abolitionists failed to press for "immediate, unconditional, and universal suffrage...we may not see, for centuries to come, the same disposition that exists at this moment."[1] Douglass and other black equal rights activists who demanded suffrage rights confronted immense obstacles. African American males were fully enfranchised in only five New England states (Massachusetts, Vermont, New Hampshire, Rhode Island, and Maine); taken together, these states held only a small percentage of the northern black population. In New York blacks could vote only if they owned property worth at least $250; this requirement effectively excluded most African Americans in the state from participating formally in the political process. In every other northern state, whites-only clauses in state constitutions had long denied blacks suffrage rights.

Thus, notwithstanding their growing optimism that the tide of history was rapidly moving the nation in the direction of equal rights for all citizens, African Americans had few illusions about quickly or easily attaining manhood suffrage. In the midst of the war, Frederick Douglass had warned that there might be a counterrevolution in the United States similar to those that occurred in Europe after the revolutions of 1848. When William Lloyd Garrison sought to disband the American Anti-Slavery Society in 1865 on the grounds that Republicans would protect the freed people, Douglass rejected Garrison's assumption as hopelessly naive. For he and other northern blacks knew that, in order to achieve suffrage and other rights, they must bring unrelenting pressure to bear on white public opinion, especially the Republican Party. The *Christian Recorder* reminded its readers that success would be achieved only by "wrestling" their rights from whites. The *Elevator* made this point more emphatically: "We cannot expect our rulers to thrust favors upon us, unless we show that we desire them. We are neglectful of our duty to ourselves, to our country, and to posterity, if we do not appreciate our political rights enough to demand them."[2]

From late in the Civil War until the ratification of the Fifteenth Amendment in 1870, northern blacks devoted their energies to gaining manhood suffrage rights. Convinced that this issue was, in the words of the PSERL, "the all important subject of our deliberations and united action," they at times exaggerated the importance of the franchise as a means of advancing their interests and protecting themselves from hostile whites. As the *Christian Recorder* declared, "It is upon the ballot-box that our freedom rests"; meanwhile, Douglass warned darkly in 1866 that only suffrage would prevent African Americans "from being thrust back into slavery." Yet blacks were not alone in investing the vote with enormous value; native-born whites and immigrants alike clearly understood the importance of having a voice in shaping the policies that vitally affected their lives. Moreover, African Americans frequently expressed the realistic concern—eloquently stated in 1865 by Michigan blacks in a petition requesting political rights—that "in a republican country, where general suffrage is the rule, personal liberty, and all other rights, become mere privileges held at the option of others, where we are excepted from the general political liberty."[3]

The Case for Suffrage Rights

Northern African Americans presented broad-ranging and sophisticated arguments on behalf of suffrage rights. Although they differed at times on tactics, timing, and the language that should be incorporated into suffrage legislation, they were in full agreement that both justice and morality demanded political equality. In making their case for suffrage rights, they were perhaps most determined to challenge the accusation that political equality would lead to demands for social equality. This charge was repeatedly leveled by the Democrats, but many Republicans held similar views. Blacks realized that this issue was a potent weapon for opponents of political equality—and equal rights generally—for in a society that was rigidly segregated along racial lines and where the possibility of miscegenation was so feared by whites that many northern states prohibited interracial marriage, any move toward racial equality might breach those barriers and threaten white supremacy. Thus, African Americans were especially intent on allaying the fears of Republicans, who were at least open to the possibility of enacting equal rights legislation.[4] They unequivocally denounced the tendency to conflate political and social equality as "superlative nonsense," "a hideous phantom," and "ridiculous and absurd."[5] A black convention reflected the thinking of most African Americans when it demanded equality before the law, not special privileges.[6] Likewise, when Democrats resorted to the assertion that social equality would open the door to interracial marriage, blacks turned the argument against their accusers by noting, as the *Christian Recorder* did in an 1866 editorial, "We had never supposed that there was such a strong affinity between Democrats and black men and women, as to make such marriage possible."[7]

Yet in vocally condemning the charge that they desired social equality with whites, black equal rights activists seemed willing to accept laws and customs that denied them equal access to many public facilities as well as privately owned businesses. Indeed, they would not add to the equal rights agenda a demand for such access until after black male suffrage rights were embedded in the U.S. Constitution. Some blacks even acknowledged that they were not the social equals of the most educated and "enlightened" whites. Much as they had done prior to the war, they frequently urged African Americans to cultivate moral and religious habits and to acquire wealth and intelligence. Otherwise, the *Christian Recorder* warned in 1866, "We will be ever despised, set aside, and denied our rights among the people of this country." Northern African Americans, especially inclined to view the freed people as culturally and socially inferior to middle- and upper-class whites (and, for that matter, many northern blacks), often lectured them on the virtues of industry, frugality, education, morality, and religion.⁸ Nevertheless, northern black spokesmen were quick to deny that the freed people's—or their own—low social and economic status and limited education justified the denial of equal rights. Instead, they maintained that virtue and patriotism were more important requisites for voting than social and educational achievements. In a thinly veiled reference to many southern—and some northern—whites who had fought against the Union yet now enjoyed suffrage rights, a speaker at an Indiana meeting used the role of black troops in the Civil War to make the point that "if we have virtue and intelligence enough to fight on the right side, certainly we will not vote on the wrong side." Moreover, they often pointed out that African Americans had already made progress in the face of enormous adversity and would continue to do so. In his lecture on "Citizenship and the Ballot," John Mercer Langston underscored the "surprising advance" that blacks had made, while Douglass told a Detroit audience in 1868 that his people's "capacities are great" and that the equal rights cause would "develop him faster than any race was ever developed before."⁹

Most suffrage activists, however, devoted far less attention to denying that they lacked sufficient intelligence to vote or desired social equality with whites than they did to the premise that, as American citizens, they unquestionably deserved suffrage rights. The numerous arguments they set forth on behalf of political rights were part of a broader strategy: to educate and inform white Americans on the relationship between the demands of the equal rights movement and the core values that most whites at least gave lip service to; to gain a favorable hearing among Republican politicians—and any Democrats who were willing to listen to their pleas—and thereby apply irresistible pressure on the political system to enact the desired legislation; and to mobilize the black community for the purpose of moving whites to act on this issue.

The language contained in the documents disseminated by the Syracuse Convention in 1864 served as the model for northern blacks during the six-year struggle for manhood suffrage rights. The movement's national officers sought to guide the campaign by publishing the proceedings of its annual meetings and dispatching Langston to deliver lectures on the suffrage issue. In addition, the NERL recruited a national delegation in 1866 to lobby federal officials to extend the franchise to black males. Yet especially in the mid-1860s, when the struggle focused largely on persuading state legislatures to remove whites-only clauses from state constitutions, the state leagues and their local auxiliaries often took the lead in addressing the issue.

Throughout the campaign for suffrage rights, the dominant message was that, as the *Christian Recorder* declared in 1867, blacks were Americans in language, manners, and customs and thought and debated as Americans. In arguing their case, they especially sought to contrast their plight as American citizens without political rights with immigrants, who could enjoy those very rights after living in the United States for only five years. While they often based their claims to the franchise on lofty principles, such as Michigan blacks' assertion in a petition to the state legislature that "if freedom is good for any, it is good for all," suffrage activists at times resorted to anti-immigrant rhetoric to substantiate their demands.[10] They especially targeted Irish immigrants, who consistently voted Democratic and were frequently hostile toward blacks. The *Elevator,* for example, referred to Irish Americans as "ignorant and disloyal," while, in a statement that had racial overtones, a speaker at a Newark meeting claimed that "blacks do not vote like a machine, as another class of people do, but like white men." On at least one occasion, blacks' anger toward the Irish for helping to defeat suffrage initiatives led them to call for a boycott of Irish-owned businesses.[11] Anti-immigrant arguments were also occasionally employed by California blacks to rebut the Democrats' contention that black suffrage would open the door to political rights for Chinese immigrants, whose numbers had grown rapidly during the previous decade and a half. Bell, the editor of the *Elevator,* was particularly outspoken on this matter, asserting that, unlike African Americans, the Chinese did not intend to become citizens, would remain apart from other groups, and were "only sojourners" who cared little for Christianity or "American habits and aspirations."[12]

For northern African Americans, any doubts that blacks had proven themselves worthy of enjoying political rights had been shattered by the sacrifices of nearly two hundred thousand black troops during the war. Although they consciously focused on the Civil War experience, they also repeatedly reminded whites that blacks had fought in every American war since the Revolution. Thus, they insisted that whites were obligated to secure suffrage rights for both northern and southern black men. To refuse to do so, the *Weekly Anglo-African* editorialized, would "dishonor the nation in the sight of God and man." It is not surprising that black Civil War veterans played an integral role in the campaign for suffrage rights, for they had been profoundly politicized by their military service. They now transformed their demand for equal pay in the army into an insistence on equal rights. They saw themselves, and were accepted by other blacks, as special advocates for the African American community on this issue. Black veterans therefore believed that it would be difficult for whites to ignore their moral authority. On a few occasions, they organized their own conventions for political rights. For example, at a meeting held by seven hundred troops of Iowa's 60th U.S. Colored Infantry in October 1865, they resolved that "he who is worthy to be trusted with the musket can, and ought to be trusted with the ballot." They also spoke out forcefully and eloquently at many state and local meetings organized by civilian leaders. In 1866, northern and southern African American veterans carried their crusade for the franchise to the national level by forming the Colored Soldiers' and Sailors' League. At these and other meetings, they and other blacks repeatedly reminded whites that, unlike most southern, and a minority of northern, whites, African Americans had never falsely sworn to the government or taken up arms against it.[13]

The courage and patriotism of black soldiers, equal rights activists believed, stood as indisputable proof that African American men deserved "manhood" rights. Prior to the Civil War, American citizenship rights were interpreted as "manhood" rights for whites only; in most of the free states, black males were placed in a dependent category with women and children and were therefore viewed as less than men. Many black men enlisted in the Union Army in part because they clearly understood that this act would—as many opponents of black enlistment indeed feared—significantly strengthen their claim to equal rights and destroy the racist stereotype of black men as childlike or feminine. Black recruiters therefore often employed the rhetoric of action and will and of enlistment as a means of securing manhood and freedom. Coming out of the Civil War, black suffrage advocates consciously and emphatically connected voting rights to manhood, for they realized that politics was considered an exclusively male domain and a proving ground for male identity. As a speaker at a Kansas convention declared in 1866, to deny a black man political rights and access to power was "to take from him one of the essential elements of his manhood," thereby rendering him "less than a man."[14]

Northern blacks also frequently looked back to the Revolutionary era in making their case for suffrage rights. They repeatedly emphasized that African Americans had fought for the American cause in the Revolution because they understood that the stated ideals of that struggle resonated with Americans as much as those that emerged in the recent Civil War. At times they employed the language of the Declaration of Independence almost verbatim in declaring that the right to vote was "inherent and natural" and "as sacred and inviolable as the right of property, liberty or life." Likewise, they appealed in the name of republican principles, especially the Constitution's guarantee of a republican form of government in the states. Convinced that all states that denied African Americans political rights on the grounds of race or color violated this guarantee, an Illinois suffrage convention charged: "An aristocracy of race or color is as repugnant to the principles of republicanism, as one of birth or wealth would be."[15]

They also invoked the Revolution's rallying cry of "no taxation without representation" to impress upon whites the fact that blacks willingly paid taxes even though they were denied a voice, either directly or indirectly, in shaping public policies that profoundly affected their lives. Langston expressed this grievance forcefully when he told an Indiana audience in 1865 that taxation and representation were inseparable and constituted "the bond of union, and the bond of obligation between the Government and the citizen."[16] In emphasizing this point, Langston did not mean to imply that such a gross violation of their rights might lead blacks to contemplate severing their ties to the government. But their anger and frustration did lead some to warn white lawmakers that, so long as they withheld the franchise from African Americans, agitation and protest would remain a disruptive force in society. In a resolution he presented at the New England Convention of Colored Citizens in 1865, George Downing predicted that disorder and turmoil might occur if the demand for suffrage and other rights were not realized. Until the struggle for equal rights came to fruition, he warned whites in an unmistakable reference to the antebellum battles surrounding the slavery issue, agitation and conflict as intense and widespread as that which had occurred during the antislavery crusade would damage the economic interests of the nation.[17] Some blacks indeed went so far as to warn explicitly that divine retribution would be visited upon those who perpetuated injustice. In response to Ohio Governor David Tod's assertion that blacks did not deserve the franchise, an Ohio veteran stated ominously:

"There is a day of retribution coming when justice will be meted out to those dangerous and political aspirants. A Cromwell will be found who will secure eternal justice to our oppressed race."[18]

Means of Persuasion

Northern black activists marshaled a broad array of sophisticated and powerful arguments on behalf of manhood suffrage rights; they also employed a wide variety of methods to disseminate their arguments and bring pressure to bear on white politicians and voters. Coming out of the Civil War, black suffrage activists at all levels of the movement—from the national officers in Philadelphia to the local auxiliaries—appear to have agreed that they must take action primarily at the state level because they realized that nearly all Americans assumed that the states had sole authority to determine suffrage rights. Members of the state and local leagues were generally pragmatic in selecting the combination of means they believed held out the best chance of success in any given situation. Relatively little disagreement seems to have developed over which tactics would be most effective. An exception to this pattern emerged in California in 1867, where followers of Philip Bell and Peter Anderson—editors of the *Elevator* and the *Pacific Appeal,* respectively—differed sharply on whether African Americans should agitate the suffrage issue while the Democrats controlled the legislature. Bell's allies insisted the effort must continue and that it was possible to influence Democratic legislators. But Anderson and his loyalists, deeming such efforts fruitless, preferred, in the name of racial pride and manhood, to "wait and combat the popular prejudice against our race, than whiningly to seek that boon" from the Democrats.[19]

Northern black rights activists established state organizations whose structures varied from state to state. The organizational structures that emerged in California and Illinois were quite different. In California, a centralized structure was created in which authority was concentrated in the hands of a statewide executive committee. At the Fourth California State Convention in 1865, which Bell termed "the most important assembly of colored men that ever met on the Pacific Coast," the delegates passed a series of resolutions, presented an address to the public, sent petitions and memorials to the legislature, and called for sending lobbyists to

Sacramento. Throughout the mid- and late 1860s, the executive committee controlled the agenda of the suffrage cause in the state; Bell, whose *Elevator* was designated as its organ, dominated the committee.[20] In Illinois, on the other hand, a more complex and decentralized organizational structure developed, within which various rights organizations cooperated in furthering the suffrage cause. African Americans, led by John Jones and other activists, held three suffrage conventions following the Civil War. The most important of these meetings, convened at Galesburg in 1866, called for the creation of a thirteen-person State Central Suffrage Committee with one member from each congressional district and a general agent who would canvass the state, establish auxiliaries, circulate petitions, collect money, and mobilize the people. Jones, who served as the state agent for the Illinois Equal Rights League, was also selected as general agent for the newly formed State Central Suffrage Committee. In preparation for his presentation to the state legislature and later to the state constitutional convention, a committee of five men was appointed to draft resolutions. Beyond this, suffrage leagues were established at the county level throughout the state.[21] While the organizational structure that emerged in Illinois dispersed power and participation more widely than did that in California, both allowed for important input from local activists. Moreover, both states employed very similar methods to disseminate the equal rights message and to pressure whites to support their objectives.

One of the methods that suffrage activists most frequently utilized was petitioning state legislatures and state constitutional conventions. Some of these petitions, which circulated in black communities across the North, were signed by hundreds of men and women even where there was a small black population. In many cases, sympathetic Republicans agreed to submit the petitions to the appropriate legislative or convention committees.[22]

In addition to sending petitions and memorials to government leaders and lobbying in the state capitals, northern blacks wrote letters to Republican newspapers and especially to the black press. Black-owned and -edited newspapers published in Philadelphia, Cincinnati, New York, Harrisburg, and San Francisco—as well as Douglass's *New National Era,* which was published in the District of Columbia between 1870 and 1875 but circulated throughout the North—informed and shaped the views of many northern blacks on a broad range of issues. These newspapers circulated widely in the black communities because they were quite inexpensive and because northern blacks received little coverage even in the more sympathetic Republican papers. African Americans also sponsored parades, which attracted large numbers of participants and spectators. These parades drew attention to the suffrage issue and used celebrations of the Emancipation Proclamation, the British emancipation of slaves in the West Indies in 1834, and the ratification of the Thirteenth Amendment as occasions to call for the franchise.[23] Taken together, these activities represent a multifaceted assault on laws that denied most Northern blacks fundamental political rights. The suffrage activists viewed all of these tactics as integral and necessary components of the effort to shape public opinion and pressure the political parties to act.

From the movement's inception, some activists, such as Langston, a lawyer, and J. Sella Martin, a New York minister who had assisted the freed people during the war, also contemplated turning to the courts for redress of their grievances on the suffrage issue. At the ninety-third anniversary celebration of the death of Crispus Attucks, a black man who died in the Boston Massacre in 1773, Langston expressed the hope that an African American would bring suit in a federal court to strike down state laws that denied black males the franchise. He was confident that U.S. Supreme Court Chief Justice Salmon P. Chase would rule in favor of such a suit. In early 1866, Martin presented a similar case for legal action. Because the Thirteenth Amendment had made African American males eligible to vote, he declared, the federal courts should lend their support to this worthy endeavor. He therefore urged his listeners to go to the polls and, if turned away, to take the matter all the way to the U.S. Supreme Court.[24]

The New Jersey, Pennsylvania, and New York equal rights leagues soon acted on Langston's and Martin's recommendations. The New Jersey Equal Rights League developed plans in 1866 to offer their votes at several polling sites in the state and, if refused, to carry the issue into the courts. They hired lawyers, and Charles Sumner and other leading Radical Republicans offered to serve as counsel. A meeting in Newark then established the State Executive Committee, which was instructed to raise money and institute legal proceedings in the state and federal courts. Two of the parties then filed suit when registrars refused to enroll them as voters. That the Pennsylvania league's executive board soon decided to cooperate with the New Jersey group in this endeavor indicates that, where federal action was deemed relevant and important, state leagues chose to combine forces for maximum effect. In 1866 the PSERL selected a five-man committee, authorized a circular soliciting contributions for the litigation, and decided to seek assistance from the Pennsylvania Anti-Slavery Society as well as Congressman William D. Kelley and Thaddeus Stevens. Five members of the league were delegated to test the right of Pennsylvania blacks to vote, but a motion to raise $5,000 for the legal effort was rejected, probably because of budget constraints. For reasons that are not entirely clear—though limited funds appear to have been a decisive factor—neither the New Jersey nor the Pennsylvania initiative produced tangible results.[25]

Yet those who sought redress in the courts achieved one notable victory when a suit brought by an African American in Wisconsin led to a definitive ruling on the suffrage issue by the state's supreme court. Blacks' efforts to gain the vote had failed in 1849 and 1857. In 1865, black leaders in Milwaukee—probably associated with the Wisconsin Equal Rights League—called a mass meeting in which it was declared that the courage and sacrifice of African American soldiers during the war necessitated the enactment of black manhood suffrage. Following this meeting, two blacks attempted to vote in order to force the issue into the courts for a reconsideration of the 1849 referendum. Black manhood suffrage had been approved in that referendum, but such a small percentage of the electorate voted on the issue that the state decreed that the referendum had failed to meet the constitutional standard of majority approval. Following the 1865 vote, a Milwaukee man, whose request that his ward's board of registry enroll him as an elector was rejected on the grounds of his skin color, filed suit in the County Circuit Court. When his suit was rejected, he appealed to the Wisconsin Supreme Court, which ruled that blacks had wrongly been denied the franchise since the 1849 referendum because a majority of voters casting ballots at the time had in fact supported the suffrage measure.[26]

Nevertheless, between 1865 and 1869 the victory in Wisconsin stood nearly alone in the northern black struggle to gain the franchise. Only in Iowa and Minnesota, where African Americans constituted a tiny percentage of the population, was black manhood suffrage enacted by a vote of the legislature or the electorate. Even in these states, success came only after long and contentious struggles. Notwithstanding a vigorous petition and lobbying campaign by African Americans in Minnesota, black manhood suffrage referenda were defeated in 1865 and 1867. A black suffrage provision was finally enacted in 1868—and then largely because, in order to make its passage more likely, the Republicans decided that the vote on whether to delete the word *white* from the state constitution should be placed on the presidential, not a separate, ballot. In Iowa, the process was especially cumbersome, for amendments to the state constitution required approval in two consecutive legislative sessions before submission to a popular vote. A black manhood suffrage provision was passed overwhelmingly in 1866 and 1867; then, with black Iowans continuing to apply pressure, it was finally enacted in 1868.[27]

In all other northern states—except for five of the New England states and for those New York blacks who owned property valued at $250 or more—where the issue of black manhood suffrage was either discussed within the Republican Party or was voted on by a legislature, a state constitutional convention, or the electorate, it was decisively rejected. In 1865, Connecticut voters defeated an attempt to remove the whites-only clause from the state constitution, while Republican leaders in Ohio, Pennsylvania, New York, New Jersey, Indiana, and Michigan prevented the issue from coming to a popular vote. Then, in 1867, political rights for black males were denied in Ohio, Kansas, and Connecticut and, a year later, in Michigan and New York.[28] Thus, three years after the Syracuse Convention, the drive for suffrage rights had stalled, and the prospects for progress at the state level appeared bleak. Black activists' arguments had seemingly fallen on deaf ears, and their tactics had changed relatively few minds. Indeed, a powerful white backlash had routed their white allies in key northern states. These developments above all underscored the reality that African Americans could not count on the Republican Party to mobilize its supporters on behalf of an issue that stood at the very center of the equal rights agenda.

Complicated Relations with the Republican Party

Any explanation for the numerous setbacks suffered by northern blacks in their efforts to strike the word *white* from northern state constitutions must take into account the deep-seated and pervasive racism among whites. If anything, racial prejudice among northern whites may well have been intensified by the fear of black migration to the North following emancipation. Such prejudice was forthrightly acknowledged by E. L. Godkin, editor of the *Nation,* who wrote in 1865: "We do not fully and heartily believe that the Negro is a man. We could not act or reason as we do unless this were the case." Democrats were especially inclined to appeal to voters' racial prejudice for political gain. They repeatedly asserted that ignorant blacks would be duped and controlled by Republicans, that the United States was a white man's republic in which only whites were citizens, and that political equality would inevitably lead to demands for social equality. Their blatant racism, which was evident in all parts of the North, was manifested clearly in the minority report presented by Democratic legislators on the Connecticut General Assembly's Committee on Constitutional Amendments in 1865: "This race, so inferior in the highest qualities of manhood to our own cannot in our view be benefited by the right of suffrage."[29] Long the target of the Democrats' pandering to racist sentiment, northern blacks had no illusions about converting the party faithful to the cause of black suffrage. They viewed Democrats as the enemy and generally attributed the party's political success not to their stated principles but rather, as the *Christian Recorder* stated, to their conscious decision "to pander to the low tastes of the vilest part of the population."[30]

Their relationship with the Republican Party was much more complicated. Most Radicals in the party felt strongly that African American males were fully entitled to the vote. Thus, blacks could generally count on them to present petitions and resolutions on behalf of suffrage rights to state legislatures and constitutional conventions and to vote for such proposals and urge the electorate to do so in referenda.[31] A growing percentage—often a majority—of northern Republicans in fact came to support blacks in their quest for political rights.[32]

Yet leading Radicals were painfully aware that many Republicans thought differently. For example, in 1865 Thaddeus Stevens, a leading Radical in the House of Representatives, informed Charles Sumner, the most influential Radical in the Senate, that large numbers of Republicans, including some Radicals, considered black suffrage "heavy and premature." Likewise, George W. Julian, an Indiana Radical who vigorously supported black manhood suffrage, accurately observed that party members everywhere were deeply divided on the issue. Many Republicans, according to Julian, feared that because the issue might help restore the Democrats to power, the party must wait until public opinion became more favorable before it committed itself.[33]

Some powerful Republicans, such as Governor Jacob Cox of Ohio, as well as the editor of the *Indianapolis Journal,* indeed pointedly warned that it would be disastrous for both the party and northern blacks if it embraced political rights for African Americans. Many more Republicans were profoundly ambivalent on the issue. While Republicans tended to embrace the concept of legal equality, they feared the political consequences of endorsing suffrage rights. In nearly all of the northern states from Connecticut to California where the issue came to a vote, it lost by a decisive margin, even where Republicans constituted a majority of the electorate or controlled both houses of the legislature.[34]

Coming out of the Civil War, northern blacks occupied a vulnerable position, as their destiny lay in the hands of Republicans, many of whom were ambivalent and unreliable allies. Nevertheless, it is not clear whether a viable alternative existed to African Americans' decision to agitate for inclusion in the mainstream of American society. During the grim years of the 1850s, many African Americans had seriously considered emigration as a solution to their plight. But this course was not financially feasible for most blacks, and it ran the risk of further marginalizing them while doing virtually nothing to change white racial attitudes. In the late 1860s, as watershed events unleashed by the war seemed to be moving the nation inexorably toward a new era of equality and democracy, they were not prepared to turn their backs on what seemed a unique opportunity to realize their dream of full citizenship. Because they constituted a mere 2 percent of the northern population, they had no choice but to look to the Republican Party to enact suffrage and other rights.[35]

Yet northern blacks' conviction that there was no viable alternative to urging Republicans to stand on principle in support of political equality provided little solace. In fact, they were often dismayed and angered by the party's cautious and expedient course. William D. Forten expressed the profound sense of betrayal felt by many African Americans when he complained bitterly in 1865: "We have been deserted by those whom we faithfully supported, and *insolently informed that this is a white man's country, though it required the strong arms of over 200,000 black men to save it,* and that the elective franchise is not now a practical question, and we must find homes in some Territory separate to ourselves, as white and black men cannot live together upon terms of equality." In similar vein, a New York rights activist denounced the decision by many Connecticut Republicans to oppose a suffrage referendum in 1865 as "unreasonable, unjust, and the result of cruel prejudice." These activists especially resented that, while most southern rebels had regained political rights and, by 1867, the freedmen were promised franchise rights, the vast majority of northern blacks still could neither vote nor hold office.[36]

Many old abolitionists, such as Theodore Tilton, Horace Greeley, and members of the Boston-based Impartial Suffrage League, actively worked for black manhood suffrage. But northern blacks were particularly disturbed by William Lloyd Garrison's decision in 1865 not to agitate for suffrage rights. They regarded Garrison's position as an indication of most northern whites' inability or unwillingness to develop a genuine appreciation of the importance of black manhood suffrage. As Charles Lenox Remond, a New York activist, lamented: "It is utterly impossible for our white friends, however much they have tried, fully to understand the black man's case in this nation."[37]

Yet notwithstanding Remond's and other blacks' sense of alienation, they realized that there was no real alternative to working with the Republicans to achieve their objective. They could not imagine voting for the Democrats, and their occasional warning that continued Republican opposition to black suffrage would eventually destroy the party held out little promise of forcing the hand of the party's leadership. Thus, the best they could hope for was that, under pressure from black and white proponents of suffrage, the party would come to its senses. "We vote that ticket," the *Christian Recorder* stated with an air of resignation, "just as a hungry man would vote to have bread and a thirsty man, water."[38]

Perhaps motivated by the desire to convince themselves and others in the movement that they must continue the struggle, no matter how difficult and prolonged it might be, a few African Americans expressed confidence that suffrage rights would soon become a reality. As the Social, Civic, and Statistical Association of the Colored People of Pennsylvania stated confidently in 1867, "This is well nigh a settled question with large numbers of intelligent white people"; meanwhile, the *Pacific Appeal* predicted that black suffrage would inevitably be enacted in all of the northern states.[39] But whatever optimism they and their white allies managed to muster was shattered by the devastating defeats in the 1867 northern state elections. Voters in twenty states went to the polls that year, and the Republicans lost ground in nearly all of them, including Ohio, Pennsylvania, and New

York—all swing states with many electoral votes. Even worse for African Americans, in every state where a black suffrage amendment appeared on the ballot, it was decisively defeated. Once again, though a majority of Republicans supported these suffrage initiatives, enough party members either chose not to vote or joined the Democrats to ensure defeat.[40]

Taking the Fight to Washington

The convergence of circumstances—including the numerous setbacks experienced by black manhood suffrage advocates between 1865 and 1867, Republican control of both houses of Congress, and the realization that congressional legislation would perhaps bring suffrage rights sooner than attempts to change state constitutions—convinced northern blacks that they must also focus their attention on Washington. Even before the war ended, a few northern blacks had begun to call for an agent or a group of lobbyists to reside in the nation's capital for the purpose of urging Congress to act on the suffrage issue and other matters. In a speech before the Indiana Conference of the African Methodist Episcopal Church in February 1865, John Jones, who headed the lobby that was seeking to convince the Illinois legislature to repeal the state's Black Laws, recommended that blacks in each congressional district send a representative to Washington to press urgent claims for African Americans. In the same month, the PSERL urged the national organization to hire an agent and establish a newspaper in the nation's capital; it then reiterated this plea at the NERL's first annual meeting in September 1865. The *Christian Recorder* soon endorsed these recommendations, calling on blacks in every state to send between three and six influential men to Washington to lobby Congress.[41]

George Downing probably was most instrumental in recruiting a delegation of prominent African Americans from both North and South. At the Convention of the Colored People of New England, held in late 1865, he expressed the conviction that a national delegation would attract the attention of blacks and whites alike, generate grassroots support for the cause, strengthen the hand of friends in Congress, and transform the racial attitudes of many Congressmen. The convention ultimately pledged $10,000 to sustain the delegation.[42]

The delegation that assembled in Washington in January 1866 was composed of leading northern activists such as Downing, Douglass, Langston, and Jones as well as men from Maryland, the District of Columbia, South Carolina, and Mississippi. Many states were not represented. With the exception of Downing, who was selected by the Convention of the Colored People of New England, members of the delegation appear to have been chosen by the NERL's officers. Yet these men reflected the national scope of the equal rights movement, for the North and the South were equally represented.[43] Almost immediately after they assembled, the delegation encountered racial prejudice. Although well dressed and orderly, they were denied admission to the Senate gallery. Refusing to be segregated or excluded, they asked Charles Sumner to do what he could to change the Senate doorkeeper's policy, saying that "our self respect is greater than our desire" to hear the Senate debates. Sumner's intervention appears to have prevented any more such discrimination. The national delegation encountered much the same prejudice in their meeting with President Andrew Johnson. Before Johnson moved into the White House following Lincoln's assassination, Langston and a committee of black leaders—probably members of the executive committee of the National Equal Rights League—met with the president. In his memoirs, written nearly thirty years later, Langston recalled that Johnson pledged to protect the rights of all citizens with "earnest and positive" action and to execute with vigor every law enacted on their behalf.[44]

In fact, Johnson resisted every attempt by congressional Republicans to extend legal rights to African Americans. Very early in his presidency, some black leaders naturally began to severely criticize his stance on Reconstruction. The *Christian Recorder* termed his policies "so utterly unsuccessful, as to call for the condemnation of many earnest men," while the Equal Rights League of Michigan denounced his energetic efforts to restore the southern states to the Union as "unwise, unfaithful to the colored American who has been faithful and self-sacrificing."[45]

It is not surprising that the black delegation's meeting with Johnson in early February 1866 went very badly. Hoping to move Johnson toward endorsing suffrage rights for black men, they told him they respected him as president and as a friend but insisted that blacks be protected in their rights as citizens. Downing and Douglass added that, because African Americans were subject to laws enacted by the government, they should share in its privileges. After listening to members of the lobby, however,

Johnson devoted at least forty-five minutes to what Douglass termed "a set speech"—more like a harangue. The president stated emphatically that he had been a friend of African Americans and therefore did not appreciate being challenged by those whose liberty had never been in peril. Above all, he would do nothing that might risk precipitating a race war, for poor southern whites had been injured by both slaveholders and slaves. Johnson proceeded to insist that the states, not the federal government, were empowered to determine the status of blacks and that if the freedmen were enfranchised, they would become pawns of the former slaveholders, thereby further undermining the interests of the southern yeoman class. He therefore saw no solution to the race problem except black migration from the South.[46]

Stunned by the president's tirade, Douglass attempted to reply but was immediately cut off by Johnson, who then ordered the delegation to leave his office. To make matters worse, one of the president's private secretaries reported to a friend that after the "darkey delegation" left, Johnson said: "Those d——d sons of b——s thought they had me in a trap. I know that d——d Douglass; he's just like any nigger, and he would sooner cut a white man's throat than not."[47]

Following the meeting, Douglass met with his colleagues, who considered Johnson's remarks "unsound and prejudicial to the highest interests of our race as well as the country at large." They discussed the contents of a rejoinder, to be written by Douglass, which would be published in the Washington *Chronicle,* a Republican newspaper. In this response, Douglass emphatically denied that black suffrage would lead to a race war or that black voters would become pawns of the planter class. He also asserted that enmity between southern African Americans and yeomen whites had been the product of slavery; with emancipation a reality, these groups could have similar interests and vote accordingly. Even if the hostility between them continued, the former slaves would be protected by their political rights; conversely, to keep blacks powerless would only invite continued abuse and oppression. For Douglass and his colleagues, "Peace between the races is not to be secured by degrading one race and exalting another; by giving power to one race and withholding it from another; but by maintaining a state of equal justice between all classes."[48]

Despite Johnson's insulting behavior and his obvious disdain for African Americans, some northern blacks chose to view the White House meeting as a positive development. For example, the editor of the *Christian Recorder* wrote Downing: "I think the seed sown this year by the colored delegation will produce sooner or later an abundant harvest." But, with good reason, most black activists held out no hope that Johnson would lend support to the cause. Thus, the national delegation chose to focus their lobbying efforts on congressional Republicans and other officials. In meetings over a period of several weeks in the winter of 1866, they were much more warmly received by these men, including Gen. O. O. Howard, who headed the Freedmen's Bureau; U.S. Supreme Court Chief Justice Salmon P. Chase; Charles Sumner; Thaddeus Stevens; and members of the House Judiciary Committee.[49]

When William Nesbit and other officers of the PSERL arrived in Washington a few weeks after the national delegation's disastrous meeting with President Johnson, they wisely chose to avoid the White House and met with Chase, Sumner, and other leading Republicans. The Pennsylvania delegation came to Washington especially to present a memorial to Congress urging passage of legislation granting political and civil rights to African Americans. After a few days in Washington, Nesbit declared the mission "eminently successful." But even in the midst of this concerted lobbying effort by equal rights activists, personal jealousies resurfaced. Perhaps resentful that no officer of the PSERL had been invited to join the national delegation, Nesbit boasted that African Americans in the District of Columbia had informed him that the Pennsylvania delegation was "far more effective if less noisy and demonstrative than the delegation which preceded us."[50]

Both the national and the Pennsylvania delegations, however, were in full agreement that fundamental legal and political rights for African Americans were imperative. In its memorial to Congress, the national lobby rejected any constitutional amendment that disfranchised a group of citizens on the grounds of race or color. Because nothing in the Constitution gave a state the authority to make race or color a disqualification for suffrage rights, their memorial declared, any such language would be "a real calamity." The PSERL memorial, which was broader in scope, reiterated the standard argument that African Americans had long been faithful to their government, that black men were citizens who deserved full rights, that Congress must guarantee a republican form of government in every state, and that congressional action that upheld justice and right would obviate continued conflict between the races as well as the vengeance of God. Above all, the Pennsylvania league condemned the common Republican refrain that black suffrage was inexpedient. "Expediency," it maintained, "is a pillar on which oppressors and tyrants always lean. It is the vanguard in the army of iniquitous measures and practices—it supports every political wrong, and is used as an argument against right."[51]

Black suffrage proponents supplemented these memorials with a broad array of measures designed to both pressure and assist Republican members of Congress. They raised money for Republican committee members to circulate documents and speeches favorable to suffrage rights and met frequently with leading Radicals such as Sumner, Stevens, Kelley, and Julian.[52] At times they chided their Radical allies. Douglass, for example, expressed his displeasure with Senator Henry Wilson of Massachusetts when he felt that Wilson was not sufficiently vocal in his support of political equality for black males. But much more often they lavished praise on their friends in Congress. Sumner was the principal recipient of their admiration and affection. Henry Highland Garnet expressed the sentiments of many African Americans when he wrote Sumner in 1866: "Yes, you have been the instrument in the hands of God, in removing a burden from my heart, and in enkindling most blessed hopes for the future of my people—*your people*—in my bosom."[53]

Northern blacks also held numerous public meetings—including the second annual meeting of the National Equal Rights League, held in Washington in 1866—which generated addresses and resolutions that were intended to apply direct pressure on congressional Republicans.[54] These efforts were supplemented by a vigorous petition campaign. Many of their petitions urged Congress to use the Constitution's guarantee of a republican form of government to prohibit state legislation that discriminated on the basis of race or color. These petitions often appear to have been circulated and signed by men and women from a broad spectrum of the black community, including members of churches, fraternal clubs, local equal rights league auxiliaries, and those who attended public meetings.[55]

Notwithstanding their concerted efforts to convince Republican congressmen to enact black manhood suffrage, northern blacks achieved only limited success prior to 1867. Even though a growing number of Republicans in Congress had come to focus their attention on developing a plan of Reconstruction during the last year of the war, they nevertheless organized the Montana Territory and passed the Wade-Davis Bill with no provision for black suffrage. By 1866, the situation had improved in some respects. A large minority of Republican senators now supported impartial suffrage legislation for the freedmen that would outlaw discrimination based on race or color but not necessarily on other grounds, and most Republicans embraced civil rights for blacks. In that year, Republicans in Congress indeed inserted in the Civil Rights Act some of the arguments pressed by the black delegations—especially their demands that the states and territories be prohibited from denying citizens a number of fundamental rights and privileges and that the federal courts have exclusive jurisdiction over crimes committed under the provisions of the Act.[56]

African American rights activists, however, did not succeed in gaining either protection of their rights when moving from state to state or an explicit statement condemning the violation of rights on the grounds of race or color. More important, the Civil Rights Act of 1866 included no mention of black suffrage. Most congressional Republicans in fact still believed that federally mandated political rights for African American males was too radical and therefore too politically risky and that to embrace such a demand would not only endanger party unity but also violate the concept of states' rights. Thus, Sumner's proposal for a national law establishing voting rights for all citizens in the states and territories attracted only limited support in Congress.[57]

The Fourteenth Amendment—at least with respect to the suffrage issue—illustrates the limits of many Republicans' willingness to alter the balance of power between the states and Washington in any dramatic way and of their commitment to federally mandated black manhood suffrage. In a memorial to Congress that the national delegation presented while the Senate was debating the House's version of the amendment, they declared emphatically that the insertion of any wording into the U.S. Constitution that implicitly or explicitly gave the states authority to deny the right of suffrage on account of race or color would be regarded as "a real calamity." But their earnest plea had little effect on many Republican congressmen. While the amendment established national responsibility for protecting civil rights, in its final form the compromise reached between moderate and Radical Republicans contained only a modest provision for allowing southern whites to continue denying blacks the franchise if they were willing to lose fifteen seats in the House of Representatives and equivalent votes in the electoral college. Moreover, in an effort to avoid antagonizing northern voters, the framers of the amendment included no mention of political rights for northern blacks.[58] When the amendment finally passed both houses of Congress, northern blacks applauded its sweeping language regarding legal rights but were furious that it granted only indirect and conditional rights for the freedmen and failed even to mention suffrage rights for northern African American males. They had hoped that, after months of intense lobbying and petitioning designed to sway Republican legislators on this issue, the party would exhibit far more political courage and moral commitment. Consequently, they felt betrayed and abandoned by those upon whom they were depending for the vote. The delegates to the second annual meeting of the National Equal Rights League articulated this sense of outrage when they declared that "in so far as it permits our disfranchisement it is undemocratic, illegitimate, and unjust."[59]

During the late 1860s, northern blacks would experience additional setbacks and bitter disappointments. But they would also be heartened by the inexorable movement by a growing number of Republicans toward support of black manhood suffrage. Throughout this struggle, with all of its emotional highs and lows, African Americans refused to abandon the cause. Indeed, 1867 would prove to be a momentous year for the suffrage campaign. Sweeping Republican victories in the 1866 elections had emboldened the Radical Republicans and a growing number of moderates to place the suffrage issue back on the party's agenda. At the same time, black activists across the North deserve considerable credit for maintaining relentless pressure on Congress to enact suffrage rights in the Colorado and Nebraska territories and the District of Columbia. In the Colorado Territory, they went so far as to go over the heads of the intransigent territorial Republican leadership by directly petitioning Congress for suffrage rights.[60]

Due in part to such pressure, between December 1866 and February 1867 congressional Republicans enacted black manhood suffrage in the District of Columbia and required impartial suffrage as a condition for admitting Nebraska and Colorado to the Union. During the debates on these controversial matters, Sumner and other Radicals were able to convince a number of moderates in the party to endorse federally mandated black suffrage. This helped to pave the way for the enactment of the First Reconstruction Act in March 1867, which explicitly required the southern states to enfranchise their black male citizens in the process of being reorganized.[61]

Northern blacks were heartened by these auspicious developments. Following more than two years of disappointment and frustration in dealing with Republicans in the state legislatures and Congress, this legislation seemed to constitute a watershed in the struggle for suffrage rights. The *Christian Recorder* was especially optimistic about the future. Terming Congress's actions a "noble stand in favor of human rights," the editor confidently predicted that the idea of political equality would soon prevail in the northern states, for it was "marching on in gigantic strength and speed, and he who resists it must and will be crushed."[62]

Yet the disastrous defeats of black suffrage referenda and Republican losses in crucial northern states in the 1867 elections once again reminded blacks that northern white opinion lagged far behind the party's position—however tentative and ambivalent—on this contentious issue. Many moderate Republicans blamed the Radicals for this rout and turned to Ulysses S. Grant—who had opposed enfranchising the freedmen until southern white intransigence convinced him they needed the vote to protect their legal rights—as the party's standard-bearer. At the same time, the party's leadership devised an ingenious double standard for its 1868 national platform, which called for permitting the northern states to continue to control suffrage while providing for federally mandated suffrage in the South.[63]

Especially following Grant's election, a growing number of congressional Republicans came to support a suffrage amendment to the Constitution. Nevada Senator William M. Stewart's journey from unequivocal opposition to black suffrage to vigorous support for the amendment sheds light on the path taken by many Republicans. Late in the Civil War, Stewart had rejected political equality for blacks on the grounds that they were inferior and that the United States "was made for white men." By 1866, however, his views on the issue had become more nuanced. While still unwilling to work for black suffrage, he was now opposed to turning the freed people over to their former oppressors and was willing to concede that "a loyal Negro has a better right to vote than a disloyal white man." Convinced that black suffrage was the right thing to do and that the black vote would enable the Republican Party to remain the dominant force in American politics, Stewart wrote the Senate version of the Fifteenth Amendment in 1868.[64]

Most Republicans were motivated to pass and ratify the Fifteenth Amendment by this mix of idealism and pragmatism. Many of them, especially the Radicals, feared that repudiating black manhood suffrage would weaken the party's claims as guardians of morality and increasingly realized that African Americans' arguments regarding justice, democracy, and fairness were entirely valid. At the same time, the moderate majority within the party desired to put the suffrage issue behind them in order to deny the Democrats a useful wedge issue, hoped that resolution of the matter would permit them to move on to other pressing issues, and worried that, in the near future, the party might lose control of the House of Representatives and some of the state legislatures.[65]

The pressure that African Americans directed toward Republicans on the suffrage issue reached a peak of intensity when the National Convention of Colored Men met for several days in Washington in January 1869 in the midst of the congressional debate on the Fifteenth Amendment. Although the northern states were the most heavily represented among the 130 delegates and Northerners dominated the proceedings, it was the first truly national black convention in American history. A large number of men from several southern and border states were present and played important roles in the convention's proceedings. The major business of the convention was shaped and guided by men who had stood at the very center of the equal rights movement for many years: Douglass, who served as its president; Downing, who chaired the Business Committee; and George B. Vashon, who wrote the convention's address to the public.[66]

The principal organizational issue that surfaced at the convention was the fate of the National Equal Rights League. Because it had been nearly moribund following Langston's resignation as president in 1868, two delegates presented separate resolutions calling for the creation of a new national organization. Convinced that the movement needed a national structure and effective national leadership, they recommended that a group called the National Equal Rights League of North America be headquartered in Washington. This organization would be headed by a committee consisting of one member from each state and territory and the District of Columbia; this committee could then appoint an executive committee of nine members. These resolutions were endorsed by the Business Committee, and the delegates approved the establishment of the National Executive Committee of Colored Persons, which was a far more geographically representative body than the old executive board of the National Equal Rights League.[67]

The delegates focused primarily on lobbying congressional Republicans and President-elect Grant. Langston headed the delegation that met with Grant, who expressed full support for the Fifteenth Amendment and pledged to do all that he could to ensure its passage. Another group of delegates, led by Downing, spoke at length with Republican members of the House Judiciary Committee, who assured them that they would vote in favor of the amendment.[68] The assertive mood of the delegates was reflected in their memorial to Congress, in which they stated unequivocally that, as native-born Americans, as saviors of the nation, and as loyal supporters of the Republican Party "so long as it continued to battle for righteousness and justice," they must receive the vote. This uncompromising tone was echoed a few months later by a member of a local auxiliary of the PSERL, who implored Jacob White and other league officials to act forcefully on behalf of the proposed amendment. "Give us a 'historic, denunciative, recitative, argumentative,' or in short infuse into it as some would say, the *damnation* spirit that is the life of colored preachers," he wrote White. "Let the proud caucassian feel that we do not cringe... on the demands for justice."[69]

One of the major concerns the delegates discussed with congressional Republicans in January 1869 was the language of the amendment. Since 1865 northern blacks had differed at times on whether to endorse impartial or universal manhood suffrage. Downing, Douglass, and Philip Bell, editor of the *Elevator,* among others, expressed support for impartial manhood suffrage, whereby black and white males would be required to meet the same voting qualifications, such as a literacy requirement. Bell, perhaps the most outspoken proponent of impartial manhood suffrage, asserted in 1865 that suffrage laws should exclude "the vicious and ignorant" of both races, though three years later he predicted that within ten years 95 percent of black men then under the age of thirty would have the vote.[70] Indeed, Bell and many of his fellow equal rights activists celebrated the dominant middle-class values of laissez-faire individualism and self-help. The ideology of individual uplift, which had occupied a central place in antebellum black protest thought, served to complement their emphasis on racial integration and inclusion. Peter Anderson, editor of the *Pacific Appeal,* succinctly expressed this belief when he urged whites to "give us equality before the law, and the removal of proscriptive laws, so we can run the free and fair race with the white Americans." Even Robert Hamilton, editor of the *Weekly Anglo-African,* who sometimes chided his colleagues for paying insufficient attention to the black masses, called for impartial manhood rather than universal manhood suffrage. In his study of antebellum black protest leaders, Patrick Rael has noted that the problem with this emphasis on individual merit was that many whites, who remained blind to the obstacles that hindered blacks' efforts to improve their condition—and often endeavored to maintain these barriers—might well hold northern African American leaders to their word that full citizenship should be based upon the ability to succeed in a race-neutral environment.[71]

Yet, in their defense, those who espoused impartial manhood suffrage did so at a time when virtually no Republican leaders endorsed federally mandated political rights for black males. Thus, their endorsement of this position appears to have been motivated in part by practical considerations, such as the hope that, by emphasizing individual uplift, they would gain a respectful hearing by middle-class whites, who, after all, dominated the political system. More important, by the late 1860s these men had come to urge Congress to enact universal black manhood suffrage.

Northern blacks did not agree on how the Fifteenth Amendment should be worded. Some leaders, such as William Nesbit, president of the PSERL, believed that African Americans should not insist on specific language. "Simply that we ask for the matter," he wrote Jacob White, "and let our friendly statesmen supply the *form* or *wording* of the Amendment." Others insisted that the language be inclusive, though they did not agree on what that meant. Petitions sent to the House Judiciary Committee by professors and students at Lincoln University, a black college in Pennsylvania, and by the PSERL's executive board, which Nesbit himself headed, called for an amendment that would secure to all citizens equal political rights without regard to class, creed, birth, race, or color; whereas black public meetings in Newark, New Jersey, and New York City went further in urging universal manhood suffrage that would, as stated during the latter meeting, guarantee the right to vote and to hold office to "all persons"—presumably males—both black and white.[72]

William D. Forten enunciated yet another variation on the amendment's language. He concurred with those supporters of universal manhood suffrage who asserted that, unless convicted of a crime, every male citizen 21 years of age or older should have the right to vote in all elections. But Forten, whose father had been born a slave, strenuously objected to any reference to race, color, or previous condition in the amendment, not only because of its conditional language but also, perhaps above all, because it would forever stigmatize blacks in the minds of most white Americans. The wording of Representative William Boutwell's proposed amendment, he angrily informed Sumner in early 1869, was "virtually a *bill of attainder.* We cannot have this thrust to endless days in our faces that we are a *Race of Slaves.* We want no reference to race or color, or what is worse to previous condition, engrafted on the Great National Charter to be handed down to the detriment whereby we may be Constitutionally branded with the misfortune of our fathers." This, he charged, would be "invidious" and "antirepublican." In the final analysis, Forten wanted no distinctions among American citizens to be inserted into the Constitution. "There must," he insisted, "be no color known to Americans but the national one—no race but the human race—no condition either previous or present but loyalty, patriotism, and sanity."[73]

The Question of Woman Suffrage

Northern blacks also debated whether women should be granted political rights. Many African American men believed that political concerns were part of the male domain; thus, they claimed male citizenship on the basis of an idealized manhood and what they considered "civilized" gender conventions. They were convinced that if black males were ever to gain the respect of whites, African American women must adhere to proper gender roles. However, northern black women had long played a pivotal role in black public life in the areas of moral reform, abolition, and civil rights; this continued throughout the Reconstruction era. While women generally deferred to men in the equal rights organizations, they, like their southern sisters following the war, insisted on the right to participate in the political culture, including speaking out on a broad range of issues that affected the black community.[74]

At times their determination to challenge the idea that politics was an exclusively male realm produced heated debate within the equal rights movement. An incident that occurred at a San Jose, California, meeting in 1865 illustrates the intensity of feeling on this issue. At this meeting the matter of women's political standing arose during a discussion of the recent election of delegates to an upcoming black state equal rights convention. A number of men strenuously objected to the election of a local businessman as a delegate because women had voted for him. To end the dispute, the businessman withdrew, and a new slate of delegates was proposed. But the women at the meeting were supported by the chairman, who moved that women be allowed to vote, as they had before. This produced chaos, with several men leaving the room in protest. The chair then congratulated the audience on the departure of "these relics of a past age"; subsequently, the businessman was reelected unanimously. But the moment of women's empowerment was brief, for within a week another meeting, which included large numbers of men, proceeded to declare the previous meeting null and void because women and children had participated in the election. They then resolved that women and children "are not entitled to the exercise of the elective franchise in matters pertaining to the body politic" and elected a new slate of delegates.[75]

The question of whether woman suffrage should be joined with the enfranchisement of black males was the subject of extensive debate among northern African Americans. It even divided families, such as the Purvises of Philadelphia. While Robert and Harriet Purvis strongly supported woman suffrage, their sons, Charles and Henry, as well as their son-in-law, William D. Forten, did not. In 1869, Robert went so far as to publicly chastise Charles for saying that the franchise for black men should take precedence over woman suffrage.[76] But the debate on universal suffrage was in fact more complicated than such divisions suggest, for race and gender both brought together and separated black and white men and women. Douglass, Downing, and Catto were among the prominent northern black men who had long endorsed suffrage rights for all citizens, regardless of gender. Equally important, black women had played an important role in the cause for a number of years. In 1859, two African American women held prominent positions at the New England Convention of Colored Citizens, which called for universal suffrage. Then, in 1866, several black women—including Harriet Purvis, Sarah Remond (a feminist and abolitionist), Sojourner Truth (a noted orator and Underground Railroad activist), and Frances Ellen Watkins Harper (a well-known poet and novelist)—joined other black and white men and women in establishing the American Equal Rights Association, which urged that the franchise be extended to all women. In the same year, a group of black men and women helped to organize the interracial Philadelphia Suffrage Association.[77]

Nevertheless, while Douglass, Downing, and other leading black male rights activists vigorously supported the AERA, they reflected the thinking of nearly all African American men that black manhood suffrage must take precedence over woman suffrage. Douglass believed that the claim of black men to the vote was more urgent than that of women because it represented a crucial step toward true black liberation. Although he conceded that suffrage rights for women were "a desirable matter," he insisted that black manhood suffrage was "a question of life and death," especially in the South.[78]

This argument sparked heated debate between white suffragists and northern black male activists during the mid- and late 1860s. A number of white suffragists, led by Susan B. Anthony and Elizabeth Cady Stanton, launched a campaign for woman suffrage in Kansas and other northern states, asserting that white women deserved the vote more than did black men, whom they described as degraded and oppressed, and thus incapable of exercising the franchise in a responsible manner. When George Downing asked Stanton at an AERA meeting whether she would oppose the enfranchisement of black males if women did not attain the vote, she rejected the prospect of uneducated and degraded black men making laws for her.[79] Stanton and many other white feminists were understandably angry and frustrated that, once again, women's interests would be subordinated to those of men. They were especially outraged by the decision by congressional Republicans, in drafting the Fourteenth Amendment, to extend equality before the law to all "male citizens"—the first time that the word *male* appeared in the U.S. Constitution. Yet Stanton's racist attacks on black men were both insensitive and unjustified, and they deeply offended black women as well as many white woman suffragists.[80]

In this debate, northern black women often stood between most African American men and white feminists such as Anthony and Stanton. Sojourner Truth's and Frances Ellen Watkins Harper's positions on the suffrage issue illustrate the complex and nuanced views held by many black women. Truth and Harper were a study in contrasts: Truth was an uneducated, poor woman, while Harper was a polished writer who had been educated by an uncle. But even though they came to somewhat different conclusions regarding the Fifteenth Amendment, they held rather similar views on the need for universal suffrage.[81]

Truth opposed the Fifteenth Amendment because she feared that it would place more power in the hands of black men. Indeed, Truth was reported to have said at the 1867 AERA meeting that "If colored men get their rights, and not colored women theirs, you see the colored men will be masters over the woman, and it will be just as bad as it was before." Yet she was deeply troubled by the fact that Anthony and Stanton focused on black men while seldom mentioning rights for black women. In addition, she agreed with Douglass and other black males that the hour belonged to blacks, while also favoring universal suffrage.[82]

Harper's views on race and gender were even more nuanced. She vocally supported woman suffrage but also was disillusioned and angered by many white feminists' attempts to speak for African Americans and especially by their racist remarks concerning black men. While Harper was no less aware of black women's struggle for equal rights than was Truth, she believed that the greatest obstacle for black women was not black men but white racism. At the 1869 AERA convention she argued that if the Fifteenth Amendment were defeated, black women would be less, not more, secure.[83]

In siding with Douglass on all counts, Harper spoke for most northern black women, who realized that many white suffragists were not dependable allies but also feared that if blacks enjoyed no political rights, the women's struggle was meaningless. Since white Americans could handle only one suffrage question at a time, Harper told the delegates to the 1869 AERA convention, she "would not have black women put a single straw in the way, if only the men of the race obtain what they wanted." When the issue involved race, she added, she would "let the lesser question of sex go."[84]

In the final analysis, none of the black manhood suffrage activists' petitions and memorials to Congress mentioned woman suffrage, nor did congressional Republicans ever seriously consider attaching it to the Fifteenth Amendment. While several Radical senators proposed that suffrage rights should not be denied on the grounds of race, color, nativity, property, education, or creed, there was no mention of gender. Indeed, both houses of Congress ultimately accepted a narrow form of impartial suffrage that excluded most of these considerations because they concluded that this was what would pass.[85]

The Response to the Fifteenth Amendment

Fashioned largely by moderate Republicans, who wished to alter the original federal structure while retaining its essential nature, the Fifteenth Amendment's negative phraseology essentially left the states in charge of determining the criteria for political rights, with the exception of race, color, or previous condition of servitude. Notwithstanding the conditional language in the amendment, which moderate Republicans insisted was necessary for it to be ratified by the states, the ratification process was difficult and prolonged. In several states, including California, Democratic-controlled legislatures rejected the amendment; although the Republicans eventually prevailed in Indiana, most Democratic legislators sought to block the vote by resigning their seats. Moreover, Democrats in New York rescinded an earlier Republican vote for ratification, but this move was rejected by Hamilton Fish, Grant's secretary of state. Even in some heavily Republican states the opposition was fierce. Nevertheless, driven by party loyalty, the pressure of time, and support by Grant and Colfax, Republicans were able to achieve ratification in the required three-quarters of the states by early 1870.[86]

During the ratification process, some northern blacks cautioned against attaching too much importance to the franchise. The *Elevator* urged African Americans not to be carried away by "false ideas" that the Fifteenth Amendment would dramatically change their lives, while Benjamin T. Tanner, editor of the *Christian Recorder,* warned his readers that the amendment should be viewed "as a means and not an end." Because the ballot alone could do nothing, the *Christian Recorder*'s editor wrote, African American men should not depend excessively on the vote.[87] Once ratification was achieved, however, both of these newspapers found cause for jubilation and chose to view it as a momentous watershed in the lives of African Americans. Philip Bell now judged the Fifteenth Amendment to be "the glorious consummation of a series of liberal and progressive legislations." The *Christian Recorder*'s editor was even more effusive in his response, terming ratification "the harbinger of Peace and prosperity—such peace and prosperity as has never rested upon the land." Indeed, Charles B. Ray, a New York rights activist, went so far as to proclaim the amendment a life-transforming achievement for African American men. "They are not only brought a new political status, a new relationship to the government," he exulted, "but into a new life; looking upon men and things through other mediums, with corresponding effects and feelings which are moral feelings and effects." This, he predicted effusively, would produce "a broader humanity."[88]

One might well ask why northern blacks responded so positively to a flawed amendment that did not explicitly confer suffrage rights on a single African American male. One possible explanation is the sense of relief many of them experienced following a difficult five-year struggle whose outcome had seemed quite uncertain during much of that time. Moreover, the importance of the franchise as a means of protecting the rights and advancing the interests of a group had long been taken for granted by both native-born and immigrant white males. African American men were also inclined—perhaps naively—to take the Republicans at their word that, with the Fourteenth and Fifteenth Amendments now embedded in the Constitution, the federal government would act resolutely to protect the civil and political rights of all citizens. But to expect northern blacks in 1870 to have peered into the future and foreseen, with much clarity, the return to power of the Democrats in the southern states and the U.S. House of Representatives, the Republican retreat from Reconstruction, and the resurgence of Jim Crow, with its inventive and unjust measures designed to deny blacks the vote on grounds other than race, color, or previous condition of servitude, seems both unfair and presumptuous.

With ratification of the Fifteenth Amendment, northern black activists had finally achieved what they considered the salient element of the equal rights agenda. Yet this had by no means been the sole focus of their agitation since the Syracuse Convention in 1864. Another issue to which they devoted enormous energy and attention during the Reconstruction era was segregation within—and, in many places, exclusion from—public schools across the North.

3

THE CRUSADE FOR EQUAL ACCESS TO PUBLIC SCHOOLS, 1864–1870

Although the delegates to the Syracuse Convention in 1864 focused their attention primarily on the suffrage issue, they also condemned public school systems that either provided African American children with an inferior education in racially segregated schools or denied them a public school education altogether. In their Declaration of Wrongs and Rights, they bemoaned the contradiction: blacks were "denounced as incurably ignorant" yet were "debarred from taking even the first step toward self-enlightenment and personal and national elevation" that an adequate education would provide.[1] Many of these delegates had been involved in the antebellum struggle to eradicate racial barriers to equal educational opportunities. These efforts had achieved some success, most notably in Massachusetts, where in the mid-1850s the legislature mandated the desegregation of all of the state's public schools.[2] But they were also painfully aware that very little improvement in black public education had occurred.[3]

Unlike their agitation on the suffrage issue, which drew their focus increasingly toward congressional action and national politics, northern equal rights activists' assault on racial segregation within, and exclusion from, public schools during the postwar years required that they concentrate on discriminatory laws at the state and local levels, for nearly all Americans assumed that the federal government should play virtually no role in public education. Consequently, the state and local auxiliaries of the National Equal Rights League prior to 1870 coordinated much of the campaign for equal access to the public schools.

Northern black activists considered the suffrage and school issues vital components of a broad-based assault on racial prejudice and discrimination that were undemocratic and morally and ethically wrong. They believed that the franchise would enable African Americans to exert more pressure on white politicians and school officials to end discriminatory practices, while equal educational opportunities would allow blacks to carry out their responsibilities as citizens more effectively. Equally important, they viewed an education as a valuable means of acquiring the knowledge and skills necessary for attaining social and economic mobility and improving the quality of life in the black community. A speaker at a Detroit convention in 1865 declared: "We consider the acquisition of a good education one of the most desirable of all earthly attainments without which no people can rise in the scale of social being or accomplish anything by which the political or physical condition can be advanced or improved." Philip Bell, editor of the *Elevator,* went even further, asserting that the education of black children was "the most important object for which we contend." While acknowledging that the franchise was essential to the welfare of African Americans, he concluded that nothing was as vital to the welfare of the black community as education.[4]

Barriers to Equal Integrated Education

Yet as they launched the equal rights movement northern blacks confronted formidable obstacles to the realization of their dream of equal educational opportunities. Racial segregation within, or exclusion from, public schools was the norm in nearly all northern states at the end of the war. Most whites—especially Democrats but also many Republicans—strongly supported these discriminatory laws, for they were convinced that African Americans were inferior and therefore that education could do little, if anything, to elevate them. These whites believed that the races should be separated wherever possible, particularly in the public schools, where they felt their children's welfare was most at stake.[5]

In 1865, Indiana stood at the opposite end of the public school policy spectrum from Wisconsin, Vermont, Massachusetts, Maine, and New Hampshire. While all public schools in Wisconsin and these New England states were racially integrated, no African American children in Indiana were allowed to attend the state's public schools. Because Indiana's school laws expressly stated that the public schools were open to whites only—even if blacks offered to pay their own tuition—they were forced to rely entirely on private schools.[6]

In most other northern states a complex mosaic of segregation, exclusion, and, occasionally, integration existed. There were no discernible patterns that set one particular region of the North apart from another. Nevada's arrangement largely resembled Indiana's in that there was only one school for blacks in the entire state. Nevada did permit a black school to be established if at least ten African American school-age children lived in a district, but where the quota was met local officials invariably chose not to create a separate public school. California had the same numerical requirement. Yet most black communities in the state did not meet the ten-student threshold. Another problem for black Californians was that, while local school boards could, under state law, allow black children to attend school with whites if a majority of white parents in the district did not object, such consent was never given. Pennsylvania's school laws were more exclusionary than those of Nevada or California. Black Pennsylvanians enjoyed access to the Public School Fund, but at least twenty school-age African American children were required to live in a district for a separate public school to be established. This meant that many black children in the state received no public school education.[7]

The public school policy in Illinois was even more complicated. Unlike the situation in Pennsylvania, school taxes paid by African Americans were not returned to them in districts where no public school was available to their children. A school district could admit black students if it was willing to incur the expense, but most communities, especially in the southern part of the state, did not do so. Consequently, in 1866 Newton Bateman, state superintendent of public instruction, estimated that one half of the six thousand black children in the state between the ages of 6 and 21 had no access to public education. However, in a few northern Illinois communities where whites did not object, they were admitted to the white schools. The most important example is Chicago, where, following black protests against the segregated schools in 1864 and the advent of Republican control in the state legislature and the City Council, its schools were desegregated.[8]

Much as in Illinois, most of Ohio's blacks lived in small communities in the southern areas of the state, thus making it difficult to provide separate public schools for their children. White resistance to education for blacks exacerbated this problem. Consequently, at the end of the Civil War only a fifth of all school districts in the state had separate black public schools. Yet in Cleveland and much of the rest of the Western Reserve area, where abolitionism and black protest against racial discrimination had taken deep root during the antebellum era, schools were generally integrated, and black teachers were employed in some racially mixed schools in Cleveland.[9]

The patterns that existed in southern and northern areas of Illinois and Ohio, respectively, were generally reversed in New Jersey: Most public schools in the southern part of the state were racially segregated, while integrated schools were more common in the northern areas. It is not clear why this was the case, especially since the Democratic Party, which almost invariably rejected school integration, was strong in many parts of northern New Jersey; whereas Republicans, who were more likely to support racially mixed schools, were the dominant political force in southern New Jersey. It appears that the large postwar migration by southern blacks into southern New Jersey created powerful anti-integration sentiment among Democrats and many Republicans. At the same time, the large-scale movement of European immigrants into the northern areas of the state, combined with the presence of a relatively small black population, may well have so increased ethnic diversity in the schools that racially mixed schools seemed less threatening to the white power structure.[10]

Still another permutation along the integration-segregation continuum existed in Michigan, Connecticut, and Rhode Island, where segregated public schools were found especially in the large cities, such as Detroit and Jackson; New Haven and Hartford; and Providence, Bristol, and Newport, respectively. Perhaps the most complex realities confronted African Americans in New York. Although state officials called for equal funding for black and white schools in 1864, relatively few schools acted on this directive. Moreover, larger school systems, such as those in New York City, Brooklyn, and Buffalo, maintained segregated schools, while many smaller communities integrated their schools primarily for economic reasons.[11]

The Ambiguities of Desegregation

All northern blacks vigorously condemned the exclusion of African American children from the public schools. But no consensus existed on whether school desegregation was a desirable objective. Many blacks were ambivalent about racially mixed schools; during the antebellum years and throughout the Reconstruction era, a vocal minority of African Americans argued the case for separate schools as a means of retaining a measure of control over their children's education, thereby providing for their academic, social, and psychological needs.[12]

Northern African Americans who opposed school desegregation during the postwar years were, like their antebellum predecessors, motivated by both ideological and practical considerations. Cultural nationalism clearly shaped their thinking on this matter. A group in Brooklyn, for example, accused black integrationists of being "ashamed or afraid of being known as colored persons" and charged that, by supporting black churches and fraternal organizations while opposing racially separate schools, the proponents of public school desegregation were inconsistent and deceitful.

In a similar vein, groups of black parents in Delaware, Ohio, and Detroit circulated petitions that called for keeping the separate schools open. These schools, proclaimed the Delaware group, were "the bulwark of the liberties of the colored people, and must be guarded with unflagging vigilance." Others, such as a correspondent to the *Daily Ohio State Journal*, chose to emphasize the positive academic consequences of all-black institutions, arguing that intellectual growth came from within, being "the result of exercise, and not contact merely." Thus, he concluded that, at least for the foreseeable future, schools and other institutions based on language or color would produce better results than "mixed organizations."[13]

Even many African Americans who favored public school integration were rather ambivalent on the issue. They were justifiably concerned that white students would mistreat and humiliate their black classmates in racially mixed schools. Indeed, the evidence points to a toxic environment in many such schools, with black children routinely being subjected to racist taunts, harassment, and violence.[14] They were also worried about how their children would be treated by white teachers and whether African American men and women would be hired to teach in racially integrated schools. They realized that their racially separate schools—whether public or private—and the black women and men who taught their children served as a focus of community organization and activity, especially for those who lived in scattered pockets in both rural and urban areas. Blacks in numerous northern communities insisted that, so long as segregated public schools existed, only black teachers should be hired.[15] In Poughkeepsie, a broad cross section of the black community demanded that the school board not appoint white teachers to their schools, while blacks in New York City strenuously objected to the superintendent's plan in 1865 to replace black teachers of superior ability with less capable whites.[16]

These protests were often lodged in response to the reality that in many black communities—even in Philadelphia, which had the largest African American population of any city in the North—a majority of teachers in the black schools were white. Blacks were especially fearful that white teachers would bring their racial prejudices into the classroom. As the *Elevator* warned, white teachers were unfortunately inclined to stereotype black pupils as inferior. Such concerns were often grounded in the assumption that black teachers better understood the intellectual, cultural, and emotional needs of African American students than did white instructors. For example, a group of Detroit parents asserted in a petition to the school board in 1865 that a black teacher could best understand and convey proper "deportment and principles for survival" in a hostile environment.[17]

Although most northern blacks favored the proposition that African American teachers were more effective than whites as role models for black pupils, this issue also often proved divisive. Perhaps the most acrimonious debate on who should teach their children erupted at the first annual meeting of the Pennsylvania State Equal Rights League in 1865. Angered by the Philadelphia Board of Education's treatment of blacks—especially its failure to hire African American teachers in the city's black schools over the years—the convention's Business Committee resolved that, because "experimental knowledge" indicated that black children made greater progress under the direction of African American than white teachers, they considered it their duty, "as lovers of the advancement of our race," to ensure that their schools were guided by black teachers. Some delegates angrily charged that the resolution was "ill advised and injurious in its operations" in that it appeared to make distinctions based on color, which equal rights activists had long denounced. But an amendment urging that no discrimination on account of color be employed in the appointment of teachers in the black schools was defeated.[18]

Following a prolonged and heated debate, Octavius Catto, a Philadelphia activist who taught at the privately-run Institute for Colored Youth—the only school in Pennsylvania where blacks could gain a teaching credential—offered a compromise resolution. Citing the 1854 state law that established separate schools for African Americans as well as the Philadelphia Board of Education's 1864 ruling that barred black teachers from instructing white students, Catto argued creatively that, because white teachers in the black schools were "inferior" in skills and experience, preference in appointments to those schools should be given to qualified African Americans based on education and custom. In addition, his proposal stipulated that, since the Philadelphia Normal School did not admit blacks as candidates for teacher certification, all teachers in the black schools must graduate from the Institute for Colored Youth.[19]

Catto, who endorsed the spirit of the original resolution but questioned its wording, believed that no white teacher could instruct a black child as satisfactorily as could an African American, not because of different intellectual abilities but because the black teacher would have the welfare of the students more at heart. Thus, he resolved that where black and white candidates for teaching positions were equally qualified, African Americans should be selected because they were better qualified by "conventional circumstances outside the schoolhouse."[20] In unanimously supporting Catto's resolution, the delegates—a number of whom had taught alongside him at the Institute—wished to make it abundantly clear that they deeply resented the practice of hiring unqualified white teachers, who frequently had been rejected for appointment in the white schools, to teach in the black schools. They also underscored their conviction that the shared experience and cultural values that bound black students, teachers, and the larger African American community were absolutely essential for black self-esteem, autonomy, and upward mobility in a hostile society.[21]

Black teachers in the racially separate schools, along with administrators and other personnel, were likely to be long-term residents of the communities they served. Unlike white teachers in either the black or racially mixed schools, they were generally involved in black community life, including the churches and fraternal organizations. White teachers not only frequently refused to recognize or acknowledge their African American students outside the school but also, at times, intimidated and ridiculed them in the classroom. For instance, white school officials sometimes placed black pupils in separate classrooms in mixed schools and, to avoid conflict between white and black students, seated African Americans apart from whites in the same room. Such demeaning treatment, as well as the ridicule poor black students experienced because of their shabby clothes, contributed to a high dropout rate among black children.[22]

Such pervasive racism among white teachers and students was deeply disturbing, even to those African Americans who espoused school integration. The *Elevator,* for example, editorialized in 1870 that, because black students seldom received the same advantages as white children in racially mixed schools, "as long as the prejudice exists which forces us into the negro pews in churches and the backseat in school houses, so long will we need colored churches and separate schools." This grievance was echoed by a group of Illinois blacks in the same year. According to Newton Bateman, superintendent of public instruction for the state, these African Americans informed him that they preferred racially separate schools because they did not desire, and would not permit, their children to attend schools where they would be exposed to "unfeeling taunts and insults." Conversely, northern blacks who questioned the wisdom of school desegregation pointed out that the self-image of students who were taught by African Americans in all-black schools was not damaged, for they were the leaders and active participants in every phase of school life; therefore, the sense of inferiority and unjust treatment or neglect were seldom present.[23] Moreover, when black schools were closed in communities where integration occurred, African Americans were left with no schools they could call their own and with little or no voice in shaping the policies that affected their children's education. Consequently, black parents often confronted a difficult dilemma: either lose what little control they had over their schools (and possibly jeopardize their children's emotional well-being) or send their children to higher-quality, racially mixed schools.[24]

Many northern blacks were also troubled by the fact that, when the public schools were desegregated, black teachers invariably lost their jobs.

Indeed, white-controlled school boards frequently warned African American teachers that they would be retained only if the schools remained segregated. These discriminatory policies sparked vigorous protest in Brooklyn, New York City, and Albany, New York; Keokuk, Iowa; and other northern communities, with black women often leading the way. Such policies posed an especially serious threat to black women's professional opportunities, for in many communities they outnumbered black men in the teaching ranks. School desegregation proved to be a double-edged sword for black women: it enabled a growing number to achieve a higher level of education and, with it, access to the teaching profession, but the closing of black schools also threatened to eliminate one of the few professional opportunities available to them.[25]

Black Teachers, Black Schools

Because teaching was probably the highest paid and most prestigious profession available to educated African Americans, it is not surprising that some blacks who were instructors in racially separate public schools, or were related to them, at times spoke out against integration.[26] Although Henry Highland Garnet generally favored integration, that his wife served as principal of one of three remaining black schools in New York City in the late 1870s appears to have motivated him, at least in part, to urge that, since the school board had decreed that African Americans could not teach or be administrators in racially mixed schools, these schools should be kept open as long as the number of students in attendance justified their continuation.[27]

Perhaps no one sparked more heated debate on this matter than Solomon Day, a black teacher in Dayton, Ohio. In a letter to the editor of the *Daily Ohio State Journal* in 1878, Day warned that desegregation of the public schools in the state would have a devastating effect on black teachers and students alike. While he agreed with the principle that all children should attend school together, he predicted ominously that the closing of black schools in Ohio would cost more than five hundred African American teachers their jobs, thereby either reducing them to "penury or want" or forcing them to seek employment in the South, where they would become victims of "Southern cruelty and barbarism."[28]

Black advocates of school integration condemned Day's arguments as self-serving and injurious to African American children. Rev. James Poindexter, a black Columbus activist who played a prominent role in the Ohio Equal Rights League, presented the most sweeping criticism of Day's position, claiming that many black teachers were not as well qualified as white teachers and that only a few blacks would lose their jobs as a result of desegregation. More important, according to Poindexter, because white children in a segregated educational setting adopted the false idea that their skin color made them superior to black children, the loss of black teachers' jobs would be far less destructive than the continuation of inferior black schools. Another critic went so far as to accuse Day of allowing his selfishness to prejudice him against the potential benefits of school integration. In a letter to the editor of the *Daily Ohio State Journal,* he stated contemptuously that Day and other like-minded black teachers simply would not deign to perform "honest" manual labor.[29]

Yet, unlike Day and Garnet, some African Americans who did not depend on separate public schools for their livelihood also wondered whether integration was worth the loss of black employment in the school systems. Philip Bell cautioned in 1865 that school desegregation might well mean that someday there would be no incentives for black men and women to enter the teaching profession; consequently, no such role models or sources of pride would exist for African American adults and children alike. Only when black men of piety, learning, judgment, and ability were admitted to the teaching and other professions because of their merit, he stated, would black schools, churches, and newspapers cease to exist.[30]

For African Americans who took pride in all-black institutions and were, at the very least, ambivalent about the consequences of school desegregation, the black school system in Cincinnati stood forth as a symbol of black identity and aspirations. Prior to the Civil War, Cincinnati blacks, who had long been excluded from, or suffered systematic discrimination within, white-dominated institutions, created their own churches, fraternal and sororal lodges, mutual benefit societies, an antislavery society, literary societies, and private schools. Following years of lobbying by black Cincinnatians, the Ohio legislature passed a law in 1856 that applied only to that city. This law, which gave a significant degree of control to the black community over the management of its schools, was highly unusual in the North. Even in Boston, New York, and Philadelphia, which had relatively large black populations, whites controlled the school boards and served as superintendents, while African American teachers and principals in the black schools were powerless to shape policy.[31]

White authorities in Cincinnati continued to determine the appropriation of taxes for all of the city's schools. But blacks oversaw the operation of their four district schools, an intermediate school, a high school, a normal school, a night school, and two colony schools. In addition, they not only served as superintendent of the system and principal of the high school; at a time when few northern blacks could vote, an elected black school board established policy for the system. Moreover, Cincinnati blacks played an important political role in patronage matters related to the educational system.[32]

Cincinnati's black school system remained a source of pride among the city's African American residents until whites seeking to curtail the role of blacks in the city's politics resumed control in 1873, for they considered these schools vehicles for social and economic mobility, equality, and assimilation into the larger society. Black teachers and administrators, unlike those in most other northern cities, earned salaries comparable to those of whites, thus helping to establish an economically viable group within the black community. These men and women also either headed or influenced a broad range of voluntary organizations that strengthened the fabric of black Cincinnati. Equally important, the system provided employment for carpenters, janitors, and others who maintained the school buildings and sent teachers into other northern communities and the South. Finally, graduates of the intermediary and high schools dominated the professions in Cincinnati's black community. Indeed, the city's white schools were in fact less successful in creating such opportunities for poor and working-class whites.[33]

Under the leadership of men like William Parham, who served as superintendent of the black public school system for a decade, and Peter H. Clark, the principal of Gaines High School for two decades, the system was managed efficiently and professionally. These and other black educators showed a genuine concern for the students, regularly visiting them in their homes, seeking to determine why attendance was often low, and training and mentoring those who decided to enter the teaching profession. They and the members of the school board also tried their best to provide schools that were conveniently located for students and to develop curricula comparable to those for white pupils.[34]

Cincinnati's black public school system served as such a potent model of efficiency and relative autonomy that other northern African Americans sought to emulate it. In the late 1860s, black equal rights leaders in Columbus urged the Ohio legislature to amend the special law for Cincinnati so as to include their own racially separate schools.[35] Likewise, in Indiana, which excluded blacks from the public schools until the late 1860s, an appeal by the Indiana Convention of Colored Men called on the legislature to establish schools that would function under the supervision of a board elected by African American males.[36] Though unsuccessful, these efforts indicate that many blacks yearned for a greater degree of control over the schools in their communities.

Yet it is instructive that Peter Clark, the longtime principal of the black high school in Cincinnati and at times an outspoken defender of all-black public schools, was painfully aware that, because the white power structure established funding levels for the black system, their schools, like nearly all other separate black schools across the North, were inferior to the white schools in nearly every respect. Even though the physical plant and equipment in the black system were often antiquated and inadequate, the white city council routinely denied funds for improving the existing structures or building new schools in the inner city. In some districts, the older black schools were replaced by abandoned white schools, which then stood as symbols of inferior black education. Moreover, notwithstanding the efforts by black education officials to locate schools near the black neighborhoods that were found in ten of the city's twenty-five wards, inadequate funding severely limited the number of black public schools. Indeed, a primary school as well as both the intermediate and high schools were housed in one building. Consequently, class sizes tended to be high; overcrowding was a constant problem.[37]

A significant disparity also existed between the curricula at Gaines High School and the white high schools in Cincinnati. While Gaines offered a three-year course of study, the white high schools provided four years. In addition, a number of courses were not taught at Gaines, in part because blacks were not trained to teach them. Not surprisingly, inferior facilities, equipment, libraries, and curricula meant that black students lagged behind their white counterparts academically, and far more whites than African Americans were found in the higher grades.[38]

These harsh realities forced Clark to confront a difficult dilemma. On the one hand, he was concerned about the potentially negative impact of school integration on the black community, especially on black children who might well be subjected to white prejudice in racially mixed schools, and he fully understood that desegregation would cost him and his black colleagues their careers as educators. On the other hand, he acknowledged that, notwithstanding the herculean efforts of black educators, Gaines High School could not begin to compare, either quantitatively or qualitatively, with the white high schools in the city. In the end, he was prepared to sacrifice his position for the advantages that racially mixed schools offered and was confident that most African Americans in Ohio favored school integration.[39]

Strategies to Achieve Equality

In their assault on racially segregated public schools (and, in some states, exclusion from the public schools), Clark and other equal rights activists developed a multifaceted and sophisticated set of arguments, which they hoped would persuade white public officials and voters to end discriminatory policies. Much as they did in their campaign for suffrage rights, they appealed to whites in the name of patriotism, republican principles, morality, and basic fairness. But on the school issue, they also emphasized a number of practical considerations in a calculated effort to convince whites that public school integration would benefit both races.

Perhaps the most sweeping assertion of equal educational rights was grounded in the conviction that the public schools existed for the benefit of all Americans, without artificial barriers or agendas. The *Christian Recorder* emphatically declared in 1870: "*We want no colored schools....* Our country must be homogeneous. No schools for race or sect ought to be tolerated much less provided for. Let the nation be the instructor of all her children." Racially separate schools, the editor concluded, were "inspired by the stupid devilish monster prejudice—a monster who has neither eyes, nor ears, nor taste, nor feeling."[40] Others focused on more specific benefits that would accrue from school desegregation. A contributor to the *Pacific Appeal* asserted that, while "class schools" always provided a defective education, a concerted effort to mingle the races would make the schools "really efficient" and create a productive spirit of competition. The *Christian Recorder* went even further in extolling the virtues of "common" schools, arguing that black and white children would come to know better the character of the other group.[41]

In their campaign against what they termed "caste schools," northern black activists looked back—much as they did in their quest for suffrage rights—to the Revolutionary era for inspiration and guidance. The *Pacific Appeal* spoke for many proponents of school integration when it charged that segregated public schools for blacks were contrary to the principles of democracy, as enunciated in the Declaration of Independence and the Constitution. For states or communities to provide an inferior education, or no education at all, based on color, condition, or nationality, they reasoned, not only created an ignorant, and therefore dangerous, element that would prove detrimental to the interests of all Americans; by distributing public benefits unequally in society, such a system also violated the constitutional guarantee of a republican form of government.[42]

African Americans consciously connected this guarantee to the Revolutionary principle of "no taxation without representation." A speaker at a convention held in Galesburg, Illinois, in 1866 proclaimed that taxation without representation was contrary to republican institutions. This assertion resonated with many northern blacks not only because it reflected their steadfast attachment to liberty and equal rights but also because it related, in fundamental ways, to their hopes and aspirations for themselves and their children. Much as in Cincinnati, white officials in many northern states and communities systematically underfunded the black schools, even though African Americans paid the same taxes as whites. It was an especially emotional issue for a large number of blacks in states such as Pennsylvania, Ohio, California, and Nevada, where they paid school taxes yet were excluded from the public schools because an insufficient number of school-age black children resided in a particular district.[43] As the *Pacific Appeal* pointedly reminded the California legislature in 1871, state authorities had forgotten that "the Public Schools are public institutions, and that all citizens are taxed in common to support them as public institutions"[44]

In Nevada and Indiana, African Americans were either completely or generally barred from the public schools. At the end of the Civil War, black Nevadans complained bitterly that, although they paid hundreds of thousands of dollars in taxes each year on real and personal property, they enjoyed no access to public school funds. A black Nevada meeting asked in 1866 whether African Americans should be compelled to pay taxes for the education of whites when their own children were doomed to grow up in ignorance.[45] In Indiana, by contrast, property owned by African Americans was exempt from taxes levied for education, but they were also denied access to the public schools. In a memorial to the legislature in 1866, the Indiana Convention of Colored Men pointed out that three thousand five hundred blacks in the state owned real estate and personal property worth millions of dollars. This property, if taxed for the support of black education, they asserted, would significantly enhance the school fund. Thus, the delegates petitioned the legislature to tax blacks at the same rates as other citizens for the purpose of educating their own children. A year later the Indiana Colored Equal Rights League convention reiterated this request and condemned the state for its "indifferent and unjust" refusal to devote a proportional amount of the public school fund to the education of African American children.[46] Determined to show that they were willing to pay taxes in support of public education as well as embarrass the legislature for refusing to act on this matter, Indiana equal rights activists agreed to levy a voluntary tax of twenty-five cents on every one hundred dollars worth of property owned by blacks in order to create a school fund that would be utilized in each county where it was collected.[47]

Northern black advocates of school desegregation also employed the taxation issue to appeal to the economic self-interest of white taxpayers. They did so by warning that uneducated or undereducated African Americans were more likely than those with an adequate education to end up in the criminal courts, state prisons, industrial schools, and almshouses, thus becoming a financial burden on society. Above all, they reminded whites of the costs associated with maintaining dual public school systems, asking whether it was practical to force taxpayers, both black and white, to educate relatively few black children in separate public schools when they could more economically be taught in racially mixed schools in their own neighborhoods. To continue such discriminatory practices, the *Pacific Appeal* declared, was to incur a "double expense in order to gratify prejudice." Peter Anderson specifically pointed to the situation in San Francisco, where taxpayers were forced to pay for the education of fifty black students in separate schools when there were nearly fifty white schools these children could be assigned to in their own neighborhoods.[48]

Newton Bateman, Illinois's superintendent of public instruction who championed education for blacks but also favored segregated public schools, concurred with Anderson on this matter. He noted that where few African American students were enrolled in a district, the cost per black pupil was five to ten times greater than that for white children. Thus, he hoped that racist policies designed to separate black and white students in districts with fewer than ten school-age black children would soon be repealed. If this were not done by white school authorities, Bateman stated in his 1874 annual report, African Americans should sue.[49]

African Americans similarly coupled practical considerations with principle in asserting that racial segregation forced their children to walk great distances to school. This problem was especially acute in rural areas of the North, where black students were often forced to walk several miles past one or more white schools on their way to the only available black public school. But this was also a common occurrence in Detroit, San Francisco, Columbus, and other cities, for concentrated African American populations had not yet developed in much of the urban North. Except in the largest cities, there generally were, at most, only a few black schools. Families who lived outside the older established sections of a city, where no designated schools existed, were the most adversely affected.[50] These realities imposed serious hardships on black students and their families. Such logistical problems, as well as the need for many children to work at an early age in order to assist their families financially, go far to explain why many children were either unable to attend school or were frequently absent. These difficulties were compounded by the taunts and threats they faced as they passed white schools en route to their segregated public schools.[51]

Northern blacks were especially angered by the inferior quality of the public schools their children were compelled to attend. Their indictment of these schools as inherently inferior to the white schools presaged, in many ways, the arguments presented by black educators such as Horace Mann Bond in the 1930s and by Thurgood Marshall and other NAACP lawyers in the *Brown v. Board of Education* Supreme Court case in the 1950s.[52] Much like the twentieth-century civil rights activists, the Reconstruction-era proponents of public school desegregation condemned numerous deficiencies in their schools, including inferior facilities, inadequate supplies, and shoddy equipment. In many communities, students were crowded into one- or two-room buildings that were cheaply constructed, unsanitary, and poorly maintained. With such limited space, a graded system according to age or ability was often impossible. In addition, meager funding frequently translated into an abbreviated school year. For example, Ohio's black schools in the late 1860s were, on average, in session one month less each year than their white counterparts. Inadequate funding also meant extremely large classes, and the lack of janitorial services often forced students to clean their own classrooms.[53] The narrow range of courses available to black students was equally insulting to many African Americans. At the Wilberforce School in Albany, students were limited to the study of the alphabet, reading, spelling, arithmetic, geography, needlework, and singing, because courses in algebra, geometry, bookkeeping, and classical subjects were not offered. Consequently, African American students were often unable to pass the annual exams required for entrance to the Free Academy—the city's high school.[54] In many other northern communities, blacks were barred altogether from gaining a high school or normal school education. In some states, such as California, African American students could not even move beyond the elementary level. These restrictions were generally grounded in the assumptions on the part of white educators and political officials that black pupils lacked the intellectual capacity for advanced studies. Even in places where African American students enjoyed access to advanced instruction, it was frequently offered either in a small room attached to a black school or at allotted times or in separate areas in a white school.[55]

In their attempt to bring their arguments before the public and to pressure state and local officials to act on behalf of equal access to the public schools, African Americans employed a broad array of tactics. In doing so, they drew from a common reservoir of methods utilized by the antebellum protest movement and those they used in the postwar campaign for male suffrage rights. Because public education was considered a state matter, they made little effort to coordinate their cause across state lines prior to the 1870s. There is no evidence that the National Equal Rights League, even when it was most active between 1864 and 1868, sought to orchestrate the education campaign, though individual delegates to its annual meetings did mention the issue. The evidence indicates that the state equal rights leagues and their local auxiliaries were heavily involved in this endeavor; in some states they cooperated with allied organizations such as the Illinois School Fund Association. The local equal rights auxiliaries often helped to coordinate the solicitation of signatures on petitions to be presented to state and local officials. These petitions, which circulated largely within the black communities, proved an effective means of mobilizing grassroots support on the school issue. Many of them articulated grievances that were germane to a particular community or state, while others expressed a generic desire to end segregation in, or exclusion from, public schools. For example, groups of black parents in Detroit and New Brunswick, New Jersey, petitioned their local school boards for admission to the high schools, while petitioners in California and Illinois demanded access to the public schools for children who were excluded by numerical requirements from establishing schools for African Americans.[56] Likewise, northern black men and women held numerous public meetings in their communities to discuss educational issues, formulate resolutions, compose memorials, and generate support for their cause. Most of these meetings were advertised and reported in the black press and in sympathetic white newspapers and were announced in the black churches. Much like the grassroots meetings convened to advance the cause of black male suffrage, these assemblages were generally dominated by middle-class professionals but also included cartmen, dyers, school janitors, and other working-class blacks.[57]

When white resistance to school integration and inclusion persisted in the face of this agitation, African Americans at times adopted more militant forms of protest. On occasion, this entailed a symbolic shift in rhetoric, such as the announcement during a Detroit public meeting in 1869 that it was now time to substitute the word *demand* for *claim* in their manifestos. On a more substantive level, they also resorted to nonviolent direct action—much like that employed so effectively by Martin Luther King Jr. and other civil rights activists in the 1950s and 1960s—to press their case. While local equal rights organizations may well have assisted in coordinating these actions, they often appear to have been planned and carried out by groups of black parents who believed it was necessary to physically confront public officials in their particular school districts. In an effort to close black public schools they considered inferior in quality to the white schools, men—and especially women, who viewed their work on behalf of their children's education as a critical component of reforms that addressed the needs of the black community—in numerous towns and cities withdrew their children from the black schools. In addition, mothers and fathers of black students marched into the offices of school superintendents and mayors to demand a hearing. Still others took their children into the white schools and insisted on a hearing, which they then occasionally used as the basis for lawsuits against white officials.[58] When their petitions, public meetings, and nonviolent direct action failed to produce the desired results, they at times mounted legal challenges to the denial of equal educational opportunities.

In the Courts and the *Workman* Case

Local and state courts served as important vehicles for attacking segregation and exclusion. Northern blacks turned to the courts for a number of reasons, including the desire to counter claims by opponents of black suffrage rights that African Americans lacked the requisite educational fitness to enjoy the franchise; their limited success in persuading state legislatures, local school boards, and city councils to repeal discriminatory policies; and the hope that Republican judges would recognize the inherent injustice of such laws and customs. During the mid- to late 1860s, northern black education activists achieved a degree of success in lawsuits filed in Iowa and Michigan on the grounds that, in denying African American children access to public schools in the districts where they lived, school boards and other local government officials were violating state laws and constitutions.[59] The first occurred in Iowa, where Alexander Clark, a prominent black leader and political activist in Muscatine, attempted to enroll his daughter in an all-white grammar school. When she was refused admission, Clark successfully petitioned a local Republican judge for a writ of mandamus ordering the school board to admit her. At the appellate level, the court ruled that, because the Iowa constitution required the state to provide an education for all children, school officials must justify, on a statutory level, any denial of equal access to the schools.[60]

In its *Clark v. Board of Directors* decision in 1868, the Iowa Supreme Court essentially agreed with the appellate court in holding that, since the Iowa legislature had not restricted admission to the public schools to whites after 1858, local school boards could not determine who could attend their schools. However, in ruling that the plaintiff's daughter must be admitted to her neighborhood school on the basis of legislative sovereignty—which the legislature could, if it wished, take away—rather than as an inherent right, the court provided little support for school desegregation on the broad principles of equal rights, due process, or justice.[61]

Unlike the *Clark* ruling, the Michigan Supreme Court's decision in *The People ex rel. Joseph Workman v. The Board of Education of Detroit* was affirmatively grounded in state law, not the absence of denial of access to all-white schools by African Americans. The developments in Detroit and at the state level that both preceded and followed this ruling in 1869 not only shed valuable light on the tactics employed by blacks to achieve racial integration in the public schools but also underscore the formidable obstacles that racist white politicians and education officials placed in the path of African Americans.

As early as January 1865, a black convention condemned segregated education in Michigan, especially Detroit. Of the many disabilities African Americans experienced, the delegates complained, "there is none more grievous to be borne than the imperfect and unjust system of public school education." While a good education was "one of the most desirable of all attainments," they asserted, in Michigan it was virtually impossible for blacks to obtain, even though they paid taxes earmarked for education at a rate equal to that paid by whites. At an annual celebration of the Emancipation Proclamation held two years later, Michigan blacks once again condemned the limited education offered to African American children as "an act of injustice and oppression."[62]

At approximately the same time, a series of events precipitated an intense struggle between the opponents and proponents of school desegregation in Michigan. This dispute, which extended over five years, pitted Republican state judicial and legislative authorities as well as Detroit's black community against the Detroit Board of Education and most whites in the city. In response to a court battle generated by a Jackson, Michigan, parent's attempt to force that city to admit his child to an all-white school in his district, the Republican-dominated Michigan legislature amended the state's general school law in 1867 to guarantee that all residents of a school district "shall have an equal right to attend any school therein." Passage of this law spurred black parents in Detroit to petition the Board of Education for their children's admission to schools in their districts.[63]

The Detroit Board's Committee on Schools subsequently urged the full board to defy the state law, insisting that the great majority of the city's residents believed the "distinctive feature" of separate schools ought to be retained. While acknowledging that the new state law intended to desegregate the state's schools and that the city's black schools "should be made equal to any in point of efficiency and adequacy of accommodation," the committee—and the larger board—claimed that because the Detroit Board of Education was the creature of a special legislative act, residents of the city should be allowed to deal with the matter as they wished.[64]

The board's members were motivated to defy state law in large part by their assumptions regarding white racial prejudice and black inferiority. Most whites in Detroit, they insisted, harbored "a strong prejudice and animosity" toward blacks; because this was frequently transmitted to children in the schools, it would inevitably engender conflict if black children were admitted to the white schools. At the same time, in remarking that most citizens must "move in humble circles" and accept "humble employments," its members appeared to contradict their stated objective of equal education by implying that all blacks could and should not try to compete with white students in racially mixed schools.[65]

In clear defiance of the recently enacted state law, the Detroit Board of Education continued to maintain a few black schools in the lower grades, which forced African Americans who lived in the more remote areas of the city to choose whether to attend those schools or go without an education. Consequently, in early 1868 Joseph Workman, a black laborer, applied for his child's admission to a white school and was refused. He then took his case before a local court, where a Democratic judge ruled for the Board of Education, even though the city's attorney upheld Workman's claim that, under the 1867 state law, black children in the state had a right to attend schools within their district.[66]

In early 1869, Detroit's black community rallied behind Workman by holding a mass meeting that included most of the city's African American men, women, and children. At this meeting, in which attendees vigorously condemned the discriminatory policies of the board, a female student recounted that she was not allowed to enroll in the high school, and several children bitterly complained that, when they were permitted to attend a racially mixed school, they were placed in separate rooms or classes. Such policies that forced African American students into "a nigger pen," the participants resolved, were the product of "an oppressive and uncalled for prejudice." Those who spoke at the meeting overwhelmingly agreed that Workman's suit must go forward, for the racial distinctions advanced by the board were clearly intended to show black children that "there is an inborn inferiority in the colored race." In its resolutions, the meeting angrily charged that the Detroit Board of Education had consciously sought to obstruct the execution of the law.[67]

A committee formed at the public meeting soon presented a petition to the board requesting that African American children be admitted to schools within their own districts and charging that the black schools were decidedly inferior in quality to those for whites. The board's Committee on Schools, however, rejected the petition on the grounds that the city's schools were now filled to capacity and that, indeed, hundreds of white children were also denied admission for lack of space. Thus, the committee resorted to a carrot-and-stick policy: it warned that if the black schools were abandoned, African Americans would receive no education whatsoever and asserted that the board had as much right to separate blacks and whites as it did to establish separate schools for boys and girls; at the same time, it urged that a new separate school for African Americans be opened in a church whenever a teacher could be hired.[68]

The Michigan Supreme Court was not prepared to accept the board's calculated moves. In his majority opinion in the *Workman* case, Chief Justice Thomas Cooley, a noted jurist, spoke for his two Republican colleagues. Cooley stated emphatically that, while local school boards were invested with broad authority, the school law passed by the legislature in 1867 in no way gave such boards the power to exclude residents from any of its schools because of race, color, religion, or "personal peculiarities." There was no doubt, he found, that the legislature had intended to give all students an equal right to attend the public schools in their districts. Thus, the court rejected the Detroit School Board's contention that it was exempt from the state law.[69]

Yet, notwithstanding the unequivocal language contained in the court's ruling, the Detroit Board of Education continued to thwart the desires of the city's black community and the will of the Michigan legislature and supreme court. While it affirmed the court's decision and the president of the board, a Republican, warned white teachers that to refuse admission to African American students probably would result in additional lawsuits and fines, Democratic members of the board used procedural tactics to prevent it from acting on the court's decision. Indeed, the board claimed that, because proportionately more black than white children were provided seats in the city's schools, it was not in violation of the court's order. Convinced that ambitious and naive Republicans in the legislature were determined to use black children as pawns in this power struggle, the Democratic majority on the board ultimately gave in and declared themselves willing to submit to the law, even as they condemned it as "ill-advised and injurious to the system of education."[70]

The Detroit School Board remained intransigent into the early 1870s, during which time it developed ingenious methods that, on the surface, signaled compliance with the court's ruling but, in reality, eviscerated its intent. Workman's child was admitted to a white school, but, soon thereafter, two other black students were denied entrance. In addition, when a black school was closed, the pupils were placed in a new racially mixed school, where two rooms were set aside for them. In a similar attempt to maintain patterns of segregation within individual schools while claiming that the system as a whole was now racially integrated, the board spent sparse funds to purchase single seats for the classrooms in the schools that were racially mixed so that no white pupil would have to sit with an African American child.[71]

The board's obstructionist tactics forced Detroit's black community to take its case back to the legislature, which responded by passing additional legislation in 1871 that unequivocally barred school segregation throughout the state. African American petitioners also continued to condemn the board's practice of assigning less qualified white teachers to the black schools than were hired in the white schools. In addition, like many other African Americans across the North, they insisted that only black teachers could instruct their children "in such deportment and principles as may best fit them for usefulness in life."[72]

Segregation is the Norm

The experience of black proponents of equal educational privileges in Detroit underscores the enormous problems northern blacks encountered in their quest for meaningful school integration, even where a sympathetic state legislature and supreme court sided with them. Black activists succeeded in desegregating some or all of the public schools in a few northern states during the mid- to late 1860s. They accomplished their objective in

Rhode Island by the mid-1860s and, with the end of school segregation in Hartford and New Haven, in Connecticut in 1869. Perhaps the most striking achievement occurred in Minnesota, which had a tiny African American population. In 1869, the Republican legislature enacted a law that banned school segregation and required that state educational funds be withheld from school districts that failed to comply.[73]

In most northern states, however, either segregation or exclusion remained the norm in 1870. For example, in Iowa, where the *Clark* decision outlawed segregated schools, communities such as Dubuque and Keokuk continued to operate racially separate public schools. The situation in Keokuk, which had the state's largest black community, shows that continuity could at times prevail over change. When the Keokuk Board of Education announced plans in 1869 to replace the black staff of the African School with a white principal and white teachers, local African Americans vigorously protested the plan and threatened to send their children to the all-white public school if their teachers were replaced. The black community ultimately prevailed. But, despite having a new school and capable teachers, segregation continued to deprive black students of a high school education and force them to walk a considerable distance to grade school. Likewise, although the Indiana legislature ended the state's longstanding policy of excluding all black residents from the public schools in 1869, in many smaller towns, where too few African Americans lived to justify separate schools, black school-age children continued to be denied an opportunity to receive a public education. A similar situation existed in California and Illinois, where many black children resided in districts where their numbers did not meet the minimum requirement for establishing a separate black public school. The situation in Pennsylvania perhaps best illustrates the persistence of school segregation outside of New England. Although a few local victories emboldened black equal rights activists to hope that "a mighty change" in public sentiment might move the school integration cause forward, the Republican-dominated legislature, fearful of a white backlash, refused to repeal the law that mandated segregated public schools in the state. Indeed, by consolidating the Pittsburgh school system in 1869 the legislature rendered it even more racially segregated than it had been.[74]

As the fierce and prolonged resistance to school integration in Detroit vividly illustrates, northern black activists could count on virtually no support from Democratic public officials during the years immediately following the Civil War. Thus, much as in their struggle to achieve male suffrage rights, African Americans made very little effort to convert Democrats to their cause.[75] Republicans, on the other hand, were often deeply divided on the school issue. A growing number of northern white Republicans—especially the Radicals—vigorously espoused school desegregation, in part because they believed that the party must stand by its stated commitment to racial justice and equal protection of the law. Indeed, in nearly every instance where school integration was enacted by legislative action or court decree, the Republicans were responsible for it. Yet, in a number of northern states, including Pennsylvania, New York, and Nevada, many Republican politicians and education officials who were philosophically opposed to school integration or fearful of offending their constituents on this controversial issue joined with the Democrats in resisting integration or only tepidly supported it.[76]

Once the Fifteenth Amendment was ratified in 1870, however, many black proponents of school integration and inclusion expressed the hope that, especially where competitive political races would enable black voters to hold the balance of power between the parties, they could effectively pressure Republicans to endorse their cause. Moreover, now that the black male suffrage issue had finally been laid to rest, they were prepared to devote most of their energies to the school issue at both the state and national levels.

4

THE EQUAL RIGHTS STRUGGLE IN THE 1870s

Having worked on attaining the franchise for so long, northern black men anxiously awaited the ratification of the Fifteenth Amendment in early 1870. Frederick Douglass exulted that this watershed event would mean "that color is no longer to be a crime; and that liberty is to be the right of all." In a similar vein, in an invitation to Wendell Phillips to attend a celebration of the amendment's ratification, Massachusetts black activists found "a smoldering enthusiasm" among African Americans as they awaited President Ulysses S. Grant's proclamation of the amendment's addition to the U.S. Constitution.[1] During the first half of the 1870s, black equal rights activists sought to use the vote as leverage to advance and expand the cause, especially by lobbying Congress on behalf of Charles Sumner's Supplementary Civil Rights Bill and by continuing to pressure state and local officials to end racial segregation within, and exclusion from, public schools.

Nevertheless, some prominent African American men were well aware of the Fifteenth Amendment's limits. For example, in criticizing San

Francisco blacks for refusing to sanction the call for a Convention of the Pacific States and Territories on the grounds that it was unnecessary in light of the amendment's ratification, Philip Bell reminded them that, because the words "or hold office" had been stricken from the final draft of the amendment, it in fact conferred only the right to vote.[2]

Northern black women, of course, had not gained even that right. During the 1870s, Sojourner Truth, Frances Ellen Watkins Harper, and other northern black women activists continued to address the issue of equal rights, particularly with regard to suffrage, from the dual perspective of a black and female identity. Unlike many white suffragists, they remained fully committed to equal rights for all citizens, for they demanded both women's right to vote and civil rights for all African Americans. Even when they adopted the strategy of the broader woman suffrage movement in calling for the vote based on the citizenship clause of the Fourteenth Amendment, or on a hypothetical Sixteenth Amendment, they emphasized the needs of black women.[3] Northern black women naturally tended to identify more with the American Woman Suffrage Association, which supported the Fifteenth Amendment while also urging suffrage and other rights for women, than the National Woman Suffrage Association, headed by Elizabeth Cady Stanton and Susan B. Anthony, which broke with the Republican Party over women's exclusion from the Fifteenth Amendment and questioned the fitness of most black males for the franchise. But, much as they had done during the suffrage debates of the late 1860s, black women often stood between most black men and white women on the issue. Truth perhaps best illustrates this tendency to occupy a middle ground. Although she spoke at AWSA meetings in the early 1870s, she also attended some NWSA meetings and lobbied vigorously for a Sixteenth Amendment, arguing that the Fourteenth Amendment must be reinterpreted in favor of women as taxpayers and citizens. In an 1872 protest, she and several other black and white NWSA members went to the polls in an unsuccessful attempt to vote.[4]

As a founder of the American Woman Suffrage Association and a major participant in its annual meetings during the early and mid-1870s, Harper was less inclined than Truth to occupy a middle ground between the two organizations. Yet, unlike most white feminists, she believed that black men needed the vote more than did white women. But she also condemned southern black men, whom she termed "ignorant and often degraded," for subjecting black women to their arbitrary authority.[5]

The Uncertain Politics of Black Male Suffrage

Northern men did not have to endure the double burden of gender and race, but they were painfully aware that virulent racism persisted among many northern whites. Convinced that the Fifteenth Amendment was as much a statement of an ideal as a concrete addition to their legal rights, Douglass pointed, with genuine alarm, to the escalation of Ku Klux Klan violence and intimidation in the South as well as the substantial control over voter qualifications that the amendment gave the states. He was particularly troubled by the abundant evidence that most white Americans had not forgotten the lessons derived from hundreds of years of slavery. "A bitter contest, I fear, is before us," he informed Charles Sumner in 1872, for 250 years of slavery had taught most whites to hate the skin color of African Americans, and the Fifteenth Amendment had not taught them to love it.[6] Other African Americans shared Douglass's concerns regarding the long-term viability of the Fifteenth Amendment in a racist society. While James Poindexter was convinced that African Americans would never abuse their political rights, he warned that, "should it appear that we cannot enjoy our liberty without putting theirs in jeopardy," whites would not hesitate to revoke the amendment.[7] His anxiety was not entirely unwarranted, for between 1860 and 1870 whites in only two northern states—Minnesota and Iowa—had actually voted to grant suffrage rights to black males. That the Democratic Party, almost to a man, had rejected every initiative that sought to extend equal rights to blacks was especially ominous. Charles Lenox Remond spoke for virtually all northern blacks when, in 1872, he bitterly charged that the party "is down with the Negro, down with Negro equality, and covered all over it is the blood drawn by the slaveholders' lash, the teeth of merciless blood hounds, the overseers' bludgeon during the two hundred and forty years of slavery, the murdered heroes of Fort Pillow, the victims of the New York mob, the barbarous cruelties of the Ku Klux during and since the war."[8]

Not surprisingly, following the ratification of the Fifteenth Amendment, which northern Democratic state legislators overwhelmingly rejected, Democrats in a number of northern states resorted to delaying tactics, legal challenges, intimidation, and violence to prevent blacks from voting. Many of these incidents involved local party officials who simply denied the legitimacy of the constitutional mandate. For example, in 1870 blacks in Circleville, Ohio, complained in a petition to Republican Senator John Sherman that "Copperhead" election judges had committed "a high-handed outrage" by refusing to receive their votes on the grounds that the Democratic governor had never issued a proclamation announcing the adoption of the amendment. Even after a black Ohioan successfully sued in federal court under the first Enforcement Act when he was denied the right to vote, local election officials in the state continued to deny the ballot to African Americans.[9]

Similar tactics were employed by Democratic officials in California, New York, Michigan, and New Jersey.[10] The Democratic press often encouraged—even applauded—these efforts to suppress the black vote. The *New Jersey Daily Journal* spoke for many Democrats when it called on whites to combat attempts to give blacks the balance of power in politics or to make them "the rulers over the white race." Based on its racist assumption that many African Americans were not entitled to vote because they had committed crimes, the paper urged Democrats to intimidate blacks who tried to vote by recording their names and addresses and checking their qualifications. Inspired by such provocative appeals, a white mob in Camden, New Jersey, attacked blacks who had just voted in the 1870 elections. More serious violence occurred in Indianapolis in the 1872 presidential election, when whites shot at blacks' homes, and in the 1876 mayoral elections, when Irish Democrats killed one black man and wounded several others.[11]

Philadelphia, which had the largest black population of any northern city, witnessed the worst political intimidation and violence directed toward blacks in the North. Even before the Fifteenth Amendment was ratified, a committee appointed by a black meeting in the city's fourth ward had warned Congress that, without legislation protecting their voting rights, "the disorderly element" in the ward would seek to prevent them from exercising their suffrage rights. Indeed, in the 1870 municipal elections, officials in the seventh ward required African Americans to have two white citizens vouch for their eligibility before being allowed to register; at one polling place in the fifth ward, all whites were permitted to vote before any blacks could cast their ballots. Many Philadelphia blacks voted early in the day in this election so as to avoid violent resistance by Democratic toughs; when a disturbance occurred, the Democratic mayor headed off a confrontation by calling in the state militia. Unfortunately, in the 1871 election the militia was unable to prevent a mob from attacking blacks and killing three men, including Octavius Catto, who had played an important role in the equal rights movement since its inception. None of the rioters in this deadly incident was ever prosecuted.[12]

The vast majority of northern African Americans supported the Republican Party because they knew very well what their interests were and who their friends and enemies were. A black New Jersey resident forcefully expressed the widely held conviction among blacks that generations of oppression had forced them to distinguish carefully between those who wished them harm and those who did not. Self-protection, common sense, and reason, he stated, dictated that blacks would not vote for those who hated them.[13] Other blacks were utterly contemptuous of those who assumed that African Americans' knowledge of political affairs had begun only with the ratification of the Fifteenth Amendment. William Howard Day, editor of *Our National Progress,* a black newspaper in Harrisburg, Pennsylvania, bluntly informed white politicians that to assume blacks were naive and uninformed concerning their true interests was "a very grave mistake." Peter Anderson fully agreed with Day. Giving gratuitous advice to black voters, he wrote, was both unnecessary and demeaning because, having contended against so much prejudice, they were as capable of discerning political realities "as those who pretend to teach them."[14]

Northern blacks aligned themselves with the Republican Party for a number of ideological, personal, and practical reasons. The most obvious and powerful ideological connection was the Republican Party's commitment to the principle of equal rights for all American citizens. Most northern black leaders also had long shared with white Republicans an attachment to temperance, morality, and law and order.[15] In addition, blacks often cited the very personal factor of manhood in choosing to cast their lot with the party. In frequently returning to the themes of honor and pride, they asserted that one's manhood depended, as Benjamin Tanner stated matter-of-factly in the *Christian Recorder,* on their working within the Republican ranks to ensure the death of the Democratic Party "by the popular gallows." To shirk this responsibility, John Jones asserted in 1872, would be shameful, for the Republican Party had consistently recognized blacks' manhood, in contrast to "the whips and chains of the pro-slavery party."[16]

There were also eminently practical considerations that motivated northern blacks to vote Republican. They were moved in part by the realization that the party was solely responsible for whatever rights and privileges they enjoyed. Consequently, as a Virginia City, Nevada, activist declared, African Americans were "under a never-to-be-forgotten debt of respect and gratitude" to the party. The other side of this coin, of course, was the prospect of losing these gains if the Democrats returned to power. Douglass articulated this fear most graphically when he warned his *New National Era* readers in 1871: "The day the rebel Democracy regain possession of the Government, if the calamity should ever again befall the country, every right secured by the colored man by the ten years of struggle we have just passed through will be at an end."[17] A more prosaic—albeit no less practical—consideration, especially for the black leadership, was that the party appeared to be a vehicle for self-esteem, ambition, personal prestige, political consciousness, and even employment for its loyal followers.[18]

Thus, it is not surprising that most northern blacks were profoundly troubled by the defection of several leading Republicans in 1872 to the Liberal Republicans, who supported civil service reform and a more lenient policy toward the South. They repeatedly condemned the Liberals for seeking to destroy the Republican Party and thus endangering the rights that African Americans had so recently achieved. The Pennsylvania State Equal Rights League denounced the Liberals as "the foes of a righteous government and of liberty," while Douglass pointedly informed a leading Liberal that "I had better put a pistol to my head and blow my brains out than lend myself in any wise to the destruction or the defeat of the Republican party."[19]

Agitation for Sumner's Bill

Northern blacks were keenly aware that their only hope of retaining and, with any luck, building on their rights as citizens lay with white Republicans, especially Radicals such as Charles Sumner. Thus, Sumner's decision to join the Liberal revolt was especially shocking to African Americans, for he had long been the leading Senate advocate of civil and political rights for blacks. Yet his decision, which was fueled primarily by his alienation from President Grant, did not lessen either his commitment to equal rights for blacks or their determination to work with him toward that objective. Throughout the first half of the 1870s, they vigorously lobbied for passage of his civil rights bill.[20] While they at times delicately implored Sumner to remain true to his principles, they frequently corresponded with him and other leading Republican congressmen and used them as conduits for their petitions and memorials on behalf of the bill. Indeed, the evidence suggests in 1870 John Mercer Langston assisted Sumner in crafting the civil rights legislation, which sought to enshrine in national law the Fourteenth Amendment's guarantee of legal equality by banning racial discrimination in public accommodations and transportation, churches, public amusements, restaurants, juries, cemeteries, and especially public schools.[21]

The five-year campaign by African Americans for the passage of Sumner's bill was national in scope. With the creation of the National Executive Committee of Colored Persons in 1869 and the launch of their crusade for sweeping federal legislation, equal rights activists throughout the country experienced a revived sense of being part of a truly national movement. The executive committee, which was headquartered in Washington, played a leading role in coordinating this effort. Led by veteran activists such as George Downing and Langston, it acted as a permanent lobby, meeting periodically with President Grant, congressional Republicans, and other federal officials. The committee also circulated blank petitions for activists to sign and then send to Congress and composed memorials to Congress and addresses to the American public. Perhaps most important, it sponsored national conventions in 1873 and 1875 that brought heightened pressure to bear on congressional Republicans as they debated Sumner's bill. The National Convention of Colored Persons, which met in Washington in December 1873, included delegates from as far away as Mississippi, Texas, California, and Oregon. At this convention, a delegation headed by Downing met with Grant and numerous congressional Republicans. Unlike the national delegation's contentious meeting with President Andrew Johnson in 1866, this group received a warm welcome at the White House, where Grant assured them that he would urge Congress to pass the bill. On the eve of the final debate on the civil rights bill in early 1875, another national convention was held in the city primarily for the purpose of pressuring congressional Republicans to retain the school integration clause in Sumner's bill.[22]

Yet this campaign was not entirely orchestrated by the National Executive Committee in Washington. The equal rights leagues in Pennsylvania, Illinois, New York, and other states also mobilized their members on behalf of the civil rights bill. For example, at each of its annual meetings from 1870 to 1875 the Pennsylvania State Equal Rights League, which in 1874 declared that Sumner's bill was "a measure of paramount importance," urged its local auxiliaries to rally behind the bill, sent petitions to Congress, and published addresses to the public. In 1873, the PSERL established a central committee to coordinate the state campaign, and it appointed delegates to the 1873 and 1875 national conventions.[23]

In their letters to the black and white press, petitions, memorials, newspaper editorials, speeches, resolutions at state and national conventions, and personal contacts with Republican politicians, northern blacks sought to counter a number of charges leveled by the bill's detractors. Many of its opponents believed that the Fifteenth Amendment should signal the end of federal efforts to protect the rights of African Americans. They therefore concluded that it was now time for blacks to stand on their own. Federal enforcement of unfettered access to public facilities, they insisted, would unfairly confer a special status on blacks. These critics also repeatedly charged—as they had done in the debates leading up to the passage of the Fifteenth Amendment—that African Americans in fact sought to achieve an artificial social equality based not on individual worth but on legislation.[24]

The lightning rod for much of the criticism was the bill's provision for integrating the nation's public schools. With some fairness, Democrats charged that northern white Republicans were hypocritical in pushing for federal desegregation of the public schools because most northern states—including some where Republicans were the dominant political force—continued to operate racially separate schools. Moreover, all Democrats and many northern Republicans warned that a mandate for racially mixed schools would destroy the infant school systems in the South because southern whites would refuse to allow their children to associate with African American children. Birdsey Grant Northrup, superintendent of public schools in Connecticut, reflected the thinking of many northern white Republicans when he asserted that the school clause would therefore "prove most disastrous to the colored people themselves."[25]

In response to these charges, black equal rights activists went on the offensive by insisting that such legislation was both just and necessary. They were especially adamant in denying the charge that, since African Americans already enjoyed fundamental legal rights under the Fourteenth and

Fifteenth Amendments, they desired that Congress legislate social equality. Much as they had done in the face of such accusations by the opponents of suffrage rights, blacks scoffed at such talk. Some, such as Philip Bell, contemptuously dismissed this charge as "a bug-bear" to excite ignorant people. "Those whom we would not associate with on any terms," he charged, "are the ones who most fear the contamination of social equality." Others chose to respond to this accusation by carefully explaining that blacks consciously drew a clear line between rights and social relations. An 1872 meeting of black leaders held in Washington asserted: "Legal rights and privileges accorded us, we propose to stand upon our worth, satisfied that society will regulate itself according to the instincts, the tastes, the judgment, and interests of mankind."[26]

This did not mean that northern black leaders were motivated to agitate for Sumner's bill more by their belief that gaining unfettered access to public facilities would allow the black elite to achieve individual success in a competitive society and to protect "respectable" African Americans from harassment by working-class whites than by their desire to improve the everyday lives of all blacks.[27] Prominent black activists indeed at times sounded elitist. They deeply resented white prejudice directed toward African Americans who were cultured and respectable, for it appeared to confirm their fear that, no matter what they had accomplished or how upstanding they were, whites would never accept them as their equals. Langston informed a black meeting in 1872 that if a black man were well dressed and well behaved and able to afford a train ticket or hotel room, he should receive the same treatment as any white man. In a rather similar vein, Peter Anderson complained bitterly about the "deadly hate" shown by whites when an African American "exhibits the qualities of gentility, or his family exhibits the proper or ordinary degree of refinement." The implication that blacks who, in James Poindexter's words, had "more mind, more culture, better morals and better manners" especially deserved better treatment and were particularly sensitive to discrimination was probably not lost on many in the black community.[28]

In fact, the leading men in the movement were not isolated from the black masses. They often attended the same churches, sent their children to the same schools, and read the same newspapers. Moreover, they mingled with a broad spectrum of the black community at mass public meetings and joined them in signing petitions and boycotting racially separate black schools. Many working-class and middle-class blacks also had reason to use urban transportation, visit amusement parks, or seek a quality education for their children. It was not as if the black masses were immune to the indignities heaped upon them by whites or were without aspirations and dreams. While a class and cultural divide certainly existed within the northern black community, it did not obviate the reality that all African Americans shared a deep-seated resentment of, and instinctive anger toward, racist laws and customs. Even Downing, one of the wealthiest northern blacks, clearly understood that nearly all blacks supported the school integration clause in Sumner's bill. "The feelings of the most ignorant colored man, in the poorest log cabin," he wrote in 1874, "is most intensely wrought upon this matter." A mass meeting of Chicago blacks called to celebrate the third anniversary of the ratification of the Fifteenth Amendment expressed, in even more forceful language, the widespread sense of indignation in the black community toward racial discrimination when it demanded "a discontinuance of the barbarous practices which refuse them those general accommodations without which they are subject to untold inconveniences and repeated indignities."[29]

Middle-class and working-class blacks alike were keenly aware that their enfranchisement did not mean they enjoyed, in the words of Langston, the "usual access to accommodations, facilities, and privileges." Langston added that, "legally considered," the black man's condition was "nondescript." Delegates to the 1873 National Convention of Colored Persons likewise pointed out that the partial recognition of their rights made the withholding of the rest "even more intolerable" for five million African Americans. This situation, which outraged and insulted African Americans every day, William D. Forten informed the PSERL's local auxiliaries, could only be rectified by "a real civil rights bill...with such penalties as will teach humanity to the imbruted, and compel the tyrant to loose his hold on the poor."[30]

Most northern blacks believed that the ubiquitous discrimination they experienced in the public sphere must be eradicated by federal legislation. Given their limited success in persuading state officials to enact equal rights legislation, they quite logically concluded, as the Pennsylvania State Equal Rights League asserted in 1873, that "The evil is national; the remedy must also be national." While some blacks were not entirely convinced that Congress had the requisite authority to protect all legal rights of American citizens, most agreed with the emphatic declaration by the National Executive Committee of Colored Persons that Congress had "supreme and unquestioned control" over the states in prohibiting racial discrimination.[31]

Because northern blacks agreed with Philip Bell's conviction that "we meet the greatest barrier when we present our children at the public school and are rejected," they naturally focused much of their attention on the school integration clause in Sumner's bill. In concert with their emphasis on an expansive federal authority under the Constitution, they articulated the themes of nationalism, shared purpose, and a common citizenship in asserting the need for a uniform national policy of public school desegregation. In an 1872 speech, Langston forcefully underscored the importance of a common education in the nation. "Being citizens of a common country, interested in the conservation of one government," he stated, "their feelings and purposes should be the same." A year later, the National Convention of Colored Persons echoed this sentiment in urging Congress to state unequivocally that all American citizens must be taught in the public schools and that they are a part of one nation, with a common identity and a strict adherence to the principle of equality before the law. Therefore, it added, there should be no barriers to admission to the public schools anywhere in the United States.[32]

Their relentless lobbying on behalf of Sumner's bill—especially its school integration clause—met with little success during the early 1870s. Even though Republicans controlled both houses of Congress, many party members opposed such sweeping legislation on constitutional grounds, feared a white backlash, or believed that the Fourteenth and Fifteenth Amendments provided sufficient protection for African Americans' rights. The ability of these Republicans to block passage of a federal civil rights bill led Peter Anderson in 1873 to grumble that, while the South was "thoroughly reconstructed, and is all right on the subject" of equal rights, the "Republican North" was not.[33] Yet these setbacks did not deter northern black equal rights activists from pursing their objectives. Indeed, the ratification of the Fifteenth Amendment had energized them to intensify their pressure on the Republican Party at both the state and national levels. They were inclined above all to connect the Fifteenth Amendment to their demand for unfettered access to the public schools, for they were deeply concerned that their newly-won political rights would have little meaning if African American children were denied equal educational benefits.

Unless their children were permitted to acquire an education that would enable them to enjoy these and other rights, the *Pacific Appeal* editorialized in 1872, the amendment "will be virtually defeated and shorn of all practical or lasting benefit to our race."[34]

Northern blacks' campaign for equal rights bore fruit in several states during the early 1870s. Progress was achieved on the school integration issue in New York, Ohio, Pennsylvania, Connecticut, and Illinois. Several cities in New York—including Albany, Geneva, Troy, New York City, Poughkeepsie, Lockport, and Buffalo—either moved toward or adopted school integration. In Poughkeepsie, for example, black parents—especially mothers—forced the issue by taking their children into the white schools. Following several confrontations, the chair of the city's Board of Education agreed in 1873 to admit black students to the white schools, in part because of the civil rights law but especially because of the financial burden on taxpayers the dual system imposed. The struggle in Lockport was more contentious. Angered by the Board of Education's resistance to integration, black residents petitioned and held public meetings in the early 1870s. When these tactics failed to produce the desired results, they boycotted the black schools and forced their way into the district's white schools. Ultimately, in 1876 the combination of the expense of operating a dual system and the effects of the ongoing boycott of the black schools led the board to integrate the school system.[35]

The struggle for public school integration and inclusion achieved similar breakthroughs in a few other northern states. Perhaps the most noteworthy triumph occurred in Toledo, Ohio, where blacks and their white allies, including the editor of the *Toledo Commercial,* waged a sustained battle for school desegregation from 1869 to 1871. Working- and middle-class African Americans in the city launched the cause by holding a public meeting in 1869 that condemned the gross inequalities in the city's public schools as "an injustice to a common humanity." When additional pressure failed to move the Board of Education to close the separate black school, a wealthy black man sued it for refusing to admit his daughter to a white school. Finally, following two years of black agitation that gradually altered white public opinion in the city and also instilled a growing awareness among whites of the cost of maintaining a dual school system, the board integrated the public schools in 1871.[36]

During the early and mid-1870s, a few other northern cities, including Pittsburgh and New Haven, followed Toledo's example by permitting African American students to attend previously all-white schools.[37]

Moreover, Illinois, which had denied black children a public education in districts where their numbers fell short of the requirement for establishing a separate school, included in its new constitution in 1874 a provision that guaranteed "a thorough and efficient system of free schools, whereby all children of this state may receive a good, common school education." State Superintendent of Schools Newton Bateman hailed this provision "with unspeakable satisfaction." Following his lead and confronted with mounting pressure from black activists, the legislature then directed school districts to provide an "equal education," though not racial integration, in all of the state's public schools.[38]

Following the ratification of the Fifteenth Amendment, northern blacks also lobbied legislatures in a number of northern states to strike whites-only suffrage clauses from their constitutions. Although the Amendment established, albeit in rather conditional language, suffrage rights for black males in all elections, they viewed such clauses as powerful symbols of racial prejudice that stigmatized and demeaned them. During the first half of the 1870s, their efforts to repeal these clauses succeeded in a number of states—including California, Pennsylvania, New Jersey, Iowa, Indiana, and Connecticut.[39] Another part of their equal rights agenda was the enactment of state civil rights laws. Even though Congress failed to pass Sumner's bill during the early 1870s, in 1873 New York blacks drafted legislation modeled on Sumner's proposal, which they then urged the legislature to enact. African Americans from across the state sent petitions to the legislature, and several prominent blacks lobbied in Albany. While the bill was being debated, the New York Citizens' Civil Rights Committee, which had been established by a state convention, also sponsored meetings in Buffalo, New York, and other cities across the state. At these meetings speakers demanded a guarantee of full and equal enjoyment of public facilities and services. The bill, which included a key provision that prohibited discrimination on the basis of race or color in the assignment of children to the public schools, was enacted by the legislature in 1873.[40]

At the Polls

The black vote was partly responsible for these gains on the equal rights front. On the eve of the Fifteenth Amendment's ratification, Douglass had predicted optimistically, "It will be a bitter pill for the proud democracy to realize that the despised Negro's vote was the weight thrown to turn the scale and change their past triumphs to defeats."[41] A very high percentage of northern black men voted during the 1870s; in places where elections were closely contested, even a relatively small number of black voters tipped the balance in favor of the Republicans.[42]

Even though some northern white Republicans reacted to black male suffrage by sitting out elections or defecting to the Democrats, Republican losses were more than offset by the addition of African American votes. These gains occurred where the Republican vote increased after black males were granted suffrage rights, where the black vote was larger than the Republican margin of victory, and where Democratic majorities decreased. A few examples will suffice. In San Francisco, the black vote helped to defeat the Democrats in the 1870 and 1872 municipal elections; in the latter year it was larger than the Republican margin of victory. A similar impact was felt in Harrisburg, where black voters were instrumental in shifting the city from a Democratic to a Republican stronghold during the 1870s. The city's eighth ward, where the largest number of African Americans lived, moved from a 63 percent Democratic majority in 1869 to a 53 percent majority for the Republican mayoral candidate the following year; the ward continued to contribute significantly to Republican victories in mayoral elections throughout the 1870s.[43]

The Republican Party in Philadelphia also depended heavily on the black vote. With 5,400 eligible voters in the city in 1871, they contributed mightily to the party's triumphs in mayoral elections throughout the decade. African American voters also played a crucial role in electing Republican governors in Pennsylvania in 1872 and 1875 as well as a state treasurer in 1873.[44] In New Jersey, where the Democrat-controlled legislature rejected the Fifteenth Amendment, the impact of the black vote was felt almost immediately, when the Republicans made sizable gains in the 1870 elections. In seven of the eleven counties where African Americans represented more than the statewide average of 3.4 percent of the population, the Republicans did better than they had in 1868. This pattern also prevailed in Connecticut, where the miniscule black vote enabled the Republicans to win numerous closely contested elections during the 1870s. The black vote was equally critical in Ohio, where closely contested elections were the norm. Because their vote total was often greater than the Republican margin of victory, African Americans were able to play a decisive role in gubernatorial elections from 1873 through 1883. For example, with 15,000 black voters in the state, the Republicans won the governorship by 5,000 votes in 1875; in 1879 the black electorate of approximately 20,000 exceeded the Republican margin of victory of 17,000. Likewise, the Republican margin of 7,516 in Ohio was smaller than the black electorate in the 1876 presidential election. And, though they represented only 1 percent of Cleveland's population, they often swung elections to the Republicans in that city. Perhaps the most dramatic reversal of political trends that resulted from the black vote occurred in Cairo, Illinois, where three thousand African Americans lived. Whereas the city had generally been controlled by the Democrats prior to 1870, the black vote enabled the Republicans to be the dominant political force there from 1870 until the early twentieth century.[45]

Inside the Republican Party

Yet because of their small numbers, racial prejudice, and the absence of a viable alternative to the Republican Party, the influence of northern blacks was often limited in party circles, as was their ability to achieve significant gains on the equal rights front. But these obstacles did not deter them from devoting considerable attention to developing strategies to maximize their leverage within the party. One issue that they wrestled with was how and to what degree—and even whether—to occupy an independent position within the party's organizational structure. The most extensive and contentious debate on this matter occurred shortly before the Fifteenth Amendment was ratified. At its 1869 annual meeting, the Pennsylvania State Equal Rights League debated a resolution stating that, because the organization had achieved its primary objective of gaining the franchise, its constitution should be amended so as to dissolve the league and essentially make it an arm of the Republican Party. Opponents of the resolution claimed that retention of a separate organization was necessary in order for blacks to speak with a unified voice and to vote intelligently. Some of these delegates also cautioned that white Republicans viewed black male suffrage above all as a vehicle to serve their own political interests. For their part, those who favored a close formal relationship with the party insisted that changing times dictated the transformation of the league's character and that the party had already done much to advance blacks' interests.[46]

In the end, the delegates appointed a committee to propose amendments to the league's constitution that would reflect impending changes in its members' political status. When the committee presented its recommendations shortly after the Fifteenth Amendment was ratified, William Nesbit, the league's president, urged that the organization continue to exist in order to ensure that all rights and liberties were protected. Following debate on several resolutions that called for changes in the league's statement of purpose, a compromise was ultimately adopted that stated that no alteration of the constitution or the character of the organization was necessary "except such as will make the League an efficient instrumentality obtaining for us an equal distribution of the school funds and school privileges." Thus, it would remain a separate entity but its primary objective would now be to procure equal educational benefits, largely through the desegregation of the state's public schools. At the same time, however, the league's members realized that this objective could only be achieved by working with white Republicans. Thus, it remained primarily a political organization throughout the 1870s.[47]

A few black activists in other northern states were likewise convinced that the time had come to disband their separate equal rights organizations. Following the passage of the New York civil rights act in 1873, a black leader asserted that, at least in his state, the need for such separate groups was "now happily past and gone I trust forever." Other prominent activists, such as Philip Bell, acknowledged that such separate organizations might well be unrepublican and repugnant to many blacks because they tended to engender caste feelings and foster prejudice. Nevertheless, most northern blacks appear to have endorsed separate black Republican clubs because they believed they would promote a sense of racial pride and identity and would prove an effective means of pressuring white party leaders to enact equal rights legislation. The Ohio Conference of Colored Men articulated this view when it warned in 1871 that, while they were loyal members of the party, they must retain sufficient autonomy to ensure that the party "go forward and not backward."[48] Even Bell feared that the party would never grant full rights to blacks unless they retained their independence within the Republican ranks. As long as African Americans had to contend for fundamental rights and privileges, he wrote, they must have their own organizations and institutions. A New York City activist expressed this thought most succinctly when he wrote: "We think that we can take better care of ourselves by maintaining our own associations."[49]

The political arithmetic associated with the black vote and the pressure that African Americans exerted on the party's leadership to recognize them as an important constituency within the Republican ranks bore fruit in the form of nominations for office and patronage jobs. White Republicans in Ohio, for example, attempted to incorporate blacks into the party by rewarding them for their loyalty. The clearest evidence of this may be seen in Cleveland, where John P. Green, a lawyer, was elected justice of the peace in 1873, thus becoming the first elected black official in the city's history. Green was reelected several times until 1881, when Republicans elected him to the state legislature. In addition, Peter Clark of Cincinnati showed that assertive blacks could at times win concessions from both parties when his threat of political independence leveraged a Republican nomination of an African American for the state legislature and prompted the Democrats to tone down their racist rhetoric.[50]

Some Illinois blacks achieved even more impressive gains within the party's ranks. In Cairo, blacks employed the threat that they would not vote for any ticket unless it included a black man to pressure white Republicans to appoint them as delegates to county conventions and as postmasters, county coroners, election judges, clerks, jailers, and constables. Others ran for elective office, including the Board of Aldermen. Likewise, even though African Americans constituted only 2 percent of Chicago's population, John Jones was twice elected county commissioner, and another black man was elected to the state legislature. Several other Chicago blacks served as delegates to Republican conventions and were appointed to a variety of government jobs.[51]

In Detroit, where close elections and a convention system in which party caucuses chose delegates to nominating conventions enabled blacks to be nominated for "balanced" tickets without first having to appeal to the electorate, African Americans were frequently selected to serve as delegates to city, county, and state Republican conventions. Moreover, beginning in 1870 at least one black served as a deputy sheriff in each Republican city administration, while others were appointed as postal clerks and carriers, clerks and inspectors in the customs house, city hall janitors, the city physician, the county coroner, and the deputy city clerk.[52] Blacks also held a variety of public offices and government jobs in Philadelphia, Camden, New Jersey, New Haven, and other northern cities.[53]

Yet, in the final analysis, northern African Americans received relatively few nominations or appointments from the Republican leadership, and most of those that were dispensed at the local, state, and national levels were on the lowest rungs of the patronage system. These limits existed in part because, even in those urban wards where a critical mass of black voters resided, they often represented a small minority of the electorate; in many cities they were also scattered across a number of voting districts. Equally important, by the time northern blacks entered Republican politics in the early 1870s, German, British, Scandinavian, and Irish Protestants were already, or were rapidly becoming, entrenched in the party's apparatus. While these groups certainly welcomed the black vote as a decisive factor in determining the outcome of various elections, they showed little inclination to share political rewards or decision-making power equitably with African Americans.[54]

These political realities prompted a growing number of northern blacks to complain that the party took them for granted and exploited their vote while refusing to reward them for their loyalty to the party and their ability to shift the balance of power to the Republicans in key states and cities. Some black spokesmen cautioned against appearing greedy or selfish in protesting too strenuously about inadequate political rewards. The *Elevator* expressed concern that blacks might become known as "a race of office seekers," while others were quick to reassure the party faithful that blacks should only be nominated for political offices or appointed to patronage jobs for which they were qualified.[55] Yet, much as with southern blacks, the sense of anger and disillusionment was deeply felt by northern African Americans, who believed that the party had reneged on its pledge to treat them in a just and equitable manner. They resented not only that little patronage was forthcoming but also that those jobs that were dispensed tended to be menial and poorly paid. They demanded respect from their white allies, as they had in their earlier struggle for the franchise. In expressing their grievances over the unjust allocation of patronage, delegates to a convention held in Philadelphia in 1870 insisted that they "be handled as men, and not as machines." In a similar vein, Douglass sought to enlighten white Republicans regarding blacks' sensitivity to such personal slights by noting that "they are *people,* and are ready to resent any undue disregard of their just expectations, and any undue partiality toward white candidates."[56]

Black Republicans often emphasized that rewards should be based on a group's loyalty to the government and Republican principles. The *Elevator* thus found just cause to complain bitterly about former members of the Confederate Army being appointed to positions in the California state bureaucracy while competent, loyal black citizens were ignored. At times their sense of outrage was so deep that they even lashed out at those who suffered similar discrimination at the hands of party leaders. Peter Anderson, for example, groused that, all too often, the freed people— "some 'Jim Crow Contraband,'" as he derisively termed them—were given preference over "more cultivated and educated" northern blacks in the rewarding of federal patronage, not because they were far more numerous but because they were "more obedient and willing to put up with the whims of the underling who may be oppressive or tyrannical in their commands."[57]

A protest meeting held in Chillicothe, Ohio, in 1873, which was organized primarily by Peter Clark, presented the sharpest and most wideranging criticism of the Republican Party's record. Clark and one hundred other delegates charged that the virtual absence of blacks in state and local government positions in Ohio was tantamount to a denial of full citizenship and "unjust discrimination." They were especially angered by the party's refusal to adequately protect African Americans from "the most flagrant violation of their rights." The party's record on these issues produced among the delegates a palpable sense of urgency and insecurity. Clark reminded the convention that they had assembled in order to "ask, and not only ask, but demand of them that they give us our rights," while the president of the convention warned that blacks must receive their full rights now, for the Republican Party might someday disappear and "leave us in the ditch."[58]

The speeches presented at the Chillicothe Convention reflected a growing conviction among northern blacks that the party's leaders were unwilling to act on their avowed commitment to defend and advance equal rights and privileges for all citizens. They were increasingly disturbed by the federal government's failure to move aggressively to stem the tide of violence and intimidation directed toward the freed people. During the late 1860s, they had occasionally expressed sympathy and support for southern blacks as they sought to adapt to their newly-won freedom but had largely focused on their own struggle to gain equal rights. Indeed, though northern and southern African Americans had at times come together to lobby the president and Congress on behalf of suffrage rights, some Northerners had been envious that the Reconstruction Act of 1867 paved the way for suffrage rights for the freedmen before northern blacks achieved them. But as they came together in national conventions to lobby for the Fifteenth Amendment and, in the early 1870s, to work for the passage of Sumner's Civil Rights Bill, they found that they had much in common, especially a deep-seated desire to have their rights as citizens fully protected under the U.S. Constitution. Moreover, news of a concerted campaign of violence and intimidation against southern blacks and the unraveling of Reconstruction in the South deeply troubled northern African Americans.

Under the Reconstruction Act of 1867 the southern states had been required to write new constitutions before being readmitted to the Union. The state constitutional conventions established the political parameters and government frameworks of the new Reconstruction order. These constitutions were quite innovative in that they laid the foundations of the southern public school system, provided protection for all citizens' civil rights, funded railroad construction, and established the basis for a new system of free labor. Yet the new southern Reconstruction governments experienced enormous problems from their very inception. Above all, the Democratic opposition never acknowledged the legitimacy of the Republican Party, especially because it was imposed by a northern Congress and relied largely on the support of the freed people. The Republican Party constantly reached out to southern whites in order to acquire legitimacy, but to little avail. In the late 1860s a resurgence of violence and intimidation that primarily targeted blacks was unleashed by the Ku Klux Klan and other white vigilante groups, with the principal objective the destruction of the Republican Party. These attacks posed a serious problem for the Reconstruction governments: If the loyal black militia units took vigorous action to defend these governments, it risked racial warfare and still more white defections to the Democratic Party. In all of this, the Republican Party was increasingly riven by serious factional strife; by the early 1870s, it was predominantly a black party.[59]

In the early 1870s, a growing number of southern Democrats adopted a "New Departure" strategy in hopes of minimizing northern military intervention. But their decision to eschew violence, accept the finality of

Reconstruction, and acknowledge the reality of black suffrage generally failed to persuade Republicans to fuse with them. Thus, by the mid-1870s the Bourbon Democrats came to power by emphasizing racial polarization and denouncing rising taxes under the Republican governments. This political strategy included organized terror and intimidation by groups such as the KKK, the White League, and the Rifle Clubs, which sought to spread fear among black Republicans. The Colfax Massacre in Louisiana in 1873, in which approximately one hundred blacks were murdered, as well as numerous other assaults on black and white Republicans, demoralized the party and drove most of its few remaining southern members into the Democratic ranks. By the mid-1870s, especially in the Deep South, the rallying cry of white supremacy had defeated Reconstruction.[60]

As the situation in the South steadily deteriorated during the early 1870s, the federal government generally avoided intervening in southern affairs so long as the state constitutions and labor laws did not infringe on federal statutes. Racial segregation persisted in many areas of southern life, but that was also true in most parts of the North. Although President Grant occasionally acted to restore order, he was increasingly reluctant to intervene in order to save failing Reconstruction governments, which he considered incapable and unworthy of being sustained. Indeed, in many respects he reflected northern whites' growing unwillingness to remain involved in southern Reconstruction.[61]

Even though most northern blacks admired President Grant, they wondered why he did not act more forcefully to crush the Ku Klux Klan and other white vigilante groups, which they considered a band of murderers who should be hanged. "Too long already," the *Christian Recorder* complained as early as 1871, "has the Government allowed its own authority to be despised and made to run riot." Thus, if Grant did not deal harshly with these criminals, the people should be made aware of this fact. Similarly, a few years later an Indianapolis convention demanded that the president provide protection for the Republican government in Louisiana against "treasonable mob violence" and urged the federal government to intervene militarily on behalf of Mississippi blacks who were threatened by the White League.[62] As the level of antiblack violence escalated in the South, the *Christian Recorder* became so frustrated by the unwillingness of federal officials to take decisive action that it tacitly endorsed a Tennessee black convention's call for an all-black state to be carved out of Tennessee,

Kentucky, and Mississippi. Such a proposal should not be criticized out of hand, the editor asserted, because neither northern nor southern whites really wished to be associated with African Americans. The editor was particularly outraged by white Americans' "placid" response to the Colfax massacre, charging that the nation "has shown neither pity nor wrath—pity toward the slain, wrath toward the slayer."[63]

By the mid-1870s, Benjamin Tanner's feelings of betrayal and disillusionment had become so intense that his denunciation of northern whites at times took on the tone of the jeremiads delivered by black activists on the eve of the Civil War. "God may be asleep as it were," he warned northern white preachers and editors, "but in the words of Sojourner Truth, He is not dead. And sooner or later, this nation will be called to judgment, as it was in 1860." He went so far as to charge that northern Republicans had stood by while southern blacks were murdered and disfranchised during the previous few years because "the North still hates the Negro; at least it does not regard him." Such "Negro-phobia," the editor concluded ominously, "will yet prove the death of this government."[64]

Applying the Fourteenth Amendment

Although most northern blacks did not share the sense of impending doom articulated by the *Christian Recorder*'s editor, they were increasingly dismayed by the fact that only New York, Massachusetts and Kansas had passed comprehensive civil rights laws. Moreover, while the slow progress made by equal rights activists in removing whites-only suffrage clauses from state constitutions can be explained in large part by nearly unanimous Democratic opposition as well as cumbersome amendment provisions, some Republican legislators also contributed to delays in bringing state constitutions in line with the Fifteenth Amendment. In addition, the Indiana legislature chose to retain key elements of its Black Laws, which African Americans condemned as "barbarous" and a denial of their rights as citizens.[65]

Even in New York, the civil rights law had been enacted in 1873 in part because its provisions were watered down sufficiently to attract Democratic support. As some blacks had predicted at the time it was passed, the fifty-dollar fine did little to deter whites from violating the rights of

African Americans. Moreover, because the law was not well enforced by Democratic, and some Republican, officials, segregation persisted in many public places, particularly the public schools. In Brooklyn, for example, the Board of Education rejected blacks' petitions that urged it to close the racially separate schools, while in Newburgh, blacks achieved school integration in 1873 but education officials responded by placing African American children in separate rooms.[66]

The effort to desegregate the public schools was even less successful in several other northern states. Although Republicans in the Pennsylvania Senate passed a bill in 1874 that would have repealed the 1854 law requiring segregated public schools, several Republicans joined with Democrats in the lower house of the Assembly to kill the bill. Likewise, a bill passed by the Kansas legislature in 1874 exempted the public schools from penalties for segregating students along racial lines. The situation that unfolded during the 1870s in Oregon, which had a tiny black population, was only somewhat more promising. Although the Portland school district decided to end its dual school system for financial reasons, the Pendleton district denied blacks admission to a white school, then opened a subscription school for whites only. When the sole black family moved away a few years later, the district chose to reopen the public school.[67] School officials in Elizabeth, New Jersey, pursued a somewhat similar strategy. Boycotts of the black school in the early 1870s that were intended to open neighborhood schools to black children and to force the hiring of competent teachers, irrespective of color, prompted the Board of Education to close the black school. In the ongoing struggle between black parents and the board, it reopened the school in 1872, but low attendance led to its closure the following year. The board then reopened the school in 1874, but poor attendance resulted in its closure in 1877. Consequently, for the next four years no public school education was provided for Elizabeth's black children.[68]

Even when a state mandated "equal education" for all students and prohibited districts from excluding black children from the public schools, the laws were often difficult to enforce. This was the case in Illinois, for the 1874 school law provided no penalties to compel compliance. Moreover, while Newton Bateman, the state superintendent of schools, applauded this law, he informed African Americans that racially separate schools should be retained. In California, the situation was even worse, for the black Educational Committee estimated in 1872 that at least four hundred

African American children living in districts where they did not meet the numerical requirement received no education. Even where their numbers warranted a separate school, black students were often not allowed beyond the third or fourth grade, and never beyond the primary level. The situation in Indiana was far worse. In his 1874–1875 report, the state superintendent of public instruction stated that many communities continued to provide no education for black children. The school law's reference to "such other means of education," he noted with obvious disappointment, in fact meant, especially in rural areas where few African Americans lived, "let the children grow up in ignorance."[69]

During the first half of the 1870s, northern blacks increasingly turned to the state courts for redress of their grievances in part because their lobbying of state legislatures had achieved only limited success, even in states such as Pennsylvania and Illinois, where Republicans were generally the dominant political force. They also resorted to legal action because, within the judicial system, they at least theoretically had as much opportunity as larger and more powerful groups to convince judges of the justice of their complaints, and the Fourteenth Amendment seemed to provide a firm legal basis for challenging discriminatory laws and practices.

Although many northern blacks were poor and marginalized, and no organization such as the National Association for the Advancement of Colored People existed at the time to coordinate the legal struggle against racial discrimination, they actively asserted their civil rights in the state courts. They considered the Fourteenth Amendment's guarantee of equality before the law a potentially powerful weapon, especially against segregation within, and exclusion from, the public schools. A convention held in Stockton, California, in 1871 reflected this optimism when it declared that the amendment gave African Americans full educational privileges that could not be obtained in "caste" schools. However, their hopes were dashed: legal historians have shown that, in cases related to racially segregated public schools, northern state courts during the 1870s in fact consistently foreshadowed the U.S. Supreme Court's 1896 decision in *Plessy v. Ferguson* by forging the doctrine of "separate but equal" in regard to public education.[70]

The Ohio Supreme Court's ruling in *State ex rel. Garnes v. McCann* in 1871 served as an important precedent for other northern state supreme court decisions regarding segregated public education during the 1870s.

The case was initiated by William Garnes, who applied to the courts for a writ of mandamus to compel school authorities to admit his three children to the white public schools. Garnes's attorney argued that the 1864 Ohio law authorizing a classification of students on the basis of color contravened the privileges and immunities clause of the Fourteenth Amendment. However, his claim that an equal education was a "fundamental" right was weakened by his heavy reliance on the Fourteenth Amendment as well as the justices' conviction that he did not satisfactorily prove that the black schools were inferior to the white schools. The justices—all of whom were Republicans—reacted to Garnes's plea by narrowly defining the privileges and immunities clause. Citing the broad discretionary powers enjoyed by local school boards and state precedents for classifying by race, the court asserted that equality of rights did not require educating blacks and whites in the same school. Thus, it concluded that any classification which preserved "substantially equal school advantages" was not prohibited by either the Ohio constitution or the U.S. Constitution.[71]

A year later, the New York Supreme Court consciously followed the lead of the Ohio court in its ruling in *People ex rel. Dietz v. Easton*. In his suit, William A. Dietz sought to force the Albany Board of Public Instruction to admit his children to a white school located near his residence. Much as in the *Garnes* case, Dietz did not claim that the black school was inferior to the white schools. Indeed, the court held out the prospect of ruling for Dietz's children if he had been able to prove that the black schools were "materially objectionable." Dietz's suit was also rendered problematic by the fact that, since there was only one school district in the city, it was difficult for him to claim that his children were excluded from schools in the district where he lived. In its decision, the court reiterated key sections of the *Garnes* decision nearly verbatim in rejecting the argument that the case fell within the purview of the privileges and immunities clause of the Fourteenth Amendment and in ruling that equality of rights did not mean that blacks and whites must be educated together.[72]

In the same year, the Nevada Supreme Court presented a similar argument in *State of Nevada ex rel. Stoutmeyer v. Duffy*, though the plaintiff's contention and the court's decision differed in some important respects from the *Dietz* ruling. This case was initiated by Nelson Stoutmeyer, who sued the Carson City Board of Education for excluding his son and other black children from the town's public schools. Stoutmeyer's suit claimed that the Fourteenth Amendment rendered unconstitutional the Nevada law that prohibited racially mixed schools because, even if a separate school was equal to the white schools in advantages, they "must differ essentially in their spirit and character." Unlike the *Garnes* and *Dietz* rulings, the Nevada court gave Stoutmeyer a partial victory on the grounds that, since there were few racially separate schools for African Americans, many black children were in fact denied an education. Yet, while the justices conceded that the school law was contrary to the spirit of the U.S. Constitution, they refused to cite the Fourteenth Amendment as a basis for their decision, because the state statute was "not obnoxious to the letter." Thus, the court agreed with the Ohio and New York rulings that local school boards had the authority to establish racially separate schools.[73]

A similar case came before the California Supreme Court, though the legal process not only was more prolonged but also elicited a more vigorous response from both the black press and community. The Oakland Board of Education provoked sustained protest when it refused to admit black children to its public schools on the grounds that fewer than the required number of school-age blacks resided in the city. Terming this exclusion from schools for which blacks were taxed "unbearable," the *Pacific Appeal* called in 1871 for a test case to be brought before the courts. Although the *Elevator* believed that a remedy should be sought in the state legislature because that approach would be more direct, less time-consuming, and much less expensive, Bell agreed with Anderson that, as taxpayers, blacks deserved a fair share of the educational benefits and that both the Fourteenth and Fifteenth Amendments prohibited all degrading distinctions based on color.[74]

By 1872, black Californians had launched an all-out effort to force the issue before the public. This included the decision to take the question of equal school facilities and admission to all public schools before the state supreme court. They hired a prominent white attorney and raised money throughout the state for legal expenses. The lawyer soon chose the case of Mary Frances Ward as the basis for legal action, claiming that Noah Floyd, a school principal, had violated her rights under the Thirteenth and Fourteenth Amendments when he refused to admit her to a white school. Citing decisions handed down in the *Clark* and *Workman* cases in Iowa and Michigan, respectively, in the late 1860s, he argued that boards of education could not require black students to attend separate schools.[75]

Although the *Elevator* predicted confidently in 1872 that the California Supreme Court would strike down the discriminatory school law "more from a sense of right and justice than from any political affinities," the case dragged on without a decision being rendered, and African Americans became increasingly impatient and angry. A convention held in 1873 criticized the court's temporizing as a tacit acknowledgement that it stood "on the side of unholy class proscription."[76] When the court finally presented its opinion in *Ward v. Floyd* in 1874, its decision—deeply influenced by the *Garnes* and *Dietz* rulings as well as the U.S. Supreme Court's 1873 ruling in the *Slaughterhouse* cases, which declared that the privileges and immunities clause of the Fourteenth Amendment did not apply to citizens of a state—asserted that the right to attend California's public schools was a privilege of state, not national, citizenship. Yet, at the same time, the justices, concurring with the plaintiff's contention that access to education was a right protected under the Fourteenth Amendment's equal protection clause, held, much like the Nevada court had argued in the *Stoutmeyer* ruling, that state authorities could not exclude students from the public schools merely because of their African descent.[77]

Not surprisingly, black Californians gave the court's decision a mixed review. The *Elevator* chose to focus on the justices' conclusion that all children had the right to an education and that districts that provided inadequate separate schools must admit black children to white schools, while the *Pacific Appeal* praised the court for acknowledging the importance of the postwar constitutional amendments in decreeing that African Americans were now entitled to attend white schools where no separate schools existed. However, both black San Francisco newspapers found much in the opinion to decry. They were especially critical of the court's decision to uphold the constitutionality of racially segregated schools, which the *Pacific Appeal* condemned as a compromise intended to "satiate the prejudice of colorphobia."[78]

While black Californians were critical of certain portions of the *Ward v. Flood* ruling, Indiana blacks were incensed by the Indiana Supreme Court's decision in *Cory et al. v. Carter* in the same year. In one of the many Indiana communities where not enough black school-age children lived to warrant a separate school, Carter sought to enroll his children in a white school, but they were denied admission. The Marion County Superior Court accepted his contention that the 1869 state law mandating separate schools violated both the Indiana Constitution and the Fourteenth Amendment. But when the Carter case reached the state supreme court in 1874, the Democratic majority—relying heavily on its own decision in *State v. Gibson* in 1871, which asserted that the regulation of marriage was exclusively under the control of the state, as well as the U.S. Supreme Court's opinion in the *Slaughterhouse* cases—emphatically rejected the contention that the 1869 Indiana school law violated the state constitution, the Thirteenth or Fourteenth Amendments, or the Civil Rights Act of 1866. Underscoring their deep-seated attachment to the states' rights doctrine, the justices declared that, even if the Fourteenth Amendment required the admission of African Americans to white schools, the courts could not, without legislative authority, confer the right upon them, for the Indiana legislature had not provided for mixed schools. The 4–1 Democratic majority on the court then gratuitously proceeded to warn blacks that, if the 1869 law were held unconstitutional, they would be left with no provision for their education.[79]

Black Indianans were deeply offended by the tone and substance of what was arguably the most constitutionally extreme northern court decision rendered against equal rights for African Americans during the 1870s. In response to the ruling, they petitioned the U.S. Senate to have a proper legal officer of the government appeal the opinion to the U.S. Supreme Court. They were particularly troubled that the ruling encouraged white school officials to expel black children from racially mixed schools in a number of Indiana communities. Yet, because of a lack of funds and the realization that the *Slaughterhouse* decision obviated any real hope of success, they ultimately chose not to appeal *Cory et al. v. Carter*.[80]

All in all, the record of Republican state judges on the school issue was certainly far more supportive than that of their Democratic counterparts. Nevertheless, many Republican state officials agreed with the Democrats that the Fourteenth Amendment did not mandate the end of racially separate public schools. Even Newton Bateman, a staunch Republican proponent of equal education for African Americans, cited the *Garnes* decision in his 1874 report on the public schools in Illinois as evidence that separate schools for blacks were "reasonable, practical, and just—tending to secure the best actual results."[81]

Break with the Republicans?

This refusal by northern state supreme courts to apply the Fourteenth Amendment to the public school segregation issue was part of a much broader Republican retreat from Reconstruction during the 1870s. This retreat—especially among the moderates in the party—manifested itself in a number of ways: their states' rights orientation in interpreting the Fourteenth Amendment, their willingness to compromise on crucial issues related to Reconstruction, their fear of losing white support if they seemed overly zealous about protecting blacks' rights, and what appeared to be an emerging vision of a society and party in which blacks receded ever further into the background.[82] While many old white abolitionists and Radical Republicans remained committed to the equal rights cause, a growing number had either died or chosen to retire from public life; and, with the dissolution of the American Anti-Slavery Society in 1870, northern blacks had no organized group of sympathetic whites to align themselves with. Even some staunch Radicals saw fit to urge blacks to curtail their demands for additional rights and legal protection. The *Cleveland Leader*, which had long endorsed equal rights for all citizens, counseled African Americans in 1873 "to await the gradual work of time in allaying prejudice against their race and raising them to an equal condition of education and intelligence."[83]

Such gratuitous advice only served to intensify northern blacks' concerns regarding the Republican Party's failure to fully embrace the equal rights agenda at the state level, especially on the school issue, or to enact Sumner's Civil Rights Bill in Congress. As their level of frustration mounted, some leading African Americans began to question their devotion to the party. Many of these discontented black Republicans showed little inclination to bolt the party, but their anger was palpable. A correspondent to the *Pacific Appeal* complained bitterly that no other group as politically important as African Americans would have remained loyal to a party that refused to confer upon it equal educational opportunities. Peter Anderson was even harsher in his denunciation of the party for ignoring the interests of its most loyal constituency, asserting that African Americans were "fast becoming subserved and set aside, or conserved in the interests of men and measures to the great detriment of the colored citizens of all the Northern States by proscription or otherwise."[84]

Some northern blacks were indeed prepared to entertain the possibility of breaking with the Republican Party. By 1871, Downing had concluded that he would not stand in the way of those who chose to pursue an independent political course. If an African American decided not to support the Republican Party, he informed Charles Sumner, "it would require consideration on my part before I should feel at liberty to condemn him, unmeasurably, for not doing so." A short time later, Downing was much less circumspect in his criticism of white Republicans, declaring angrily that the party was inclined to treat the black man as "a political slave—a slave to be grateful for such pitiful allowance of privilege as the owner may be pleased to dole out to him."[85]

Peter Clark was even more outspoken in his endorsement of an independent political course during the early 1870s. He had long been critical of Republicans for their equivocation on the equal rights issue, and even flirted for a time with the Liberal Republicans before returning to the Republican fold in 1871. By 1873, his peripatetic search for respect and acceptance in a white-dominated society and party led him to propose that dissident Ohio blacks meet for the purpose of declaring independence from the Republicans. Clark and most of his fellow delegates at the Chillicothe Convention were especially angered by the party's failure to pass a civil rights bill both in Ohio and at the federal level. The depth of his disaffection with the party was such that when the president of the convention referred to "the party to which we belong," Clark corrected him by suggesting that it was "the party to which we are attached." In the end, the delegates concurred with Clark's sentiment, resolving that blacks did not consider themselves "under eternal obligations to a party which favors us as a class, only in proportion as it is driven by its own necessities." They then urged Ohio blacks to refrain from unconditionally pledging their support for the party's nominees.[86]

Other prominent northern blacks shared Downing's and Clark's determination to distance themselves from the Republican Party. In 1874, William Still and Robert Purvis, both wealthy and influential Philadelphians long active in the struggle for equal rights, broke with the party and supported an independent candidate—who was also endorsed by the Democratic Party—in the Philadelphia mayoral election. Still and Purvis were denounced by many in the city's black community as traitors to their race. In response to these attacks, Still vigorously defended his refusal to support the Republican candidate, insisting that African Americans would not advance their cause by simply voting the Republican ticket "as a matter of 'gratitude,' *nor* by waiting for offices from the Republican Party—never." Instead, he posited that blacks could only advance through their own efforts as well as the independent judgment of black voters who rejected the "political tyranny" of whites.[87]

Still and Purvis found support among some Philadelphia blacks who believed that their independent course represented a vindication of the rights guaranteed by the Constitution. In a speech defending his position, Still pointed to men who insisted that blacks were "at perfect liberty to make such a departure." Although it is impossible to calculate the percentage of northern blacks who were prepared, or at least threatened, to bolt the Republican Party, it is clear that their ranks extended beyond a few leaders. James Poindexter and Peter Anderson, for example, frequently reminded white Republicans that eight hundred thousand black voters throughout the United States could, if they wished, swing quite a few elections to one party or the other. Poindexter even suggested in the *Daily Ohio State Journal* in 1873 that disgruntled black voters were prepared to do just that if the party's leadership did not change its ways, warning ominously that black voters, "preserving the harmlessness of the dove, will not forget the wisdom of the serpent."[88] In a similar vein, delegates to a New Jersey convention vented their anger at "political tricksters" by announcing that they were "unalterably determined not to be guided by party dictation or party tactics in our judgment"; meanwhile, in 1872, a Fort Scott, Kansas, meeting held the Republican Party "responsible for all the embarrassments under which we labor" and hinted at the possibility of sitting out the upcoming presidential election.[89]

Still other northern blacks went so far as to vote for Democratic candidates. These men were motivated by a complex mix of anger toward the Republican leadership for failing to act on the party's stated principles and concerted efforts by "New Departure" Democrats—who constituted a minority within the party—in New York, Michigan, New Jersey, Ohio, and other northern states to entice blacks into their ranks. Concerned that the black vote might well shift the balance of power in favor of the Republicans in crucial elections, these Democrats accepted black suffrage as an accomplished fact, appealed to African Americans' sense of independence, jettisoned some of their most racist rhetoric, occasionally supported civil rights legislation, and selectively dispensed patronage to blacks.[90]

While relatively few northern blacks defected to the Democratic ranks, the evidence indicates that those who did resided in several northern states and that their numbers grew during the decade. A white New York City Democratic ward leader certainly engaged in hyperbole when he claimed that a large number of black leaders in the city were members of the party and predicted that as many as half of the city's black voters might support the Democrats in 1873. But several African Americans in the city in fact publicly endorsed the Democratic slate.[91] In addition, in Detroit dozens of blacks voted Democratic in the early 1870s, while several Cleveland blacks consented to be nominated for office by the party. A similar movement toward the Democratic ranks also occurred in San Francisco, Rochester, and various communities in Massachusetts, and several prominent northern blacks attended the National Convention of Colored Democrats held in Louisville in 1872.[92]

Most black Republicans reacted angrily to those who steered an independent course or moved into the Democratic camp. Sometimes they questioned the defectors' principles or forced them out of the party. More often, they branded them as traitors to their race and actively sought to shun and stigmatize them. For example, the Pennsylvania State Equal Rights League insisted in 1873 that black voters make sure that no black man associated himself with "the politically accursed whose hand, red with the blood of the law, was still lifted and ready to assault the temple of liberty." Occasionally, black Republican stalwarts, fearful that these rebels might well enable the Democrats to come to power once again, threatened violence. In Philadelphia, they not only boycotted William Still's coal business but even threatened to lynch him; Still was ultimately forced to call upon the police to protect his home from attack.[93]

Yet the differences that separated the large majority of northern blacks who chose to remain loyal to the Republican Party and the relatively small number who either adopted an independent stance or aligned themselves with the Democratic Party were often nuanced and subject to change. Frederick Douglass's evolving views on the relationship between African Americans and the Republican Party are a case in point. Soon after the ratification of the Fifteenth Amendment, he sparked an angry reaction when he asserted that blacks should vote as they saw fit because each person should decide which men and measures were preferable. In making such a suggestion, he exposed a central dilemma for African Americans:

Should they remain loyal to the party that had liberated the slaves and granted blacks fundamental legal rights or use the vote to further their own interests? Some black leaders condemned Douglass's suggestion as reckless. But at the same time, Douglass harshly criticized a black man who voted Democratic as "a social outcast, a fugitive and a vagabond, a Judas Iscariot, and an enemy of his race."[94]

Douglass could identify with the pain that Downing and many other blacks experienced in being marginalized within the party. Because of white Republicans' racial prejudice, he wrote in the *New National Era*, African Americans were "the ugly child of our political family, and he is put in the back room when company comes to the house; but he does get a peep at the company once in a while and may someday be admitted into society shocking the public taste. Until this good time comes, he will be snubbed, ignored, and slighted." He also conceded that the Republican Party was "grossly at fault" for not doing more for blacks. Yet he sternly took Downing to task on several counts. He denied that the lack of offices and honors for blacks reflected an absence of principle on the part of white Republicans and even lectured African Americans on the need for "wisdom, nerve, and honesty" to prove that they were worthy of such political rewards. But he was particularly offended by Downing's assertion that the two parties were quite similar, labeling this charge "repulsive, scandalous, and shocking."[95]

The debate between Philip Bell and Peter Anderson regarding blacks' relationship with the Republican Party was even more complicated, with both men shifting positions on the issue in an effort to locate an elusive balance accommodating pragmatism, principle, and political independence. At an 1873 convention Anderson told the assembled California black delegates that, since black voters had given Grant the margin of victory in the 1872 election, if California Republicans did not soon end school segregation and exclusion it would be proper to inform the party that there would be no more black Republicans. Convinced that Anderson's speech was both reckless and premature, Bell asked that the address be tabled. Anderson eventually withdrew his speech. But, in fact, in 1871 Bell had thrown his support to a Democrat for San Francisco fire commissioner. Three years later he and a few other California black leaders formed a new organization that proceeded to issue a manifesto of political independence. They would "go for themselves," they stated, in order to protect blacks' civil and political rights. For his part, Anderson, seemingly less disenchanted with the party, denounced Bell's organization in 1876 as an obstacle to moving African Americans into the political mainstream.[96]

That Downing and Douglass as well as Anderson and Bell—whatever their differences on political strategy and rhetoric—were all increasingly discontented with the Republican Party's unwillingness to commit itself unequivocally to the cause of equal rights illustrates the depth of disappointment and anger among northern black Republicans.

The Fate of Sumner's Bill

Perhaps the most devastating setback for the northern black equal rights movement occurred when, after years of relentless lobbying by African Americans on behalf of Sumner's Civil Rights Bill, congressional Republicans decided to remove the crucial school integration clause—which northern blacks had long considered its most essential provision—and a few other clauses from the bill in order to ensure its passage before the Democrats assumed control of the House of Representatives in 1875. Equally disturbing for African Americans was the message from many party leaders that they had grown tired of dealing with issues related to Reconstruction. The *Washington National Republican* spoke for many white Republicans when it editorialized in 1874 that "the negro question, with all its complications, and the reconstruction of the Southern States, with all its interminable embroilments, have lost much of the power, which they once wielded, to rally the voters of the North to the support of the party." The prevailing impression was, the paper concluded, that "we have done almost enough." Such sentiments go far to explain why many moderate Republicans continued to resist any substantial expansion of federal authority, especially if it entailed public school desegregation.[97]

As it became painfully clear that the House of Representatives planned to omit the school clause from Sumner's bill, some northern African Americans, though bitterly disappointed, chose to point to substantial gains in what remained of the emasculated bill. James Poindexter, for example, reported that many of his fellow activists hoped the right to travel on public transportation, stay in hotels, and serve on juries on equal terms with whites would secure for blacks far better treatment than was currently available in many parts of the country. Others, such as Peter Anderson, were either reduced to expressing the wan hope that the exclusion of the school clause would not seriously limit the bill's value or naively suggesting that legal action in the federal courts might force school integration in states such as Pennsylvania, California, and Indiana.[98]

But many northern blacks were furious. The *Christian Recorder* condemned the decision as a "monstrous proposition" and conceded that it might be preferable to see the entire bill fail than to have such mischief embedded in law. Charles B. Purvis, Downing, Langston, and other members of the National Executive Committees of Colored Persons concurred, charging that the House's action "legalizes and tends to perpetuate color and class discrimination as to schools and education." Indeed, one Massachusetts black went so far as to conclude that it represented the death knell of legal equality for African Americans. "Concede the impropriety of the co-education of the races," he argued, "and the whole frame-work of equality before the law falls to the ground."[99]

When Congress passed the eviscerated Civil Rights Act of 1875 and Grant signed it into law, it is therefore not surprising that northern blacks' reactions were rather subdued. Downing, who had perhaps invested more time and energy than any other African American in working for the passage of Sumner's bill, merely informed his sons that it had passed, while the *Christian Recorder* cautioned against expecting or demanding too much of the law. Because racial prejudice would "continue to show its teeth," the editor wrote, the measure was important primarily for its moral effects.[100] This sentiment was echoed by James Poindexter, who urged African Americans to exercise restraint and discretion in reacting to the legislation. Instead of engaging in "a struggle for abstractions—privileges of no practical value," he stated in the *Daily Ohio State Journal,* they should agitate for rights and privileges that involved their property and happiness. Most northern blacks indeed appear to have been torn between feelings of anger and cynicism and a sense of obligation to the Republican Party. Peter Anderson, for example, advised African Americans to regard the party as redeemed, if for no other reason than the Democrats' unconditional rejection of the final version of the bill. But, at the same time, he acknowledged that few African Americans were pleased with this "defective" law and condemned the duplicity of those "hypocritical colorphobia" Republicans who had long opposed Sumner's bill but now applauded and defended it.[101]

As they looked back on the years of intense lobbying for Sumner's Civil Rights Bill, northern blacks were forced once again to address two central questions: Was it possible to sustain a viable equal rights movement? And could they ever again realistically place their trust in white Republicans to protect the fundamental rights of all American citizens?

5

The Republican Retreat from Reconstruction

Following the passage of the Civil Rights Act of 1875, the moderate Republican *New York Times* asserted that there was nothing in the legislation which was "of very great consequence to the Negro or the white race."[1] This statement was far from comforting for even the most optimistic northern black. Indeed, they faced a very uncertain future. Many congressional Republicans had ultimately chosen to place political expediency above a principled stand on the school integration clause, which was especially important to northern African Americans. The message appeared to be that Congress would pass no more civil rights legislation. Moreover, in its *Slaughterhouse* decision, the U.S. Supreme Court had made it abundantly clear that blacks could not rely on the Fourteenth Amendment for protection of their fundamental rights. There was also every indication that the next president—even if he were a Republican—would not improve on Grant's inconsistent record of protecting the rights of southern blacks, and might do far less.

Fighting Separate but Equal

The *New York Times* predicted that northern blacks would not demand strict enforcement of the civil rights bill's provisions. "As a rule the negroes in this part of the country," it stated in a condescending manner, "are quiet, inoffensive people who live for and to themselves, and have no desire to intrude where they are not welcome." The *Times,* however, underestimated blacks' determination to file suit against those who refused them access to theaters, hotels, restaurants, and other public facilities. Notwithstanding their doubts concerning the relevance of the act's provisions to their daily lives, African Americans in Illinois, Minnesota, Pennsylvania, New York, New Jersey, California, Indiana, Kansas, and other states across the North during the first few years following its passage went to court in order to defend their civil rights.[2]

Black litigants were, at times, successful in cases where they had been excluded from—as opposed to being segregated within—public facilities because of their race. But such victories proved to be the exception rather than the rule. Although the Civil Rights Act granted broad powers to the federal courts, numerous obstacles stood in the path of effective legal action. The law placed the burden of court action primarily on black litigants, who generally had little political influence and few economic resources and often encountered hostile white public opinion.[3] Equally important, the number of lawsuits declined after a few years because federal attorneys often advised African Americans to take civil action rather than pursue matters in the federal courts. Many federal officials did not in fact believe that exclusion from privately owned establishments warranted prosecution under the Civil Rights Act of 1875. In fairness to these federal attorneys and judges, the 1873 *Slaughterhouse* ruling had undermined the constitutional theory that permitted federal officials to interpret their powers broadly. Consequently, they frequently limited their jurisdiction to cases involving state-sponsored discrimination. By the mid-1870s, such uncertainty regarding the scope of federal jurisdiction generally led the federal courts and the Justice Department to decide against attempting to enforce the civil and political rights of litigants.[4]

Their reluctance to prosecute those who discriminated against African Americans, in turn, increasingly discouraged aggrieved blacks from filing lawsuits and encouraged whites, including government officials, to disregard the law. Moreover, when blacks turned to the courts, they often lost. For example, in a ruling that the *Pacific Appeal* denounced as a "Judge Taney decision" (a reference to the lamentable *Dred Scott* ruling in 1857), a U.S. Circuit Court judge in California concluded that Congress could not require equal access to private businesses. Even more disturbing was the federal courts' consistent conflation of "separate but equal" with "equal." The final version of Sumner's bill—in accord with most northern state supreme court decisions on school integration—prohibited only exclusion from, but not segregation within, public facilities.[5]

The message to African Americans that they should not expect to be treated as the equals of whites came not only from Congress and the courts but also from other white officials, including those who organized the national celebration of the centennial of the Declaration of Independence in Philadelphia in 1876. Frederick Douglass was among the dignitaries—including President Grant, the secretary of state, members of Congress, governors, and representatives of foreign countries—seated on the platform at the opening ceremonies of the Centennial Exposition. Yet in a compromise struck by members of the Centennial Commission in the name of sectional reconciliation, Douglass, one of the greatest orators of his time, was not permitted to speak. The invitation to be visibly silent was, to say the least, humiliating for such a powerful speaker. To make matters worse, because the white organizers of the Exposition assumed that African Americans could not show proficiency in the arts and sciences, blacks were excluded from the Centennial's exhibits.[6]

Hayes and the Election of 1876

This very public, and painful, reminder by the Republican-dominated Centennial Commission that African Americans must not be allowed to stand in the way of reconciliation between northern and southern whites, coupled with the party's backsliding on the Civil Rights Act of 1875 and the Grant administration's failure to act vigorously to protect southern blacks from white vigilantism, led a growing number of blacks to question whether they should support Republican candidates in the 1876 elections. Some were prepared to leave the party. For example, on the eve of the elections, a group of New York blacks declared that, given the perfidy of the

Republicans, "there is only one resource left to the Negro, and that is to abandon the party that betrayed him, then to go to the Democratic Party." Others, including a number of African Americans in Detroit, argued that, in the name of fair play, blacks should at least listen to Democrats' calls for switching party allegiance. Still others, such as a group of black Liberal Republicans in Detroit, opted for an independent course. Convinced that African Americans' decision to affiliate exclusively with one party "tends to destroy their influence and injures them as a people," these Liberals resolved to support only those candidates who would best serve the interests of Africans Americans.[7]

Many northern blacks indeed remained profoundly ambivalent toward the Republican Party. Northern and southern delegates to the National Convention of Colored Citizens, held in Nashville in April 1876, expressed such conflicted feelings. The convention, which probably was organized by the National Executive Committee of Colored Persons, engaged in extensive debate on where African Americans should stand in relation to the party. Many delegates bitterly complained about the party's decision to water down the civil rights legislation and its failure to protect the rights of southern blacks. They also were deeply troubled by those white Republican politicians who talked one line and voted another, yet still expected blacks to support them. In the final analysis, most delegates were unwilling to defect to the Democrats. But their tepid endorsement of the Republican Party, after urging blacks to engage the leaders of both parties, reflected the deep sense of distrust and disillusionment that had taken root among African Americans.[8]

Some northern blacks harshly condemned the Nashville Convention. For example, a group of Columbus blacks denounced the convention's leaders as "disappointed office-seekers, sore heads and malcontents," and Peter Clark, who had distanced himself from the Republican Party during the previous several years, reported that, following the convention, the most vocal Nashville delegates had been threatened and harassed by black Republican loyalists. Clark warned that such coercion would mean that "the slavery into which we shall sink will be worse than that from which we have arisen." While Clark had moved farther than most northern African Americans toward an independent political position, blacks shared a very difficult, and recurring, dilemma: their fear of the consequences of a Democratic victory and their anger at white Republicans for betraying their trust. A Massachusetts activist articulated this quandary when, at a Boston rally for Republican candidates, he denounced the Democrats' "venomous opposition" to blacks' rights and declared that he was a Republican "from nature and on principle"; at the same time, he charged that the Republican leadership had "tragically" lowered their standards by refusing to provide political or moral support for southern blacks in their time of need. In the final analysis, most northern blacks seemed resigned to vote Republican because there was no viable alternative. Benjamin Tanner spoke to this tendency to endorse the Republican Party because it was the lesser of two evils when he stated pragmatically in the *Christian Recorder:* "A negative friend is to be preferred to a positive enemy. Such friends may not pull us up; but they will not push us down."[9]

The most pressing question that African Americans confronted in 1876 was whether to support Rutherford B. Hayes, the Republican nominee for president. For more than a decade, he had thrown his support behind equal rights for blacks. As governor of Ohio in 1867, he endorsed black male suffrage when it was unpopular with many party members. Moreover, he welcomed the ratification of the Fifteenth Amendment, informing Peter Clark of his wish that, with the Constitution now in harmony with the Declaration of Independence, "may the intelligence, virtue, and patriotism of the enfranchised people be so conspicuous in all our future history that no good citizen will ever doubt the justice or wisdom" of that amendment.[10] However, during the early and mid-1870s, Hayes, like many other northern Republicans, increasingly vacillated between supporting the progressive policies of the 1860s and reconciling with southern whites. He especially became disillusioned with Radical Republican Reconstruction policies—particularly the use of federal troops to prop up the few remaining Republican governments in the South. Thus, he came to embrace what Eric Foner has termed a "let alone policy," which would remove federal troops as an active force in the South, thereby allowing southern whites to determine the course of race relations and the status of blacks in the region.[11]

African Americans were understandably disturbed by Hayes's position, which appeared to presage the end of Reconstruction. John D. Bagwell, chairman of the Colored Republican Committee of New Jersey, which represented seven thousand black voters in the state, informed Hayes in July 1876 that, while blacks wished to support his candidacy, they could not do so intelligently without knowing where he stood with regard to equal civil and political rights and the core principles of the Republican Party. African Americans' status as citizens, he asserted bluntly, would not be fully established until their rights guaranteed by the Constitution had been attained "in complete liberty and exact equality."[12]

It is not known whether Hayes responded to this urgent request for a clear statement of his views on this matter, which Bagwell hoped would remove doubts and confusion among African Americans throughout the nation. But most blacks, fearful that the Democrats might win a close contest for the presidency—perhaps even, as the *Christian Recorder* warned, stealing the election and seeking to take control of the federal government by force—ultimately endorsed Hayes's candidacy. Even Douglass, who appealed to delegates at the Republican national convention to nominate Oliver Morton, an Indiana senator, and was troubled by the convention's refusal to recognize several southern black delegations, accepted Hayes's nomination as a reality. Indeed, during the campaign he frequently told African American audiences that the election was a contest between liberty and slavery and consciously downplayed Hayes's clear indications that he favored home rule for the South. Some northern black leaders even went so far as to endorse Hayes enthusiastically. For example, after Hayes's assurance that he would honor his pledge to protect and promote the welfare of southern blacks, John Mercer Langston, who had known Hayes since the 1850s, pledged to work "to make your election certain and triumphant."[13]

Following a prolonged constitutional and political crisis, Hayes won a razor-thin victory in the Electoral College in early 1877. The creation of an electoral commission, with a slim majority of Republican members, ultimately decided the election.[14] Once in office, Hayes continued to promise blacks that, as he informed a delegation from the African Methodist Episcopal Church, he would "care equally for all our people, and I assure you that the race represented by you will never be neglected by my Administration."[15] He also acted to strengthen his standing among African Americans by meeting with James Poindexter and Douglass while the outcome of the election was still unknown. Hayes recorded in his diary that both men approved of his "firm assertion and maintenance" of the rights of southern blacks under the Thirteenth, Fourteenth, and Fifteenth Amendments and his expressed willingness to recognize all Southerners regardless of their past actions. Moreover, he appointed Douglass as

U.S. marshal for the District of Columbia and Langston as Minister to Haiti. These appointments, which many whites—including most of his Cabinet—opposed, were welcomed by northern black leaders and cemented Douglass's support for Hayes during the rest of his term. Hayes, Douglass informed a man who congratulated him on his appointment, "is a just man, and his policy embraces the welfare of both races, and I rejoice at any evidence of support whether from the North or the South."[16]

Northern blacks urged the Hayes administration to appoint other African Americans—including Peter Clark, Henry Highland Garnet, and John Jones—to government positions, not only because they were eminently qualified but also, as the *Christian Recorder* pointedly reminded white Republicans, because the black vote had been instrumental in electing Hayes and saving the government and the party. A black laborer in Indianapolis wrote Hayes that, while he did not seek a patronage job, he wished "to see my race elevated and men of ability and character and honeste appointed to plases of trust and profit." But others, such as George Downing, emphasized more practical considerations: that these appointments would make Hayes's southern policy more palatable to northern friends of blacks and, perhaps above all, that he and other northern black leaders deserved and needed such political rewards.[17]

The Collapse of Reconstruction

Although Hayes dispensed little additional patronage to northern or southern blacks during his presidency, he continued to assure southern blacks that they would be safer than when federal troops had been present. Whites, he told a Nashville audience, had no desire to "invade" blacks' rights, and blacks would be "cheerfully accorded" every right guaranteed by the Constitution.[18] Yet it was painfully clear to most northern blacks and their few remaining white Radical Republican allies that, for all intents and purposes, Reconstruction had come to an end. Nothing upset Hayes more than the allegations that his southern policy seriously jeopardized southern blacks' civil and political rights. But his stated belief that their fundamental rights should be protected was in fact at odds with his support for sectional reconciliation and the creation of a truly national Republican Party; securing those rights would have required additional troops in the South, which white Southerners adamantly rejected and the Democrat-controlled House of Representatives would not permit. Indeed, his conciliatory approach failed to divide southern whites or attract southern Democrats to the Republican ranks, and white outrages against southern blacks inflicted no political damage on northern Democrats. Beyond this, most northern white Republicans, tired of Reconstruction, agreed with southern whites that the freed people were not prepared for equality. Thus, a broad consensus existed among white Americans that white Southerners should deal with the race issue in their own way.[19]

With the inauguration of Hayes, the South's rulers could, with no threat of federal intervention, manage the region's domestic affairs. The federal withdrawal of troops was an irreversible step, for any request for troops to quell election disturbances had to be made by state officials. All of these officials were now Democrats, who would not act. The Democrats—who termed themselves Redeemers—were committed to dismantling the Republican governments, reducing the political power of blacks, and reshaping the South's legal system for the purpose of establishing labor control and racial subordination. They proceeded to put in place new systems of class, political, and race relations. This was not accomplished immediately; southern blacks indeed continued to vote and hold office after 1877. But it became increasingly difficult for them to enjoy their rights as citizens. The new state constitutions that the Redeemers had put in place during the previous several years severely restricted the scope and expense of government, especially funding for public education for blacks. Equally important, in the Deep South and then in the rest of the region, blacks' political rights were progressively eroded through electoral fraud and the threat of violence. As a result of these developments, it became extremely difficult for southern blacks to mobilize politically. Thus, economic, political, and social oppression became the dominant reality in their lives.[20]

Hayes's southern strategy contributed significantly to this debacle. He not only remained silent when southern Republicans were brutally massacred by white vigilantes, he also appointed many more southern Democrats than Republicans to federal positions. This accelerated the demise of the Republican Party in the region, for it depended heavily on federal patronage for its existence. Thus, soon after Hayes was inaugurated, the Republican organization in the South was effectively dismantled.[21]

The collapse of Reconstruction was so painful and discouraging to northern blacks that some were reduced to fantasizing that either the "better classes" of white Southerners would someday act to protect the rights of southern African Americans or that blacks would eventually gain the respect of whites through education and uplift. Desperately seeking to understand, rationalize, and accept Hayes's southern policy, Downing shortly after the inauguration gave the president credit for "acting with good judgment" by attempting to divide white Southerners. Yet he was forced to acknowledge to Douglass that "for a time, I know not how long, there will be a continuance of confusion and outrage, including murders in the South," until the southern white elite would step forward to assist the landless and illiterate freed people. The editor of the *Christian Recorder* was even more inclined to engage in wishful thinking regarding the impact of Hayes's policy on race relations in the South. He not only clung to the conviction that Hayes would "put down all Ku-kluxism and Bull-dozing" and hold the "intelligent class" in both the North and South accountable for the way it governed but also even expressed the unfounded belief that "in the end, we will be the chief gainers thereby; even as we have been the chief sufferers in the past."[22]

Many African Americans, however, rejected such unrealistic visions of the freed people eventually advancing under the benign guidance of the southern white elites and the doctrine of self-improvement. Instead, feeling abandoned and betrayed, they proceeded to bombard the Hayes administration with complaints, organize boycotts of elections, and pass resolutions condemning the president's southern policy. As a black Ohioan angrily informed John Sherman, "Nineteen out of every twenty colored men I know believe the Republican Party wishes to unload them." A number of black Democratic clubs also were formed in response to Hayes's policy, and even the *Christian Recorder* was outraged by Hayes's decision to abandon Daniel Chamberlain, who had been elected as the Republican governor of South Carolina. This decision, Benjamin Tanner warned, would send the dangerous signal that, in the future, any elected official might be forced from office by armed mobs. Indeed, the editor soon expressed regret that Hayes had been elected. Even Langston concluded by late 1876 that, however sincere his motives, the president had effectively subordinated blacks' citizenship rights to national peace and prosperity.[23]

Some northern blacks felt so betrayed and devastated by white indifference toward the welfare of African Americans that they could see virtually no hope for a brighter future. Writing to William Lloyd Garrison as "an able, consistent and influential friend of the colored race" following the 1876 election, Downing and several other blacks in Newport, Rhode Island, poured out their pain and sadness about how northern white Republicans they trusted and respected had turned their backs on African Americans. "We are depressed," they confessed to Garrison, "things seem sadly out of joint; we are sick at heart through hope deferred. The declarations and advancement in civilization that are true of our country and that may be referred to make our condition deplorable. They make us more sensible as to the outrage we endure." While these men were all too familiar with hatred and poor treatment from whites, what distressed them most was the indifference to their rights shown by leading New England men who had once been their collaborators and friends. African Americans could, they acknowledged, endure, "with a certain degree of complacency," the insults they were constantly subjected to, but "the indifference as to the weak, as to our rights, and sympathizing with those who are outraging us...make cold chills come over us." What particularly enraged them was that, during the 1876 campaign, the Republican leadership had frequently told African Americans that the party could get along without them. In fact, it had desperately clung to the despised black man as its only hope. In light of all this, these men could foresee no other relationship with the party than "that which the South exacts of the colored man to become his defender though he is lord."[24]

The Struggle Continues in the Schools

Most African Americans probably could identify with the deep sense of betrayal expressed by Downing and his colleagues. In the wake of the *Slaughterhouse* ruling, the limited enforcement of the Civil Rights Act of 1875, the Democrats' control of the House of Representatives, and the implementation of Hayes's southern policy, they, too, had largely lost hope that the federal government would protect their fundamental rights. In a letter he wrote to Douglass two weeks after Hayes assumed office, Downing suggested that, given the mood of white Americans, blacks perhaps should become less active politically.[25] While Downing remained adamant in demanding equal rights, he indeed became less involved in the movement.

Having played a leading role in the cause for many years, he now chose not to go to Washington to lobby Congress. Other black activists likewise turned their attention away from Congress. Consequently, the National Executive Committee of Colored Persons appears to have become far less influential and active than it had been during the first half of the decade. Yet, unlike Downing, most northern blacks were not prepared to abandon their agitation for equal rights—especially unfettered access to the public schools—in their own states. Congress's decision to remove the school integration clause from the Civil Rights Act of 1875 and the Justice Department's reluctance to enforce the act's provisions meant that it was necessary to focus their energies on state and local policies. Moreover, they still enjoyed political rights, and they were determined to use the vote as leverage to pressure the political parties to end racial discrimination, especially in the public schools.

Despite their serious doubts concerning the Republican Party's commitment to equal rights for all citizens, most northern blacks remained loyal to the party. They did so in part because they realized that whatever success they had achieved on the equal rights front had come at the hands of the Republicans. At the same time, they were increasingly alarmed by the resurgence of the Democratic Party in key northern states such as Ohio, New York, and Pennsylvania. For these reasons, the Pennsylvania State Equal Rights League adopted a new constitution in 1878 that included, as a condition for membership, a pledge to support all Republican candidates. In a similar vein, Peter Anderson urged blacks to give up their separate Republican clubs and work hand in hand with whites in the party.[26] Nevertheless, blacks occasionally supported Democratic candidates in order to punish Republicans. In Philadelphia, for example, black voters, angered by white Republicans' refusal to dispense patronage to African Americans, helped to elect a Democrat as city controller in 1877. In the same year, Connecticut blacks reacted to Republicans' refusal to make black battalions regular members of the state militia by providing the margin of victory for the Democrats in municipal elections in Hartford and Bridgeport.[27]

During the last half of the 1870s, northern blacks used the vote, as well as mass meetings, petitions, and boycotts, to achieve progress on the school issue in several northern states. One of their most notable triumphs occurred in California. Undeterred by the state supreme court's ruling in *Ward v. Flood* in 1874, which upheld the constitutionality of racially separate public schools, African American parents in San Francisco launched a boycott of the city's black schools. The Board of Education resisted this pressure. However, faced with a prolonged boycott and the cost of maintaining a dual school system in the midst of an economic depression, the board opened all of the city's schools to blacks in 1875. African Americans quickly took advantage of the new policy, as shown by the dramatic drop in absentee rates for black students, from 40 percent in 1875 to 17 percent in 1880. Across the state, African Americans emulated the strategy employed in San Francisco.[28]

African Americans in Stockton pursued a similar course. Separate black elementary schools were maintained in Stockton until 1876, and a high school education continued to be unavailable to African American students. In order to delay admitting blacks to the white high school, the superintendent facilitated the admission of black pupils to the San Francisco high school. But blacks continued to press for full access to the city's public schools, holding public meetings, circulating petitions, and writing letters to both black and white newspapers in the area. They finally prevailed in the face of stiff white resistance. In 1878, Republican officials relented and permitted black students to attend the two highest grammar school grades; two years later, the Stockton Board of Education abolished separate schools throughout the city.[29]

Such pressure by African Americans had a significant impact on public officials throughout California. The state's superintendent of public instruction reported in 1880 that the number of black public schools in the state had declined from thirteen in 1876, to seven in 1878, to none at the end of the decade. In 1880, the Republican-dominated legislature acknowledged this reality by repealing all statutes that mandated separate schools for African Americans (though not for the Chinese). This move prompted the 1880 State Colored Convention to urge all black parents to send their children to the nearest schools, with the expectation that they would be admitted.[30]

There were similar successes in other states as well. In Ohio, where African Americans could determine the outcome of closely contested elections, they succeeded in 1878 in pressuring the Democrats, whose "New Departure" strategy included attempts to attract black voters, to repeal the statute excluding blacks from the public schools where fewer than twenty school-age black children resided. In addition, persistent lobbying and petitioning by African Americans in Kansas prompted the legislature in 1876 to strike the clause in the state constitution that mandated racially separate public schools.[31]

As the 1870s came to a close, northern black equal rights activists in many states could point to real progress on the school issue: no black child was prohibited by law from attending a public school, and a growing number of northern states had banned racially separate schools.[32] Yet, unlike the situation in the South, where Reconstruction effectively ended with the collapse of the last of the Republican state governments in 1877, there was no clear dividing line that pointed to the conclusion of Reconstruction in the North. Indeed, the equal rights struggle continued into the 1880s, not only on the school issue but also on state civil rights legislation.

After years of failing to convince legislators to end racial segregation in the public schools, equal rights activists in Pennsylvania, New Jersey, and Ohio finally prevailed during the 1880s. Following the lead of congressional Republicans who supported Charles Sumner's civil rights bill, Republican legislators in Pennsylvania had taken up the school issue in 1874, and the Republican majority in the state senate repealed the law that mandated racially separate schools. However, Democrats in the House, who were joined by a number of Republican legislators, chose not to vote on the bill. In spite of annual petition campaigns by the PSERL demanding an end to segregated public schools, the state legislature did not even debate the issue for the remainder of the decade.[33] The situation changed dramatically in 1881, however, when a black parent in Meadville sued school officials who refused to admit his children to a white grammar school in his district. He petitioned the County Court of Common Pleas for a writ of mandamus ordering them to admit his children, arguing that the Board of Education's policy violated his rights under the Fourteenth Amendment. School officials insisted that they were in compliance with the 1854 state law by providing an equal, albeit separate, education for black children. But the judge ruled in 1881 that, because black and white schools in Meadville were not of equal quality, the policy violated the equal protection clause of the Fourteenth Amendment. He then ordered the school directors to admit the plaintiff's children to the nearest public school. While this case was pending, the PSERL sent several petitions to the state senate calling for an end to racially separate public schools. In the end, the court ruling, black pressure, and the black vote's importance in determining the outcome of some elections help to explain why, after refusing for many years to enact a school integration law, the Pennsylvania legislature did so in 1881 by a unanimous vote in the Senate and a large majority in the House.[34]

In the same year, the black vote was instrumental in enabling New Jersey black activists to persuade the legislature to enact a school integration bill.[35] The struggle in Ohio, however, continued well into the 1880s. Here, as in Pennsylvania and New Jersey, the desire by both political parties to attract black voters played an important role in deciding the issue, though opposition from many Democrats and Republicans, especially in the southern part of the state, where most blacks lived, delayed passage of a school integration bill for several years. During the early and mid-1880s, black activists held numerous public meetings, lobbied and petitioned the legislature, and reminded both parties that the black vote could tip the balance in elections. This pressure was sufficient to convince both a Democratic governor and his Republican successor to endorse school integration in the mid-1880s. In 1887, most Republicans and some Democrats in the legislature voted to repeal the state law that mandated racially segregated public schools.[36]

Northern black equal rights activists enjoyed even greater success in their efforts on behalf of state civil rights legislation. This agitation was spurred by the U.S. Supreme Court's decision in the *Civil Rights Cases* in 1883, which declared the public accommodations section of the Civil Rights Act of 1875 unconstitutional on the grounds that the Fourteenth Amendment applied to state-sponsored discrimination, not to acts committed by individuals or groups functioning in a private capacity. Although the Civil Rights Act had seldom been enforced, with the consequence that blacks continued to be denied equal access to most public facilities and private businesses, they were outraged by the court's ruling. It was, Douglass charged, "one more shocking development of that moral weakness in high places which attended the conflict between the spirit of liberty and the spirit of slavery."[37]

Even more clearly than the congressional Republicans' decision in 1875 to remove key provisions from Sumner's civil rights bill, the court's decision signaled that blacks could not count on the federal government to protect their civil rights. But, rather than become so discouraged that they ceased to protest against racial discrimination, northern blacks launched a vigorous campaign in the mid-1880s on behalf of state civil rights laws. In every northern state, they mobilized the black community and applied relentless pressure on both parties to enact such legislation. Their efforts were quite successful: eighteen state legislatures—from New England to California—passed civil rights laws, often with broad bipartisan support. These laws closely followed the language of the Civil Rights Act of 1875: all of them applied to public accommodations, while most included provisions related to theaters, inns, and public transportation. In all, they provided more protection for African Americans' rights than had the Civil Rights Act of 1875 because few people doubted that state legislatures had the constitutional authority to enact such legislation.[38]

A divergence between these school laws and broader civil rights legislation and their application, however, often limited their ability to eliminate longstanding patterns of racial discrimination. The persistence of racially segregated schools in some northern communities can be explained in part by the steadfast support among a minority of African Americans for retaining their own separate schools.[39] However, other factors—including vaguely written or weak legislation, lax enforcement, gerrymandering of school districts, intimidation, and creative interpretations of legislation by local officials—appear to have played a far greater role in either limiting or precluding school integration and, in some cases, even access to the public schools in parts of the North.[40] The civil rights laws enacted by many northern states were also beset by problems, such as dependence on white juries to punish violators, minimal fines for offenders, haphazard enforcement, and vague language.[41]

Notwithstanding these limits, when northern blacks looked back over the years since the launch of the equal rights movement at the Syracuse Convention in 1864, they could justifiably be proud of their accomplishments. Though constituting a mere 2 percent of the northern population, the black community had aggressively challenged the pervasive and deeply rooted patterns of racial discrimination. As a result of their relentless pressure on the white power structure at all levels of government, they had persuaded Congress to enact suffrage rights for black men as well as a sweeping civil rights act. Moreover, the campaign they waged from the 1860s to the 1880s against segregation within, and exclusion from, the public schools had produced impressive results in numerous northern states. Finally, in the 1880s they vigorously responded to the U.S. Supreme Court's evisceration of the Civil Rights Act of 1875 by convincing a majority of northern state legislatures to enact far-reaching civil rights laws. Their struggle indeed stands as the most important African American crusade for full citizenship rights prior to the modern civil rights movement of the 1950s and 1960s.

Epilogue

The northern black struggle for full citizenship rights continued through the late nineteenth and early twentieth centuries. New leaders, such as Timothy Thomas Fortune, publisher of the *New York Age,* and W. E. B. DuBois, a prominent intellectual and activist, emerged as forceful advocates for black civil and political rights. Moreover, African American women collaborated more actively with men in the cause and established the women's club movement to agitate for suffrage and other rights for all blacks. But the movement also drew heavily on the Reconstruction-era cause for leadership, organizational structure, and inspiration. Douglass, Langston, and many other veterans of the post–Civil War crusade for equal rights remained active into the 1890s and, in some cases, beyond the turn of the century. In addition, the Afro-American League, the Afro-American Council, the Niagara Movement, and the National Association for the Advancement of Colored People—created by black activists between the late 1880s and 1910—were, in many ways, modeled on the National Equal Rights League. Finally, these activists were inspired by the core principles and objectives of the earlier struggle for political and legal equality. Thus, northern Reconstruction remains essential to understand how the postwar black crusade for equal rights shaped and influenced the later civil rights movement.[1]

Northern blacks' efforts to protect the fundamental rights of African Americans during the post-Reconstruction years encountered enormous obstacles. While the southern Jim Crow system was far more brutal and rigid than the system that took root in the North around the turn of the century, racial segregation increased significantly in the North due in part to whites' hostile reaction to the large-scale northern migration of southern blacks. The U.S. Supreme Court sanctioned such segregation by invoking the doctrine of "separate but equal" in its *Plessy v. Ferguson* decision in 1896. At the same time, the Republican Party became the dominant political force in much of the North between the 1890s and the 1930s; with fewer close elections in which blacks could determine the outcome, the party's leadership felt little need to consider the black vote—and with it blacks' interests—in their political calculations.[2] In this hostile environment, black civil rights organizations enjoyed far less success than the Reconstruction-era equal rights movement. Indeed, with few resources and white allies and little political leverage, they were largely unable even to stem the rising tide of segregation and oppression.[3]

Only with the New Deal, World War II, the growth of a postwar black middle class, changing white racial attitudes, and other significant developments did the modern civil rights movement emerge in the mid-twentieth century. This movement was, like the Reconstruction-era cause, national in scope, with northern black activists playing important roles from its inception. Both movements emerged during a time of sweeping social and economic change that, following decades of unrelenting white oppression, held out the hope of a brighter future for African Americans. Both sought to take advantage of these propitious developments by launching a vigorous assault on deeply rooted patterns of racial discrimination. Both also enlisted widespread support within the black community. Their relentless pressure on the white power structure produced impressive gains in the areas of civil and political rights, though both movements encountered white opposition and indifference that ultimately limited their accomplishments. The Reconstruction-era equal rights movement and the modern civil rights movement represent defining moments in the longstanding African American struggle to pressure white Americans to give real meaning to the ideals of equality, justice, and democracy they so often celebrated.[4]

NOTES

Preface

1. See, Eric Foner, *Reconstruction: America's Unfinished Revolution, 1863–1877* (New York, 1988); John Hope Franklin, *Reconstruction After the Civil War* (Chicago, 1961); Kenneth M. Stampp, *The Era of Reconstruction, 1865–1877* (New York, 1965); Robert Cruden, *The Negro in Reconstruction* (Englewood Cliffs, N.J., 1969); Rembert W. Patrick, *The Reconstruction of the Nation* (New York, 1967); Allen W. Trelease, *Reconstruction: The Great Experiment* (New York, 1971); W. R. Brock, *An American Crisis* (New York, 1963). W.E.B. DuBois's classic revisionist study, *Black Reconstruction in America: An Essay Toward a History of the Part Which Blacks Played in the Attempt to Reconstruct Democracy in America, 1860–1880* (New York, 1935), likewise makes only brief reference to northern blacks.

2. Foner, *Reconstruction;* 192; Franklin, *Reconstruction After the Civil War,* 43, 74, 109–10, 140–41, 172; Stampp, *The Era of Reconstruction,* 47n, 141.

3. Thomas J. Sugrue, *Sweet Land of Liberty: The Forgotten Struggle for Civil Rights in the North* (New York, 2008), xiii-xlv; Robert O. Self, *Babylon: Race and the Struggle for Postwar Oakland* (Princeton, 2003) 1, 10–11, 331–32; Matthew J. Countryman, *Up South: Civil Rights and Black Power in Philadelphia* (Philadelphia, 2006), 1–4. See also Jeanne F. Theoharis and Komozi Woodward, eds., *Freedom North: Black Freedom Struggles Outside the South, 1940–1980* (New York, 2003).

4. Leslie A. Schwalm, *Emancipation's Diaspora: Race and Reconstruction in the Upper Midwest* (Chapel Hill, 2009), 5, 115, 266.

5. Andrew Deimer, "Reconstructing Philadelphia: African Americans and Politics in the Post-Civil War North," *Pennsylvania Magazine of History and Biography* 133 (January 2009): 29–58;

David Quigley, *Second Founding: New York City: Reconstruction, and the Making of American Democracy* (New York, 2004).

6. In addition to works by Schwalm, Deimer, and Quigley, see, for example, David A. Gerber, *Black Ohio and the Color Line, 1860–1915* (Urbana, 1976); Ira V. Brown, *The Negro in Pennsylvania History* (University Park, Pa., 1970); Davison M. Douglas, *Jim Crow Moves North: The Battle over Northern School Segregation, 1865–1954* (Cambridge, Eng., 2005); Elmer R. Rusco, "*Good Time Coming?" Black Nevadans in the Nineteenth Century* (Westport, Ct., 1975); Emma Lou Thornbrough, *The Negro in Indiana* (Indianapolis, 1957); Eugene H. Berwanger, *The West and Reconstruction* (Urbana, 1981); Roger D. Bridges, "Equality Deferred: Civil Rights for Illinois Blacks, 1865–1885," *Journal of the Illinois State Historical Society* 74 (Summer 1981): 82–108; Edward R. Price, Jr., "Let the Law be Just: The Quest for Racial Equality in Pennsylvania 1780–1915" (Ph.D. diss., Pennsylvania State University, 1973); Arthur O. White, "The Black Movement Against Jim Crow Education in Buffalo, New York, 1800–1900," *Phylon* 30 (Winter 1969): 375–93; Marion Thompson Wright, "Negro Suffrage in New Jersey, 1776–1875," *Journal of Negro History* 33 (April 1948): 168–224.

7. Schwalm, *Emancipation's Diaspora,* 317n2.

8. See Steven Hahn, *A Nation Under Our Feet: Black Political Struggles in the Rural South from Slavery to the Great Migration* (Cambridge, Mass., 2003); Ira Berlin, ed., *Freedom: A Documentary History of Emancipation, 1861–1867,* series 2, vol. 1 (Cambridge, Eng., 1982); Steven Hahn, Steven F. Miller, Susan E. O'Donovan, John C. Rodrique, and Leslie S. Rowland, eds., *Freedom: A Documentary History of Emancipation, 1861–1867,* series 3, vol. 1 (Chapel Hill, 2008).

Chapter 1

1. See, for example, Vincent Harding, *There Is a River: The Black Struggle for Freedom in America* (New York, 1982), 117–19; Jane H. Pease and William H. Pease, *They Who Would Be Free: Blacks' Search for Freedom, 1830–1861* (New York, 1974), 144–45, 174–92, 284–85; Leon Litwack, *North of Slavery: The Negro in the Free States, 1790–1861* (Chicago, 1961), 66–77, 903–95; and James Oliver Horton, *Free People of Color: Inside the African American Community* (Washington, D.C., 1993), 151–52.

2. See, for example, Howard Holman Bell, ed., *Minutes of the Proceedings of the National Negro Conventions, 1830–1864* (New York, 1969), 11–15; James Brewer Stewart, *Holy Warriors: The Abolitionists and American Slavery,* 2d ed. (New York, 1996), 134–38; Jane H. Pease and William H. Pease, "Negro Conventions and the Problem of Black Leadership," *Journal of Black Studies* 2 (September 1971): 29–30; Pease and Pease, *They Who Would Be Free,* 144–49, 152–53, 156–57, 164–68, 192–93; David E. Swift, *Black Prophets of Justice: Activist Clergy before the Civil War* (Baton Rouge, La., 1989), 276–79; Thomas A. Sanelli, "The Struggle for Black Suffrage in Pennsylvania, 1838–1870" (Ph.D. diss., Temple University, 1977), 102–3, 118–20; James Adolphus Fisher, "A History of the Political and Social Development of the Black Community in California, 1850–1950" (Ph.D. diss., State University of New York at Stony Brook, 1972), 32–56; and Phyllis F. Field, *The Politics of Race in New York: The Struggle for Black Suffrage in the Civil War Era* (Ithaca, N.Y., 1982), 91–97.

3. See John Stauffer, *The Black Hearts of Men: Radical Abolitionists and the Transformation of Race* (Cambridge, Mass., 2002); Leon Litwack, "The Emancipation of the Negro Abolitionist," in *The Antislavery Vanguard: New Essays on the Abolitionists,* ed. Martin Duberman (Princeton, N.J., 1965), 137–38; and James Oliver Horton and Lois E. Horton, "The Affirmation of Manhood: Black Garrisonians in Antebellum Boston," in *Courage and Conscience: Black and White Abolitionists in Boston,* ed. Donald M. Jacobs (Bloomington, Ind., 1993), 142.

4. Harding, *There Is a River,* 125–26.

5. See Stewart, *Holy Warriors,* 128–31; and Benjamin Quarles, *Black Abolitionists* (New York, 1969), 47–51.

6. Stewart, *Holy Warriors,* 131–32; Jane H. Pease and William H. Pease, "Antislavery Ambivalence: Immediatism, Expediency, Race," *American Quarterly* 17 (Winter 1965): 682–95; and Litwack, "The Emancipation of the Negro Abolitionist," 139–40.

7. Litwack, "The Emancipation of the Negro Abolitionist," 149 (quotation); Stanley Harrold, *The Rise of Aggressive Abolitionism: Addresses to the Slaves* (Lexington, Ky., 2004), 17, 93–95; and Jane H. Pease and William H. Pease, "Ends, Means, and Attitudes: Black-White Conflict in the Antislavery Movement," *Civil War History* 18 (June 1972): 117–28.

8. See, for example, Julie Winch, *Philadelphia's Black Elite: Activism, Accommodation, and the Struggle for Autonomy, 1787–1848* (Philadelphia, 1988), 109–29; Dorothy Parker Wesley, "Integration versus Separatism: William Cooper Nell's Role in the Struggle for Equality," in *Courage and Conscience,* ed. Jacobs, 214; Jane H. Pease and William H. Pease, *Bound with Them in Chains: A Biographical History of the Antislavery Movement* (Westport, 1972), 178–79; and Waldo Martin, *The Mind of Frederick Douglass* (Chapel Hill, N.C., 1984), 165–67, 172–85, 219–20, 281–82. On northern blacks' attachment to middle-class values, see Patrick Rael, *Black Identity and Black Protest in the Antebellum North* (Chapel Hill, N.C., 2002), 52–53, 119–20, 125–38, 198–99.

9. Litwack, "The Emancipation of the Negro Abolitionist," 155 (quotation); and Pease and Pease, *Bound with Them in Chains,* 175–83.

10. Bell, ed., *Minutes of the Proceedings of the National Negro Conventions, 1830–1864;* Stewart, *Holy Warriors,* 134–38; and Pease and Pease, *They Who Would Be Free,* 144–49.

11. See, for example, Sanelli, "The Struggle for Black Suffrage in Pennsylvania, 1838–1870," 38–90, 100–103, 118–20; Pease and Pease, *They Who Would Be Free,* 144–49, 152–53, 164–68, 174–92; and Swift, *Black Prophets of Justice,* 273–79.

12. Pease and Pease, *They Who Would Be Free,* 255–57, 264–67, 270. On the black rights organizations, see Horton and Horton, *Free People of Color,* 61–62; Litwack, *North of Slavery,* 260–67; and Robert J. Chandler, "Friends in Time of Need: Republicans and Black Civil Rights in California during the Civil War Era," *Arizona and the West* 24 (Winter 1982): 320–22. On the rights that were available to northern blacks, see Paul Finkleman, "Prelude to the Fourteenth Amendment: Black Legal Rights in the Antebellum North," *Rutgers Law Journal* 17 (Spring and Summer 1986): 417, 450–51; see also Kenneth C. Kusmer, *A Ghetto Takes Shape: Black Cleveland, 1870–1930* (Urbana, Ill., 1976), 28, 30–31; Robert J. Cottrol, *The Afro-Yankees: Providence's Black Community in the Antebellum Era* (Westport, Conn., 1982), 78–79; John Roy Squibb, "Roads to Plessy: Blacks and the Law in the Old Northwest: 1860–1896" (Ph.D. diss., University of Wisconsin, 1992), 14–15; and David A. Gerber, "Education, Expediency, and Ideology: Race and Politics in the Desegregation of the Ohio Public Schools in the Late Nineteenth Century," *Journal of Ethnic Studies* 1 (1973): 3–4.

13. For treatments of the developing sectional crisis during the first half of the 1850s, see Holman Hamilton, *Prologue to Conflict: The Crisis and Compromise of 1850* (Lexington, Ky., 1964); Don E. Fehrenbacher, *The South and Three Sectional Crises* (New York, 1980); Stanley Campbell, *The Slavecatchers: The Enforcement of the Fugitive Slave Law* (Chapel Hill, N.C., 1970); James Rawley, *Race and Politics: "Bleeding Kansas" and the Coming of the Civil War* (Philadelphia, 1969); William W. Freehling, *The Road to Disunion: Secessionists at Bay, 1776–1854* (New York, 1990); and Robert W. Johannsen, *Stephen A. Douglas* (New York, 1973).

14. See Don E. Fehrenbacher, *The Dred Scott Case: Its Significance in American Law and Politics* (New York, 1978); and Robert W. Johannsen, *The Impending Crisis, 1848–1861* (New York, 1976).

15. See Eric Walther, *The Shattering of the Union: America in the 1850s* (Wilmington, 2004); Kenneth M. Stampp, *America in 1857: A Nation on the Brink* (New York, 1990); Walter Ehrlich, *They Have No Rights: Dred Scott's Struggle for Freedom* (Westport, Conn., 1979); Litwack, *North of Slavery,* 261–67; and David W. Blight, "They Knew What Time It Was: African-Americans and the Coming of the Civil War," in *Why the Civil War Came,* ed. Gabor S. Boritt (New York, 1996), 57–66.

16. See Floyd J. Miller, *The Search for a Black Nationality: Black Emigration and Colonization, 1787–1863* (Urbana, Ill., 1975), 93, 127–28, 134; and Harding, *There Is a River,* 134, 151, 172–76. For studies of the African Civilization Society, see Joel Schor, "The Rivalry Between Frederick Douglass and Henry Highland Garnet," *Journal of Negro History* 64 (Winter 1979): 34–35; Earl Ofari, *"Let Your Motto Be Resistance": The Life and Thought of Henry Highland Garnet* (Boston, 1972), 80–83; and Richard MacMaster, "Henry Highland Garnet and the African Civilization Society," *Journal of Presbyterian Church History* 48 (Summer 1970); 90–112. V. P. Franklin argues that the emigrationists appealed especially to the black masses and the black culture of resistance as a viable alternative to the black elite's desire for equal rights. Franklin, *Black Self-Determination: A Cultural History of African American Resistance* (Brooklyn, N.Y., 1984), 100–102. But Harry Reed points out that most northern blacks could not afford to emigrate. Reed, *Platform for Change,* 165. See also Litwack, *North of Slavery;* Leonard P. Curry, *The Free Black in Urban America, 1800–1850: The Shadow of the Dream* (Chicago, 1981); and V. Jacques Voegeli, *Free But Not Equal: The Midwest and the Negro during the Civil War* (Chicago, 1967).

17. Winch, *Philadelphia's Black Elite,* 4–5, 129; Harding, *There Is a River,* 121, 158–67; Swift, *Black Prophets of Justice,* 260–65; and Pease and Pease, *They Who Would Be Free,* 206–32, 245, 251–52.

18. *Weekly Anglo-African,* 30 March 1861. Debra Jackson notes that the paper enjoyed considerable influence in New York City's black community. Jackson, "A Cultural Stronghold: The *Anglo-African* Newspaper and the Black Community in New York," *New York History* 85 (Fall 2004): 331–36.

19. *Christian Recorder,* 20 April 1861. For similar sentiments, see *Weekly Anglo-African,* 27 April, 24 August 1861.

20. *Weekly Anglo-African,* 14 September 1861; also 5 October, 28 December 1861.

21. David W. Blight, "'For Something beyond the Battlefield': Frederick Douglass and the Struggle for the Memory of the Civil War," *Journal of American History* 75 (March 1989): 1156–78; and *Weekly Anglo-African,* 3 January 1863.

22. *Weekly Anglo-African,* 28 February 1863; Swift, *Black Prophets of Justice,* 321–22; Miller, *The Search for a Black Nationality,* 262–64; and Henry Louis Gates Jr. and Evelyn Brooks Higginbotham, eds., *African American National Biography,* vol. 3 (New York, 2008), 55.

23. *Weekly Anglo-African,* 17 January, 7 March 1863; see also Gates and Higginbotham, eds., *African American National Biography,* 7:414–15; minutes of the executive committee, February 1863, Records of the Social, Civic, and Statistical Association of the Colored People of Pennsylvania, Leon Gardiner Collection on Negro History, Historical Society of Pennsylvania; E. R. Williams to Richard Yates Sr., 9 February 1863, Yates Family Collection, Illinois State Historical Library; Sumner to (unknown), 26 July 1863, Leo Julian to Gen. Augur, 19 January 1864, George T. Downing Papers, Moorland-Spingarn Research Center, Howard University; *Weekly Anglo-African,* 17 January 1863; Ofari, *"Let Your Motto Be Resistance,"* 110–11; J. Harlan Buzby, *John Stewart Rock: Teacher, Healer, Counselor* (Salem, N.J., 2002), 55–56; and Allen C. Guelzo, *Lincoln's Emancipation Proclamation: The End of Slavery in America* (New York, 2004), 246–47. For a treatment of the connection between military service and citizenship rights for African Americans, see Christian G. Samito, *Becoming American under Fire: Irish Americans, African Americans, and the Politics of Citizenship during the Civil War Era* (Ithaca, N.Y., 2009), 45–76.

24. Benjamin Quarles, *The Negro in the Civil War* (New York, 1953), 184–94; and Harding, *There Is a River,* 239–40.

25. George T. Downing to Charles Sumner, 19 February 1863, Charles Sumner Papers, Harvard University; *Weekly Anglo-African,* 13 February 1864; and Edwin S. Redkey, ed., *A Grand Army of Black Men: Letters from African-American Soldiers in the Union Army, 1861–1865* (Cambridge, Eng., 1992), 208–9 (quotation); see also Jim Cullen, "'I's a Man Now': Gender and African

American Men," in *Divided Houses: Gender and the Civil War,* ed. Catherine Clinton and Nina Silber (New York, 1992), 82–84; David W. Blight, *Frederick Douglass's Civil War: Keeping Faith in Jubilee* (Baton Rouge, La., 1989), 157–66, 181–82; and Herman Belz, "Law, Politics, and Race in the Struggle for Equal Pay during the Civil War," *Civil War History* 22 (September 1976): 197–222.

26. *Weekly Anglo-African,* 21 March 1863.

27. Michael Vorenberg, *Final Freedom: The Civil War, the Abolition of Slavery, and the Thirteenth Amendment* (Cambridge, Eng., 2001), 82–85; *Weekly Anglo-African,* 26 September 1863 (quotation); and Guelzo, *Lincoln's Emancipation Proclamation,* 180.

28. James M. McPherson, *The Negro's Civil War: How American Negroes Felt and Acted during the War for the Union* (New York, 1965), 249–50.

29. See, for example, James Fisher, "The Struggle for Negro Testimony in California, 1851–1863," *Southern California Quarterly* 51 (December 1969): 313–24; Chandler, "Friends in Time of Need," 326–29; J. William Snorgrass, "The Black Press in the San Francisco Bay Area, 1856–1900," *California History* 60 (Winter 1981/82): 307–8; and Quintard Taylor, *In Search of the Racial Frontier: African Americans in the American West, 1528–1990* (New York, 1998), 91–92.

30. Chandler, "Friends in Time of Need," 332–34; also Sacramento *Union,* 5 October 1864; *National Anti-Slavery Standard,* 24 December 1864; and Ella Forbes, *African American Women during the Civil War* (New York, 1998), 150.

31. *Christian Recorder,* 9 July 1864; *National Anti-Slavery Standard,* 2 July 1864; *Weekly Anglo-African,* 2 July 1864; Andrew Diemer, "Reconstructing Philadelphia: African Americans and Politics in the Post–Civil War North," *Pennsylvania Magazine of History and Biography* 133 (January 2009): 37, 41; Jane E. Dabel, *A Respectable Woman: The Public Roles of African American Women in Nineteenth-Century New York* (New York, 2008), 142–43; Leslie A. Schwalm, *Emancipation's Diaspora: Race and Reconstruction in the Upper Midwest* (Chapel Hill, N.C., 2009) 193, 203–4; and Taylor, *In Search of the Racial Frontier,* 92–93. For black protest in New York City, see Forbes, *African American Women during the Civil War,* 151–53; in Boston and Cincinnati, see *Liberator,* 17 February 1865; in Chicago and Indianapolis, see John Roy Squibb, "Roads to Plessy: Blacks and the Law in the Old Northwest: 1860–1896" (Ph.D. diss., University of Wisconsin, 1992), 47–54. See also Margaret Hope Bacon, "'One Great Bundle of Humanity': Frances Ellen Watkins Harper (1825–1911)," *Pennsylvania Magazine of History and Biography* 113 (January 1989): 21–43.

32. John Jones, *The Black Laws of Illinois and a Few Reasons Why They Should be Repealed* (Chicago, 1864), 3, 5; *Illinois State Register,* 14 January 1865; *Weekly Anglo-African,* 14 January 1865; Charles A. Gliozzo, *John Jones and the Repeal of the Illinois Black Laws* (Duluth, Minn., 1975), 1–8. For Republican support for repeal, see *Illinois State Journal,* 2, 23 January 1865; and "The Illinois Black Laws," *Chicago History* 8 (Spring 1967), 65–75.

33. *Weekly Anglo-African,* 7 March 1863 (quotation); and McPherson, *The Negro's Civil War,* 274. On blacks' efforts to amend the constitution in New Jersey, see Marion Thompson Wright, "Negro Suffrage in New Jersey, 1776–1875," *Journal of Negro History* 33 (April 1948): 198–99, 202; in Michigan, *Weekly Anglo-African,* 7 March 1863, 23 January 1864; in New York, *Journal of the Assembly of the State of New-York: At Their 87th Session* (Albany, N.Y., 1864), 32 (6 January 1864), 487 (12 March 1864); in Connecticut, *Journal of the Senate of the State of Connecticut, May Session, 1864* (New Haven, Conn., 1864), 25 May 1864, 130, 526; *Journal of the Senate of the State of Connecticut, May Session, 1865* (Hartford, 1865), 22 May 1865, 152, 197.

34. Robert Purvis, *Speeches and Letters* (1898), 3–4 (quotation); *Proceedings of the National Convention of Colored Men, Held in the City of Syracuse, October 4, 5, 6, and 7, 1864; with the Bill of Wrongs and Rights, and the Address to the American People* (1864), 24; see also Margaret Hope Bacon, *But One Race: The Life of Robert Purvis* (Albany, N.Y., 2007); and Buzby, *John Stewart Rock,* 56.

35. See, for example, Catherine M. Hanchett, "George Boyer Vashon, 1824–1878: Black Educator, Poet, Fighter for Equal Rights: Part Two," *Western Pennsylvania Historical Magazine*

68 (October 1985): 335; William Edward Farrison, *William Wells Brown: Author and Reformer* (Chicago, 1969), 394; and Vorenberg, *Final Freedom,* 157–58.

36. William Cheek and Aimee Lee Cheek, *John Mercer Langston and the Fight for Black Freedom, 1829–65* (Urbana, Ill., 1989), 425–26; Joel Schor, *Henry Highland Garnet: A Voice of Black Radicalism in the Nineteenth Century* (Westport, Conn., 1977), 202; and John S. Rock to Charles Remond and George T. Downing, 19 April, 15 July 1864, Ruffin Family Papers, Moorland-Spingarn Research Center, Howard University.

37. John S. Rock to Henry Highland Garnet, 15 July 1864, Ruffin Family Papers. Opposition to Garnet's African Civilization Society among blacks in the District of Columbia was sufficiently strong to deny him election as a delegate to the Syracuse Convention, thus forcing him, at the last minute, to attend as a representative of the society in New York City. Cheek and Cheek, *John Mercer Langston and the Fight for Black Freedom, 1829–65,* 426–27.

38. John S. Rock to Henry Highland Garnet, 23 July 1864, Ruffin Family Papers; and *Weekly Anglo-African,* 20 August 1864.

39. *Christian Recorder,* 15 October 1864.

40. George Ruffin's Report, 1864, Box 81-1, Folder 58, Ruffin Family Papers; *Weekly Anglo-African,* 1 October 1864 (quotation); and *Christian Recorder,* 15 October 1864.

41. *Proceedings of the National Convention of Colored Men, Held in the City of Syracuse, October 4, 5, 6, and 7, 1864,* 4; *Weekly Anglo-African,* 15 October 1864; *National Anti-Slavery Standard,* 15 October 1864; Cheek and Cheek, *John Mercer Langston and the Fight for Black Freedom, 1829–1865,* 428–29; Hahn, *A Nation under Our Feet,* 106–7; and Gates and Higginbotham, eds., *African American National Biography,* 2:217.

42. *Proceedings of the National Convention of Colored Men, Held in the City of Syracuse, October 4, 5, 6, and 7, 1864,* 2–4.

43. Ibid., 9.

44. Ibid., 23–24, 58.

45. Ibid., 61, 36.

46. Ibid., 41–42, 46–51, 59; and *National Anti-Slavery Standard,* 15 October 1864.

47. *Proceedings of the National Convention of Colored Men, Held in the City of Syracuse, October 6, 5, 6, and 7, 1864;* and Harding, *There Is a River,* 247–48.

48. *Proceedings of the National Convention of Colored Men, Held in the City of Syracuse, October 4, 5, 6, and 7, 1864,* 33–34. On manhood during the Civil War, see E. Anthony Rotundo, *American Manhood: Transformations in Masculinity from the Revolution to the Modern Era* (New York, 1993), 232–33; Cullen, "'I's a Man Now,'" 85; and Michael Kimmell, *Manhood in America: A Cultural History* (New York, 1996), 73–75, 77–90. Unfortunately, many whites did not consider the military contributions of black soldiers proof of black manhood. Mia Bay, *The White Image in the Black Mind: African American Ideas about White People, 1830–1925* (New York, 2000), 88.

49. Schor, *Henry Highland Garnet,* 205; *Proceedings of the National Convention of Colored Men, Held in the City of Syracuse, October 4, 5, 6, and 7, 1864,* 37–38; and *National Anti-Slavery Standard,* 15 October 1864.

50. *Weekly Anglo-African,* 29 October 1864; see also *National Anti-Slavery Standard,* 15 October 1864.

51. *Weekly Anglo-African,* 29 October 1864; George Ruffin's Report, 1864, Ruffin Family Papers; and Lois Brown, *Pauline Elizabeth Hopkins: Black Daughter of the Revolution* (Chapel Hill, N.C., 2008), 181.

52. *Weekly Anglo-African,* 19 November 1864.

53. Schor, *Henry Highland Garnet,* 167, 178, 182, 202–4.

54. *Proceedings of the National Convention of Colored Men, Held in the City of Syracuse, October 4, 5, 6, and 7, 1864,* 26–27; and *Weekly Anglo-African,* 29 October 1864.

55. *Proceedings of the National Convention of Colored Men, Held in the City of Syracuse, October 4, 5, 6, and 7, 1864,* 27–28; and *Weekly Anglo-African,* 29 October 1864.

56. *Proceedings of the National Convention of Colored Men, Held in the City of Syracuse, October 4, 5, 6, and 7, 1864,* 28.

57. Ibid., 18–19.

58. Cheek and Cheek, *John Mercer Langston and the Fight for Black Freedom, 1829–65,* 434; *Christian Recorder,* 15 October (quotation), 3 December 1864; and *Weekly Anglo-African,* 26 November 1864.

59. William Cheek and Aimee Lee Cheek, "John Mercer Langston: Principle and Politics," in *Black Leaders of the Nineteenth Century,* ed. Leon Litwack and August Meier (Urbana, Ill., 1988), 114; C. Peter Ripley et al., eds., *The Black Abolitionist Papers. Volume V. The United States, 1859–1865* (Chapel Hill, N.C., 1992), 304. In his autobiography, which he wrote many years later, Langston made no mention of his work as president of the National Equal Rights League. *From the Virginia Plantation to the National Capitol: An Autobiography* (Reprint, New York, 1969). On the creation of the state organization in Ohio, see *Weekly Anglo-African,* 1 February 1865; in Massachusetts, see *Weekly Anglo-African,* 4 February 1865; in New Jersey, see *Proceedings of the State Convention of Colored Men of the State of New Jersey, Held in the City of Trenton, New Jersey, July 13th and 14th, 1865* (Bridgeton, N.J., 1865), 4, 13–14; in New York, see *Weekly Anglo-African,* 8 April 1865; in Indiana, see *Indianapolis Daily Journal,* 9 November 1866; in Michigan, see Philip S. Foner and George E. Walker, eds., *Proceedings of the Black State Conventions, 1840–1865. Volume I: New York, Pennsylvania, Indiana, Michigan, Ohio* (Philadelphia, 1979), 209–10; in the southern states, see Eric Foner, *Forever Free: The Story of Emancipation and Reconstruction* (New York, 2005), 89; and Hahn, *A Nation under Our Feet,* 108–9.

60. For a study of the Pennsylvania State Equal Rights League during the Reconstruction Era, see Hugh Davis, "The Pennsylvania State Equal Rights League and the Northern Black Struggle for Legal Equality, 1864–1877," *Pennsylvania Magazine of History and Biography* 126 (October 2002): 611–34. On White, see Gates and Higginbotham, eds., *African American National Biography,* 8:250. According to the 1870 census, Pennsylvania's sixty-five thousand blacks represented only 1.9% of the state's total population. U.S. Bureau of the Census, *Negro Population, 1790–1915* (Washington, D.C., 1918), 51. The PSERL records include the minutes of its executive board's meetings and the correspondence of its Recording Secretary, Jacob C. White Jr. In addition, the columns of the *Christian Recorder,* a Philadelphia African Methodist Episcopal Church newspaper that served as the PSERL's official organ from 1865 to 1868, include valuable information on the organization's activities.

61. Minutes of the executive board, 14 October 1864, 1–3, 5–6, 19–20, Records of the Pennsylvania State Equal Rights League (hereafter, Records of the PSERL), Leon Gardiner Collection on Negro History, Historical Society of Pennsylvania.

62. *Christian Recorder,* 4, 18 February 1865.

63. *Christian Recorder,* 7 January 1865. On the formation of local auxiliaries, see *Christian Recorder,* 8 February, 15 April, 18 November 1865, 20 January 1866; minutes of the executive board, 6 September 1865, 7 January, 13 March 1866, Records of the PSERL, Jacob C. White Collection, Moorland-Spingarn Research Center, Howard University; *Christian Recorder,* 4, 18 February 1865, 124–35. On the first annual meeting of the PSERL, see *Christian Recorder,* 31 March 1865; and *Liberator,* 3 March 1865.

64. For such claims, see Fishel, "Repercussions of Reconstruction," 332–35; and Heather Cox Richardson, *The Death of Reconstruction,* 133–34. Steven Hahn and other historians of southern Reconstruction have shown that the freed people responded assertively to Reconstruction by playing a major role in the new state governments, voting in large numbers, building new political relationships and institutions in their communities, and resisting Democratic threats and overtures.

Moreover, black veterans—many of whom had been slaves—played important roles in the postwar southern black community. Although a majority of the delegates to the freedmen's conventions were from the bourgeoisie, they came to see their destinies as inextricably linked to those of the rural masses. See Hahn, *A Nation under Our Feet,* 121–23, 164–65, 177–85, 193–98, 207, 210; Hahn et al., eds., *Freedom,* 59–60, 67, 190, 455–57; Howard N. Rabinowitz, ed., *Southern Black Leaders of the Reconstruction Era* (Urbana, Ill., 1982); Joel Williamson, *After Slavery: The Negro in South Carolina during Reconstruction, 1861–1877* (Chapel Hill, N.C., 1965); Edmund L. Drago, *Black Politicians and Reconstruction in Georgia: A Splendid Failure* (Baton Rouge, La., 1982); and Donald R. Shaffer, *After the Glory: The Struggles of Black Civil War Veterans* (Lawrence, Kans., 2004), 32.

65. See, for example, Carlson, "The Black Community in the Rural North," 86; David M. Katzman, *Before the Ghetto: Black Detroit in the Nineteenth Century* (Urbana, Ill., 1973), 147–51; David Quigley, *Second Founding: New York City, Reconstruction, and the Making of American Democracy* (New York, 2004), 73–74; Richard M. Valelly, *The Two Reconstructions: The Struggle for Black Enfranchisement* (Chicago, 2004), 34–35; and Samito, *Becoming American under Fire,* 45–76.

66. W. H. Messick to Jacob C. White Jr., 14 December 1868, Jacob C. White Collection; and *Christian Recorder,* 4 November 1865. On the membership of the PSERL, see minutes of the executive board, 14 March 1866, Records of the PSERL.

67. See, for example, minutes of the executive committee, 5 September, 3 December 1860, February 1863, 18 February 1867, Records of the Social, Civic, and Statistical Association of the Colored People of Pennsylvania; minutes of the executive board, 20 January 1865, 29 May, 5 June 1866, Records of the PSERL; *Christian Recorder,* 1, 29 September 1866; and *National Anti-Slavery Standard,* 3 June 1865, 31 March 1866. Black protest against Philadelphia's streetcar companies is studied in Philip S. Foner, "The Battle to End Discrimination against Negroes on Philadelphia's Streetcars: (Part I) Background and Beginning of the Battle," *Pennsylvania History* 40 (July 1973): 261–91; and "The Battle to End Discrimination against Negroes on Philadelphia's Streetcars: (Part II) The Victory," *Pennsylvania History* 40 (October 1973): 355–79; and Edward J. Price Jr., "Let the Law Be Just: The Quest for Racial Equality in Pennsylvania, 1780–1915" (Ph.D., diss., Pennsylvania State University, 1973), 56–83. Unfettered access to public transportation in San Francisco was not achieved until 1893. Taylor, *In Search of the Racial Frontier,* 93. On the pervasive racism in Philadelphia, see Sam Bass Warner, *The Private City: Philadelphia in Three Periods of Its Growth* (Philadelphia, 1968), 125–26.

68. See *Christian Recorder,* 1 September 1866; minutes of the executive board, 20 January 1865, 29 May, 5 June 1866, Records of the PSERL; *Philadelphia Press,* 30–31 January, 31 May 1865; Ira V. Brown, *The Negro in Pennsylvania History* (University Park, Pa., 1970), 46–47; Foner, "The Battle to End Discrimination against Negroes on Philadelphia's Streetcars: (Part I) Background and Beginning of the Battle," 281–82; "The Battle to End Discrimination against Negroes on Philadelphia's Streetcars: (Part II) The Victory," 361–71; William D. Kelley, *Why Colored People in Philadelphia Are Excluded from the Streetcars* (Philadelphia, 1866), 3–5; and Janice Sumler-Edmond, "The Quest for Justice: African American Women Litigants, 1867–1890," in *African American Women and the Vote, 1837–1965,* ed. Ann D. Gordon et al. (Amherst, 1997), 101–3. Soon after the enactment of the 1867 law, the Pennsylvania Supreme Court upheld separate railroad cars for blacks. But since the action being considered in this case occurred before 1867, the court was not ruling on the law's constitutionality. Price, "Let the Law Be Just," 86.

69. See W. M. Strother to Jacob C. White Jr., 5 November 1866, minutes of the executive board, Records of the PSERL; and E. N. Reynolds to Jacob C. White Jr., 15 February 1866, W. H. Robinson to Jacob C. White Jr., 25 July 1867, Oliver Reynolds to Jacob C. White Jr., 27 December 1869, Jacob C. White Collection.

70. B. J. Wilson to Jacob C. White, 11 February 1866, William E. Welch to Jacob C. White, 6 December 1868; I. Franchetti to Jacob C. White, 10 November 1868, Records of the PSERL.

71. See Foner, "The Battle to End Discrimination against Negroes on Philadelphia's Streetcars: (Part II) The Victory," 374–75 (quotation); and William Still, *A Brief Narrative of the Struggle for the Rights of the Colored People of Philadelphia in the City Railway Cars; and a Defence of William Still, Relating to His Agency Touching the Passage of the Late Bill, etc. Read Before a Large Public Meeting Held in Liberty Hall, April 8, 1867* (Reprint, New York, 1969), 1–2 17–23. See David A. Gerber, *Black Ohio and the Color Line, 1860–1915* (Urbana, Ill., 1976), 136–37.

72. *Elevator,* 22 November 1867; and *Pacific Appeal,* 26 October 1867. On the Bell-Anderson dispute, see Snorgrass, "The Black Press in the San Francisco Bay Area, 1856–1900," 308, 311; Leigh Dana Johnsen, "Equal Rights and the 'Heathen Chinee': Black Activism in San Francisco," *Western Historical Quarterly* 11 (January 1980): 59; Fisher, "A History of the Political and Social Development of the Black Community in California, 1850–1950," 135–41; and Frank N. Lortie Jr., "San Francisco's Black Community, 1870–1890: Dilemmas in the Struggle for Equality" (San Francisco, 1973), 35. In a rather similar vein, when some of Frederick Douglass's admirers in the Indiana Equal Rights League offered a resolution complimenting him in 1867, other members, recalling that Douglass had once refused to lecture for the league, managed to table the resolution, "really shouting and giving praise to God" as they voted. *Indianapolis Daily Journal,* 8 October 1867.

73. *Proceedings of the Colored Men's Convention of the State of Michigan, Held in the City of Detroit, Tuesday and Wednesday, September 12th and 13th, '65* (Adrian, Mich., 1865), 6–12, 17–18; Foner and Walker, eds., *Proceedings of the Black State Conventions, 1840–1865,* 198–207; and *First Annual Meeting of the National Equal Rights League, Held in Cleveland, Ohio, October 19th, 20th, and 21st, 1865,* 11–12, 16.

74. *Weekly Anglo-African,* 1 July 1865.

75. *Christian Recorder,* 18 August, 1 September, 15 December 1866, 2 February 1867; and *First Annual Meeting of the National Equal Rights League, Held in Cleveland, Ohio, October 19th, 20th, and 21st, 1865,* 15, 22–28.

76. Cheek and Cheek, *John Mercer Langston and the Fight for Black Freedom, 1829–65,* 434–35; *Christian Recorder,* 19 January 1867; and William Nesbit to Thaddeus Stevens, 7 February 1868, Thaddeus Stevens Papers, Library of Congress.

77. Cheek and Cheek, "John Mercer Langston," in *Black Leaders of the Nineteenth Century,* ed. Litwack and Meier, 115.

78. Parker Smith to the Social, Civic, and Statistical Association of the Colored People of Pennsylvania, 22 February 1867, Leon Gardiner Collection on Negro History; *Weekly Anglo-African,* 26 August 1865; *First Annual Meeting of the National Equal Rights League, Held in Cleveland, Ohio, October 19th, 20th, and 21st, 1865* (Philadelphia, 1865), 17; and Sanelli, "The Struggle for Black Suffrage in Pennsylvania, 1838–1870," 243; see also *Elevator,* 7 April 1865.

79. *Christian Recorder,* 25 November 1865. A similar debate occurred at black conventions in Indiana in 1866 and 1867. *Indianapolis Daily Journal,* 9 November 1866; and Emma Lou Thornbrough, *The Negro in Indiana* (Indianapolis, 1957), 256.

80. *Christian Recorder,* 25 November 1865, 23 February 1867; and *First Annual Meeting of the National Equal Rights League, Held in Cleveland, Ohio, October 19th, 20th, and 21st, 1865,* 17.

81. *First Annual Meeting of the National Equal Rights League, Held in Cleveland, Ohio, October 19th, 20th, and 21st, 1865,* 42; and *Christian Recorder,* 2 September, 26 August, 25 November, 2 December 1865.

82. *Christian Recorder,* 25 March 1865.

83. Clarence Walker, *Deromanticizing Black History: Critical Essays and Reappraisals* (Knoxville, Tenn., 1991), xvi. Likewise, John C. Rodrigue points out that much of Reconstruction scholarship since the appearance of Eric Foner's *Reconstruction* in 1989 has emphasized divisions within the southern black community. Rodrigue, "Black Agency after Slavery," in *Reconstructions: New Perspectives on the Postbellum United States,* ed. Thomas J. Brown (New York, 2006), 40–65.

Chapter 2

1. *The Equality of All Men before the Law, Claimed and Defended: In Speeches by Hon. William D. Kelley, Wendell Phillips, and Frederick Douglass, and Letters From Elizur Wright and William Heighton* (Boston, 1865), 36–37.

2. Philip S. Foner, *Frederick Douglass* (New York, 1964), 2236–37; *Liberator,* 26 May 1865; *Christian Recorder,* 2 November 1867; and *Elevator,* 20 September 1867.

3. *Christian Recorder,* 26 October 1867 (quotation); Foner and Walker, eds., *Proceedings of the Black State Conventions, 1840–1865,* 147; David W. Blight, *Frederick Douglass' Civil War: Keeping Faith in Jubilee* (Baton Rouge, 1989), 194; and *Journal of the House of Representatives of the State of Michigan,* 18 January 1865.

4. Blacks challenged laws in Indiana, Michigan, and Ohio that prohibited interracial marriage. The most significant Reconstruction-era legal challenges to miscegenation statutes occurred in Indiana, where in the early 1870s the state supreme court upheld the ban on interracial marriage. But during much of this period, northern African Americans devoted little attention to this issue, perhaps because they realized that to do so might play into the hands of racist whites. See Squibb, "Roads to Plessy," 75–77; and *Indianapolis Daily Journal,* 31 August, 22 September 1875.

5. *Newark Evening Courier,* 13 August 1867; *Christian Recorder,* 3 February 1866; and *Elevator,* 7 April 1865.

6. *Proceedings of a Convention of Colored Citizens, Held in the City of Lawrence, October 17, 1866* (Lawrence, Kans., 1866), 4. For a similar view, see *Elevator,* 7 April 1865.

7. *Christian Recorder,* 3 November 1866.

8. See *Detroit Advertiser and Tribune,* 3 February 1868; and *Christian Recorder,* 24 March, 9, 16 December 1865, 24 March 1866 (quotation); see also Gary Libman, "Minnesota and the Struggle for Black Suffrage: 1849–1870 A Study in Party Motivation" (Ph.D. diss., University of Minnesota, 1972), 54; Janice Sumler Lewis, "The Fortens of Philadelphia: An Afro-American Family and Nineteenth-Century Reform" (Ph.D. diss., Georgetown University, 1978), 214; and William Toll, *The Resurgence of Race: Black Social Theory from Reconstruction to the Pan-African Conferences* (Philadelphia, 1979), 11–14.

9. *Indianapolis Daily Journal,* 8 November 1866; Hon. John Mercer Langston, *Freedom and Citizenship. Selected Lectures and Addresses of Hon. John Mercer Langston, LL.D.* (Washington, D.C., 1883), 105; and *Detroit Advertiser and Tribune,* 3 February 1868.

10. *Christian Recorder,* 9 November 1867; and *Journal of the House of Representatives of the State of Michigan,* 18 January 1865.

11. *Elevator,* 16 June 1865; and *Newark Evening Courier,* 13 August 1867; *Journal of the House of Representatives of the State of Michigan,* 18 January 1865.

12. *Elevator,* 19 January 1866; see also 30 August 1867.

13. *Weekly Anglo-African,* 24 June (quotation), 18 November 1865 (quotation); and *Elevator,* 17 November 1865. For similar sentiments, see *Christian Recorder,* 10 June, 2 September 1865; and *Indianapolis Daily Journal,* 3 December 1866. For a discussion of the role of black veterans in the North and South, see Shaffer, *After the Glory,* 32, 67–70.

14. See Gail Bederman, *Manliness and Civilization: A Cultural History of Gender and Race in the United States, 1880–1917* (Chicago, 1995), 13, 20; George M. Fredrickson, *The Black Image in the White Mind: The Debate on Afro-American Character and Destiny, 1817–1914* (New York, 1971), 11; Cullen, "'I's a Man Now,'" 77–86; Shaffer, *After the Glory,* 1, 3–4; Schwalm, *Emancipation's Diaspora,* 108–9, 113; and *Proceedings of a Convention of Colored Citizens, Held in the City of Lawrence, October 17, 1866,* 4–5.

15. *Christian Recorder,* 1 July 1865; and *Proceedings of the Illinois State Convention of Colored Men, Assembled at Galesburg, October 16th, 17th, and 18th, Containing the State and National Addresses Promulgated by It, With a List of Delegates Composing It* (Chicago, 1867), 27; see also

Christian Recorder, 2 September 1865, 19 January 1867; and Philip D. Swenson, "Illinois: Disillusionment with State Activism," in *Radical Republicans in the North,* ed. James C. Mohr (Baltimore, 1976), 15.

16. *Elevator,* 29 December 1865; see also *Christian Times and Witness,* 25 October 1865; William D. Green, "Minnesota's Long Road to Black Suffrage, 1849–1868," *Minnesota History* 56 (Summer 1998): 79; *Christian Recorder,* 10 December 1864; and *Elevator,* 24 November 1865.

17. *Weekly Anglo-African,* 23 December 1865. For similar sentiments, see *Proceedings of a Convention of Colored Citizens, Held in the City of Lawrence, October 17, 1866,* 7; *Indianapolis Daily Journal,* 8 August 1867; and *Christian Recorder,* 14 July, 3 November 1866.

18. Edwin S. Redkey, ed., *A Grand Army of Black Men: Letters from African-American Soldiers in the Union Army, 1861–1865* (Cambridge, Eng., 1992), 292.

19. See *Pacific Appeal,* 10 (quotation), 24 October 1867; and *Elevator,* 18 October, 1, 22 November 1867.

20. See *Elevator,* 2 June (quotation), 4 August 1865; see also Lortie, "San Francisco's Black Community, 1870–1890," 8, 32; and Fisher, "A History of the Political and Social Development of the Black Community in California, 1850–1950," 93, 96–99. For a similar organizational structure in Kansas, see *Christian Recorder,* 28 October 1865; Eugene Berwanger, "Hardin and Langston: Western Black Spokesmen of the Reconstruction Era," *Journal of Negro History* 64 (Spring 1979): 105; in New York, *Christian Recorder,* 4 May 1867; and *Weekly Anglo-African,* 1 July 1865; in New Jersey, *Newark Evening Courier,* 24 July 1867; in Nevada, *Elevator,* 4 August 1865; in Indiana, *Christian Recorder,* 6 January 1866; and *Indianapolis Daily Journal,* 4 November 1866.

21. *Proceedings of the Illinois State Convention of Colored Men, Assembled at Galesburg, October 16th, 17th, and 18th,* 16–19; *Carbondale New Era,* 19 October 1869; *Christian Recorder,* 5 January 1867; and *Chicago Tribune,* 17 January 1867.

22. See, for example, *Minutes of Votes and Proceedings of the Ninetieth General Assembly of the State of New Jersey. Convened at Trenton, January 9th, 1866* (Woodbury, N.J., 1866), 18, 30 January, February 1866, 56, 140, 170; *Minutes of Votes and Proceedings of the Ninety-First General Assembly of the State of New Jersey* (Camden, N.J., 1867), 26, 28 March, 1, 4 April 1867, 793, 855, 860, 881, 971; *Journal of the Twenty-Third Senate of New Jersey, Being the Ninety-First Session of the Legislature* (Newark, N.J., 1867), 6, 7, 12, 21 March 1867, 357, 377, 391, 504; *Journal of the House of Representatives of the State of Ohio, For the Regular Session of the Fifty-Seventh General Assembly, Commencing on Monday, January 1, 1866. Vol. LXII* (Columbus, 1866), 17, 19, 30 January 1866, 44, 62, 97, 121; *Journal of the Senate of the State of Ohio, for the Regular Session of the Fifty-Eighth General Assembly, Commencing on January 2, 1867. Vol. LXIII* (Columbus, 1867), 12 March 1867, 310; *Journal of the Senate of the Twenty-Fourth General Assembly of the State of Illinois* (Springfield, 1865), 5, 6 January 1865, 72, 79; *Journal of the Senate of the Twenty-Fifth General Assembly of the State of Illinois* (Springfield, 1867), 11 January 1867, 76; *Journal of the Convention of the State of New York* (Albany, N.Y., 1867), 19 June, 24, 31 July 1867, 83, 282, 361; *Journal of the Senate, during the Sixteenth Session of the Legislature of the State of California, 1865–6* (Sacramento, 1866), 5 January 1866, 127; and Petitions to the California Legislature, 1863–1866 (7, 10, 12 January 1866), California State Archives, Sacramento, Calif.

23. See, for example, *Newark Evening Courier,* 15 August 1867; and Russell H. Davis, *Black Americans in Cleveland from George Peake to Carl B. Stokes, 1796–1969* (Washington, D.C., 1972), 84.

24. *New York Times,* 4 February 1866; and *Liberator,* 24 March 1865.

25. Wright, "Negro Suffrage in New Jersey, 1776–1875," 208–11; Sanelli, "The Struggle for Black Suffrage in Pennsylvania, 1838–1870," 228–30; Minutes of the Executive Board of the Pennsylvania State Equal Rights League, 4 September, 10 November 1866, Leon Gardiner Collection on Negro History; and *Christian Recorder,* 15 September 1866. A lawsuit sponsored by the New York Equal Rights League, which challenged a state law declaring that no person could be

placed on the register of voters in New York City and Brooklyn—where most black New Yorkers lived—unless he appeared personally before the Board of Registrars during the registration period, appears to have suffered the same fate. Block, *The Circle of Discrimination: An Economic and Social Study of the Black Man in New York* (New York, 1969), 182–83.

26. John Godby Gregory, "Negro Suffrage in Wisconsin," *Transactions of the Wisconsin Academy of Sciences, Arts, and Letters* 2 (1896–97): 94–101; and Richard N. Current, *The History of Wisconsin. Vol. II: The Civil War Era, 1848–1873* (Madison, Wisc., 1976), 570–71.

27. For studies of developments in Minnesota and Iowa, see Green, "Minnesota's Long Road to Black Suffrage, 1849–1868," 80–81; Libman, "Minnesota and the Struggle for Black Suffrage: 1849–1870," 57–60, 197–99; G. Galin Berrier, "The Negro Suffrage Issue in Iowa—1865–1868," *Annals of Iowa* 39 (Spring 1968): 253–54; *American Annual Cyclopedia of Important Events of the Year 1866* (New York, 1867), 406–7; Schwalm, *Emancipation's Diaspora,* 183–88; and Alexander Keyssar, *The Right to Vote: The Contested History of Democracy in the United States* (New York, 2000), 89.

28. For treatments of the setbacks suffered by black suffrage advocates across the North, see Gillette, *The Right to Vote,* 25–27; and Eugene H. Berwanger, *The West and Reconstruction* (Urbana, Ill., 1981), 156–59. For discussions of this issue in California, see Chandler, "Friends in Time of Need," 336–37; and Fisher, "A History of the Political and Social Development of the Black Community in California, 1850–1950," 100–102; in Illinois, see *Chicago Tribune,* 17 January 1867; *Journal of the House of Representatives of the Twenty-fifth General Assembly of the State of Illinois* (Springfield, 1867), I, 12 January 1867, 48; and Roger D. Bridges, "Equality Deferred: Civil Rights for Illinois Blacks, 1865–1885," *Journal of the Illinois State Historical Society* 74 (Summer 1981): 90–95; in New York, see *Journal of the Convention of the State of New York,* 19 June 1867, 91; Ena Lunette Farley, "The Issue of Black Equality in New York State, 1865–1873" (Ph.D. diss., University of Wisconsin, 1973), 27–33; and James C. Mohr, *The Radical Republicans and Reform in New York during Reconstruction* (Ithaca, N.Y., 1973), 234–35; in Pennsylvania, see Sanelli, "The Struggle for Black Suffrage in Pennsylvania, 1838–1870," 202–5, 215–16, 250–60; Robert Mittrick, "A History of Negro Voting in Pennsylvania during the Nineteenth Century" (Ph.D. diss., Rutgers University, 1985), 51–53; and Brown, *The Negro in Pennsylvania History,* 48–50; in Kansas, see Martha Belle Caldwell, "The Attitude of Kansas toward Reconstruction" (Ph.D. diss., Kansas University, 1933), 51–62; and Berwanger, *The West and Reconstruction,* 105–7; in Michigan, see George M. Blackburn, "Michigan: Quickening Government in a Developing State," in *Radical Republicans in the North,* ed. Mohr, 126, 130–31; in Connecticut, see *Journal of the House of Representatives of the State of Connecticut, May Session, 1865* (Hartford, 1865), 93, 132–40; and John Niven, "Connecticut: Poor Progress in the Land of Steady Habits," in *Radical Republicans in the North,* ed. Mohr, 28; in Oregon, see K. Keith Richard, "Unwelcome Settlers: Black and Mulatto Oregon Pioneers," *Oregon Historical Quarterly* 84 (Spring 1983): 47; in Nevada, see Elmer R. Rusco, *"Good Time Coming?" Black Nevadans in the Nineteenth Century* (Westport, Conn., 1975), 29; and William Hanchett, "Yankee Law and the Negro in Nevada, 1861–1869," *Western Humanities Review* 10 (Summer 1956): 243; in New Jersey, see *Journal of the Twenty-second Senate of the State of New Jersey, Being the Nineteenth Session of the Legislature* (Salem, N.J., 1866), 6 March 1866, 384.

29. Leslie J. Fishel Jr., "Northern Prejudice and Negro Suffrage, 1865–1870," *Journal of Negro History* 39 (January 1954): 9–10 (quotation); and Committee on Constitutional Amendments, Connecticut General Assembly, African Americans, 1821–1869, RG002, Box 1, 99–139, 25 May 1865, General Assembly Papers, Connecticut Historical Library, Hartford. For similar sentiments, see *Detroit Free Press,* 26 January 1865; Herbert H. Wubben, "The Uncertain Trumpet: Iowa Republicans and Black Suffrage, 1860–1868," *Annals of Iowa* 47 (Summer 1984): 419–20; and Berwanger, *The West and Reconstruction,* 107–8. On the Democrats' anti-suffrage arguments, see Lawrence Grossman, *The Democratic Party and the Negro: Northern and National Politics, 1868–92*

(Urbana, Ill., 1976), 1–4, 14–22; Jerome Mushkat, *The Reconstruction of the New York Democracy, 1861–1874* (East Brunswick, N.J., 1981), 118–27; Forrest G. Wood, *Black Scare: The Racist Response to Emancipation and Reconstruction* (Berkeley, Calif., 1968), 80–102; and Louis B. Moore, "Response to Reconstruction: Change and Continuity in New Jersey Politics, 1866–1874" (Ph.D. diss., Rutgers University, 1999), 73–74.

30. *Christian Recorder,* 12 October 1867. For similar views, see *Cincinnati Colored Citizen,* 18 January 1868; and entry for 16 March 1869, Jacob C. White Collection.

31. For evidence of Radical Republican support for black suffrage, see *Journal of the House of Representatives of the State of Ohio, for the Regular Session of the Fifty-seventh General Assembly, Commencing on Monday, January 6, 1866. Vol. LXII* (Columbus, Ohio, 1866), 24 January 1866, 9, 24, 31 January 1866, 126, 8 February 1866, 155–56, 17 February 1866, 220, 20 February 1866, 234, 21 February 1866, 244, 28 February 1866, 266, 2 April 1866, 521; Morrow B. Lowry to Isaiah C. Wears, 12 March 1869, Isaiah C. Wears Papers, Leon Gardiner Collection on Negro History, Historical Society of Pennsylvania; Richard J. Oglesby to Union Republicans of New York, 14 October 1867, Richard J. Oglesby Papers, Illinois State Historical Library, Springfield; House, *Resolutions of the Legislature of Vermont, on the Subject of Equal Suffrage,* 39th Cong., 2d Sess., 1866, H. Misc. Doc. 4; and *Detroit Advertiser and Tribune,* 22 February 1868.

32. See LaWanda Cox and John H. Cox, "Negro Suffrage and Republican Politics: The Problem of Motivation in Reconstruction Historiography," *Journal of Southern History* 33 (August 1967): 303–30; and Field, *The Politics of Race in New York,* 159–60, 218.

33. Ira V. Brown, "Pennsylvania and the Rights of the Negro, 1865–1887," *Pennsylvania History* 28 (January 1961): 51–52; Hans L. Trefousse, *Thaddeus Stevens: Nineteenth-Century Egalitarian* (Chapel Hill, N.C., 1997), 155 (quotation); and George W. Julian, *Political Recollections, 1840–1872* (Chicago, 1884), 263.

34. See, for example, Felice Bonadio, *North of Reconstruction: Ohio Politics, 1865–1870* (New York, 1970), 80, 86–87, 94–95; see also James M. McPherson, *The Struggle for Equality: Abolitionists and the Negro in the Civil War and Reconstruction* (Princeton, N.J., 1964), 33–34, 351–52; Sanelli, "The Struggle for Black Suffrage in Pennsylvania, 1838–1870," 203–16, 250–60; Robert D. Sawrey, *Dubious Victory: The Reconstruction Debate in Ohio* (Lexington, Ky., 1992), 17–19, 30–31, 33–37; Berwanger, "Hardin and Langston," 105–7; Rusco, *"Good Time Coming?"* 21–22, 46; Moore, "Response to Reconstruction," 88–90, 114–18; and Xi Wang, *The Trial of Democracy: Black Suffrage and Northern Republicans, 1860–1910* (Athens, Ga., 1997), 24–27.

35. For the debate on this matter, see Harding, *There Is a River,* 243–45; and Rael, *Black Identity and Black Protest in the Antebellum North,* 10.

36. *First Annual Meeting of the National Equal Rights League, Held in Cleveland, Ohio, October 19th, 20th, and 21st, 1865,* 39, 45–46 (quotation); and *Christian Recorder,* 21 October 1865 (quotation); see also *Pacific Appeal,* 23 November 1867. On the Reconstruction Act of 1867 and black suffrage, see Eric Foner, *A Short History of Reconstruction, 1863–1877* (New York, 1990), 120–22.

37. *Liberator,* 26 May 1865. For similar views by northern blacks, see *First Annual Meeting of the National Equal Rights League, Held in Cleveland, Ohio, October 19th, 20th and 21st, 1865,* 39; and *Newark Evening Courier,* 13 August 1867. For abolitionists' support for black suffrage following the Civil War, see *Independent,* 28 September, 26 October, 16 November 1865, 21 March, 21 April, 14 November 1867; *New York Tribune,* 12 September, 3 October 1865, 12 February 1866; *National Anti-Slavery Standard,* 19 August 1865; *Philadelphia Press,* 14 February 1865, 14 January 1866; and *The Right Way,* 20, 27 January, 28 April, 5 May 1866.

38. *Christian Recorder,* 20 March 1869; see also *Newark Evening Courier,* 13 August 1867; *Pacific Appeal,* 17 August 1867; *Elevator,* 3 August 1867; and *Cincinnati Commercial,* 23 February 1867.

39. See, for example, minutes of 22 April 1867, Records of the Social, Civic, and Statistical Association of the Colored People of Pennsylvania; and *Pacific Appeal,* 14 September 1867.

40. See, for example, Sawrey, *Dubious Victory,* 115; Michael Les Benedict, "The Rout of Radicalism: Republicans and the Elections of 1867," *Civil War History* 18 (December 1972): 340–44; Gillette, *The Right to Vote,* 26, 30–37; and Earl M. Maltz, *Civil Rights, the Constitution, and Congress, 1863–1869* (Lawrence, Kans., 1990), 136–37.

41. *Christian Recorder,* 24 February, 30 September, 2 December 1865; *First Annual Meeting of the National Equal Rights League, Held in Cleveland, Ohio, October 19th, 29th, and 21st, 1865,* 47; and William Nesbit to executive board of the PSERL, 27 September 1865, Leon Gardiner Collection on Negro History. Lewis Tappan and Gerrit Smith—two pioneer abolitionists who strongly supported political and civil rights for African Americans—were among those who contributed to sustaining a black lobby in Washington. Lewis Tappan to Frederick Douglass, 11 January 1866, George T. Downing Papers, Moorland—Spingarn Research Center; and Lewis Tappan to Gerrit Smith, 3 January 1866, Gerrit Smith Miller Collection, Syracuse University.

42. *Weekly Anglo-African,* 11 November 1865; and *National Anti-Slavery Standard,* 13 January 1866.

43. George T. Downing to Frederick Douglass, 18 January 1866, Frederick Douglass Papers, Library of Congress; George T. Downing and John Jones to Charles Sumner, 1 February 1866, Charles Sumner Papers; *Christian Recorder,* 17 February 1866; and *Chicago Tribune,* 7 February 1866.

44. George T. Downing to Frederick Douglass, 18 January 1866, Frederick Douglass Papers; and John Mercer Langston, *From the Virginia Plantation to the National Capitol: An Autobiography* (Reprint, New York, 1969), 230–31.

45. *Christian Recorder,* 12 August 1865; and *Proceedings of the Colored Men's Convention of the State of Michigan, Held in the City of Detroit, Tuesday and Wednesday, September 12th and 13th, '65,* 13.

46. *Christian Recorder,* 17 February 1866.

47. LaWanda Cox and John H. Cox, *Politics, Principle, and Prejudice, 1865–1866: Dilemma of Reconstruction America* (New York, 1963), 163.

48. Frederick Douglass, *Life and Times of Frederick Douglass* (New York, 1994), 820–22; and *Christian Recorder,* 17 February 1866.

49. James Lynch to George T. Downing, 13 February 1866, DeGrasse-Howard Papers, Massachusetts Historical Society, Boston; William Nesbit to Charles Sumner, 17 March 1866, George T. Downing and John Jones to Charles Sumner, 13 February 1866, Charles Sumner Papers; George T. Downing to Thaddeus Stevens, 8 March 1866, Thaddeus Stevens Papers; George T. Downing to Frederick Douglass, 18 January 1866, Frederick Douglass Papers; and *Chicago Tribune,* 1 February 1866.

50. William Nesbit to Charles Sumner, 17 March 1866, Charles Sumner Papers; William Nesbit to Jacob C. White Jr., 5 March 1866, Jacob C. White Papers, American Negro Historical Society Collection.

51. Senate, *Memorial of a Delegation Representing the Colored People of the Several States, remonstrating against the passage of joint resolution,* 39th Cong., 1st Sess., 1866, S. Doc. 56, serial 1239; and Memorial to Congress, February 12, 1866, Pennsylvania State Equal Rights League, 2–3, Leon Gardiner Collection on Negro History.

52. See, for example, Charles Sumner to John Mercer Langston, 2 December 1866, Charles Sumner Papers; Trefousse, *Thaddeus Stevens,* 155, 167, 199; George W. Julian to son, 8 February 1866, Julian to wife, 10, 20 February 1866, George W. Julian Papers, Indiana State Library, Indianapolis; Julian, *Political Recollections, 1840–1872,* 263–66; Elsa Holderried, "The Public Life of Jacob Merritt Howard" (Master's thesis, Wayne State University, 1950), 145–46; *Indianapolis Daily Journal,* 28 August 1867; *Chicago Tribune,* 1 February 1866; *Independent,* 16 March 1865; Ira V. Brown, "William D. Kelley and Radical Reconstruction," *Pennsylvania Magazine of History and Biography* 85 (July 1961): 321–23; and Schuyler Colfax to Cresswell, 28 September 1867, Schuyler Colfax Papers, Hayes Historical Library, Fremont, Ohio.

53. Douglass to Wilson, 12 September 1866, Frederick Douglass Papers; Henry Highland Garnet to Charles Sumner, 17 February 1866, Charles Sumner Papers; also George T. Downing to Sumner, 31 January 1865, 5 May 1866, John Jones, Downing, and others to Sumner, 13 February 1866, Frederick Douglass to Sumner, 29 April 1865, Charles Sumner Papers; and Joseph C. Bustill to Thaddeus Stevens, 22 December 1865, Thaddeus Stevens Papers.

54. House, *Address of the Colored Citizens of Chicago to the Congress of the United States*, 39th Cong., 1st Sess., H. Doc. 109, serial 1271, 1–2; *Weekly Anglo-African*, 29 July 1865; *New York Times*, 4 February 1866; *Liberator*, 11 August 1865; Charles Sumner to John Mercer Langston, 2 December 1866, Charles Sumner Papers; and *Christian Recorder*, 19 January 1867.

55. Numerous petitions calling for black manhood suffrage rights are found in Senate, Committee on the Judiciary, 40th Cong., 1st Sess., RG46; Senate, Committee on the Judiciary, 41st Cong., 1st Sess., RG46; Senate, Joint Committee on Reconstruction, 39th–41st Cong., RG128, National Archives; and 17 December 1866 meeting, Records of the Social, Civic and Statistical Association of the Colored People of Pennsylvania. David Quigley shows that many working-class black men and women agitated for suffrage rights. Quigley, *Second Founding*, 67–68.

56. See Voegeli, *Free but Not Equal*, 160–64; Maltz, *Civil Rights, The Constitution, and Congress, 1863–1869*, 8–11, 122; and Robert J. Kaczorowski, "To Begin the Nation Anew: Congress, Citizenship, and Civil Rights after the Civil War," *American Historical Review* 92 (February 1987): 49–50.

57. Kaczorowski, "To Begin The Nation Anew," 49; Kaczorowski, "Revolutionary Constitutionalism in the Era of the Civil War and Reconstruction," *New York University Law Review* 61 (November 1986): 881–82; Xi Wang, *The Trial of Democracy*, 24–25; and *Independent*, 7 June 1866.

58. See William E. Nelson, *The Fourteenth Amendment: From Political Principle to Judicial Doctrine* (Cambridge, Mass., 1988), 125–33; Xi Wang, *The Trial of Democracy*, 27–28; Kaczorowski, "Revolutionary Constitutionalism in the Era of the Civil War and Reconstruction," 882–83. A number of historians have argued that moderate Republicans, who shaped much of Reconstruction policy, were constitutional conservatives who believed that the major responsibility for protecting the rights of citizens should remain in the hands of the states. See, for example, Michael Les Benedict, *A Compromise of Principle: Congressional Republicans and Reconstruction, 1863–1869* (New York, 1974); Herman Belz, *A New Battle of Freedom: Freedmen's Rights, 1861–1866* (Westport, Conn., 1976); Harold M. Hyman, *A More Perfect Union: The Impact of the Civil War and Reconstruction on the Constitution* (New York, 1973); and Phillip S. Paludan, *A Covenant with Death: The Constitution, Law, and Equality in the Civil War Era* (Urbana, Ill., 1975). Other scholars, however, have asserted that Republicans in fact shifted authority, in some significant ways, from the states to the federal government. See especially Robert J. Kaczorowski, *The Politics of Judicial Interpretation: The Federal Courts, the Department of Justice, and Civil Rights, 1866–1876* (New York, 1985); and LaWanda Cox and John H. Cox, *Politics, Principle, and Prejudice, 1865–1866*.

59. *National Anti-Slavery Standard*, 7 July 1866; and *Christian Recorder*, 19 January 1867. For similar sentiments, see Senate, *Memorial of a Delegation Representing the People of the Several States, remonstrating against the passage of joint resolution, H.R. No. 57, proposing to amend the Constitution of the United States*, 39th Cong., 1st Sess., S. Doc. 56, serial 1239; and *Christian Recorder*, 19 May 1866.

60. George T. Downing to Charles Sumner, 31 January 1867, Charles Sumner Papers. On black activists' agitation in Colorado, see Lewis Douglass to Frederick Douglass, 29 October 1866, Frederick Douglass Papers; also Eugene H. Berwanger, "William J. Hardin: Colorado Spokesman for Racial Justice, 1863–1873," *Colorado Magazine* 52 (Winter 1975): 54–58; and Berwanger, "Reconstruction on the Frontier: The Equal Rights Struggle in Colorado, 1865–1867," *Pacific Historical Review* 44 (August 1975): 313–19, 323–25.

61. Xi Wang, *The Trial of Democracy,* 29–34, 150–53; *Independent,* 14 February 1867; and Maltz, *Civil Rights, the Constitution, and Congress, 1863–1869,* 123–30, 133–34.

62. *Christian Recorder,* 26 January, 9 March 1967.

63. See Brooks D. Simpson, *The Reconstruction Presidents* (Lawrence, Kans., 1998), 143; Gillette, *The Right to Vote,* 32–39; and Richard H. Abbott, *The Republican Party and the South, 1855–1877: The First Southern Strategy* (Chapel Hill, N.C., 1986), 200.

64. See Hanchett, "Yankee Law and the Negro in Nevada, 1861–1869," 244; and Russell R. Elliott, *Servant of Power: A Political Biography of William M. Stewart* (Reno, Nev., 1983), 32, 57–58, 62–63.

65. A number of historians have argued that the Republicans above all believed that the black vote would more than offset the effects of a white backlash, thus providing the margin of victory in a number of crucial northern states. See, for example, Gillette, *The Right to Vote,* 166–90; Squibb, "Roads to Plessy," 64–70; Abbott, *The Republican Party and the South, 1855–1877,* 205–6; Moore, "Response to Reconstruction," 56–58; Bonadio, *North of Reconstruction,* 92–97, 106; and Wubben, "The Uncertain Trumpet," 420–22. Other scholars, however, have concluded that most Republicans were committed to black manhood suffrage despite the political risks involved and that in several northern states the black vote would make little difference in the outcome of elections. See Cox and Cox, "Negro Suffrage and Republican Politics," 303–30; Field, *The Politics of Race in New York,* 159–60, 169–70, 181–83; McPherson, *The Struggle for Equality,* 333–34; Libman, "Minnesota and the Struggle for Black Suffrage," 1–5, 132–33; Berrier, "The Negro Suffrage Issue in Iowa—1865–1868," 245–46; and Current, *The History of Wisconsin: Vol. II,* 572. Still others have noted a more complex blend of pragmatism and idealism among Republicans. See William Gillette, *Retreat from Reconstruction, 1869–1879* (Baton Rouge, La., 1979), 18–19; Robert M. Goldman, *Reconstruction and Black Suffrage: Losing the Vote in Reese and Cruikshank* (Lawrence, Kans., 2001), 16–17; Simpson, *The Reconstruction Presidents,* 143; Sawrey, *Dubious Victory,* 114; Maltz, *Civil Rights, the Constitution, and Congress, 1863–1869,* 144–45; and Berwanger, *The West and Reconstruction,* 174.

66. *National Anti-Slavery Standard,* 23 January 1869; and *Christian Recorder,* 23 January 1869.

67. *National Anti-Slavery Standard,* 30 January 1869.

68. (Unknown) to Schuyler Colfax, 18 January 1869, John Mercer Langston Papers, Fisk University (microfilm); *National Anti-Slavery Standard,* 30 January 1869; and *Christian Recorder,* 23, 30 January 1869.

69. Senate, *Memorial of the Executive Committee of the Late National Convention of the Colored Men of the Country, praying the right of suffrage to be granted to all citizens without regard to race, color, or previous condition,* 40th Cong., 3d Sess., S. Doc. 44, serial 1361 (quotation); William A. Lavalette to Jacob C. White Jr., 20 July 1869, Jacob C. White Papers, American Negro Historical Society Collection.

70. *Elevator,* 15 September 1865; also 23 March 1867, 21 February 1868; *Weekly Anglo-African,* 1 July 1865; George T. Downing to Frederick Douglass, 18 January 1866, Frederick Douglass Papers; and *Liberator,* 17 February 1865.

71. *Christian Recorder,* 25 November 1865; *Weekly Anglo-African,* 1 July 1865; and *Elevator,* 15 September 1865. Douglass argued that a literacy test should be applied equally to all males. *Liberator,* 17 February 1865. See also Rael, *Black Identity and Black Protest in the Antebellum North,* 295–96; and David Gerber, "A Politics of Limited Options: Northern Black Politics and the Problem of Change and Continuity in Race Relations Historiography," *Journal of Social History* 14 (Winter 1980): 241.

72. William Nesbit to Jacob C. White Jr., 25 November 1868, Jacob C. White Papers, American Negro Historical Society Collection; petitions of 1 December 1868, 5 January 1869, House Committee on the Judiciary, 40th Cong., 3d Sess., RG46, National Archives; and *Newark Evening Courier,* 13 August 1867.

73. William D. Forten to Charles Sumner, 1 February 1869, Charles Sumner Papers.

74. Dable, *A Respectable Woman,* 129–31, 139, 156; and Schwalm, *Emancipation's Diaspora,* 5–6. On the continuing debate among historians on southern women's role in the political culture during Reconstruction, see Martha S. Jones, *All Bound Up Together: The Woman Question in African American Public Culture, 1830–1900* (Chapel Hill, N.C., 2007), 142; Foner, *Forever Free,* 131; Hahn, *A Nation under Our Feet,* 227, 230–34; Michael W. Fitzgerald, "Reconstruction Politics and the Politics of Reconstruction," in *Reconstructions,* ed. Brown, 102; Elsa Barkley Brown, "Race Identity and Political Activism: The Shifting Contours of the African American Public Sphere," in *The Black Public Sphere: A Public Culture Book* (Chicago, 1995), 111–50; and Julie Saville, "Rites and Power: Reflections on Slavery, Freedom, and Political Ritual," *Slavery and Abolition* 20 (January 1999): 81–102.

75. *Elevator,* 15 September 1865; and Jones, *All Bound Up Together,* 142–43.

76. Lewis, "The Fortens of Philadelphia," 208–9.

77. Rosalyn Terborg-Penn, *African American Women in the Struggle for the Vote, 1850–1920* (Bloomington, Ind., 1998), 19–21, 24; Marianna W. Davis, ed., *Contributions of Black Women to America, Vol. II: Civil Rights, Politics and Government, Education, Medicine, Sciences* (Columbia, S.C., 1982), 144, 147; and Paul Giddings, *When and Where I Enter: The Impact of Black Women on Race and Sex in America* (Toronto, 1984), 67.

78. See *National Anti-Antislavery Standard,* 1 June 1867, 6 February 1869; Lewis, "The Struggle for Black Suffrage in Pennsylvania, 1838–1870," 232; Elizabeth Cady Stanton et al., eds., *History of Woman Suffrage* (New York, 1882), II, 183; Rosalyn M. Terborg-Penn, "Afro-Americans in the Struggle for Woman Suffrage" (Ph.D. diss., Howard University, 1977), 79; and Martin, *The Mind of Frederick Douglass,* 156. For similar views of other African American men, see Farrison, *William Wells Brown,* 409; William E. Ward, "Charles Lenox Remond: Black Abolitionist, 1838–1873" (Ph.D. diss., Clark University, 1977), 256–57; Stanton et al., eds., *History of Woman Suffrage,* II:182–86.

79. Nell Irvin Painter, "Voices of Suffrage: Sojourner Truth, Frances Ellen Watkins Harper, and the Struggle for Woman Suffrage," in *Votes for Women: The Struggle for Suffrage Revisited,* ed. Jean H. Baker (Oxford, 2002), 49; Darlene Clark Hine, ed., *Black Women in America,* 2d ed. (Oxford, 2005), III:36–37; Giddings, *When and Where I Enter,* 67; and Terborg-Penn, *African American Women in the Struggle for the Vote, 1850–1920,* 32.

80. Lori D. Ginzberg, *Elizabeth Cady Stanton: An American Life* (New York, 2009), 116–24; and Ellen Carol DuBois, *Woman Suffrage and Women's Rights* (New York, 1998), 89–90, 93–96.

81. Giddings, *When and Where I Enter,* 65; Painter, "Voices of Suffrage," 46–50; and Jones, *All Bound Up Together,* 142–44.

82. Stanton et al., eds., *History of Woman Suffrage,* I:72–73. On Truth's views, see Giddings, *When and Where I Enter,* 65; Painter, "Voices of Suffrage," 45–47; Terborg-Penn, *African American Women in the Struggle for the Vote, 1850–1920,* 31; and Gerda Lerner, *Black Women in White America: A Documentary History* (New York, 1972), 569.

83. Giddings, *When and Where I Enter,* 66; and Terborg-Penn, *African American Women in the Struggle for the Vote, 1850–1920,* 32.

84. Nell Irvin Painter, *Sojourner Truth: A Life, A Symbol* (New York, 1996), 224–25; Hine, ed., *Black Women in America,* III:37; Giddings, *When and Where I Enter,* 68; Stanton et al., eds., *History of Woman Suffrage,* II:391–92; Carleton Mabee, *Sojourner Truth: Slave, Prophet, Legend* (New York, 1993), 176–80; and Ella Forbes, *African American Women during the Civil War* (New York, 1998), 216. Margaret Hope Bacon "'One Great Bundle of Humanity,'" 35, 39; and Ellen Carol DuBois, *Feminism and Suffrage: The Emergence of an Independent Women's Movement in America, 1849–1869* (Ithaca, N.Y., 1978), 67–70.

85. See Gillette, *The Right to Vote,* 175–76; Patricia Lucie, "The Enduring Significance of the Civil War Constitutional Amendments," in *Legacy of Disunion: The Enduring Significance of the*

American Civil War, ed. Susan-Mary Grant and Peter J. Parish (Baton Rouge, La., 2003), 179–80: Elliott, *Servant of Power,* 63; Xi Wang, *The Trial of Democracy,* 46–48; and Goldman, *Reconstruction and Black Suffrage,* 15–16.

86. See, for example, Gillette, *The Right to Vote,* 113–26, 156–57; Xi Wang, *The Trial of Democracy,* 49–50; *Journal of the House of Representatives of the State of Indiana, during the Forty-sixth Regular Session of the General Assembly* (Indianapolis, 1869), 13 April 1869; Ena L. Farley, "The Denial of Black Equality Under the States Rights Dictum: New York, 1865–1877," *Afro-Americans in New York Life and History* (January 1977): 18; Sawrey, *Dubious Victory,* 143; Blackburn, "Michigan," 130; Senate, *Resolution of the Legislature of Pennsylvania, ratifying the amendment to the Constitution of the United States known as Article XV,* 41st Cong., 1st Sess., S. Doc. 20, serial 1399, 172–79; Rutherford B. Hayes to Schuyler Colfax, 22 October 1869, Schuyler Colfax Papers; Berwanger, *The West and Reconstruction,* 177–80; and Simpson, *The Reconstruction Presidents,* 143–44.

87. *Elevator,* 12 November 1869; and *Christian Recorder,* 11 September 1869.

88. *Elevator,* 11 February 1870; *Christian Recorder,* 9 April 1870; and Florence Ray, *Sketch of the Life of Rev. Charles B. Ray* (New York, 1887), 53–54. Northern blacks held numerous public celebrations, often with Radical Republicans in attendance. See, for example, entry for 14 April 1870, Ruffin Family Papers; and Katzman, *Before the Ghetto,* 3–4.

Chapter 3

1. *National Antislavery Standard,* 15 October 1864.

2. On the desegregation of the public schools in Massachusetts, see Jacobs, "The Nineteenth-Century Struggle over Segregated Education in the Boston Schools," 80–82; George A. Levesque, "Before Integration: The Forgotten Years of Jim Crow Education in Boston," *Journal of Negro Education* 48 (1979): 113, 116–25. In the early 1850s, the Ohio legislature created a black school system in Cincinnati that would be managed largely by African Americans. Moreover, in California and Pennsylvania laws were enacted that allowed black schools to be established in districts where a sufficient number of school-age black children resided; this represented an improvement over policies that had excluded all African American children from the public schools. On the Cincinnati black schools, see David L. Calkins, "Black Education and the Nineteenth-Century City: An Institutional Analysis of Cincinnati's Colored Schools, 1850–1887," *Cincinnati Historical Society Bulletin* 33 (Fall 1975): 161–62. On developments in California and Pennsylvania, see William Warren Ferrier, *Ninety Years of Education in California, 1846–1936: A Presentation of Education Movements and Their Outcome in Education Today* (Berkeley, Calif., 1937), 17–18; and Brown, "Pennsylvania and the Rights of the Negro, 1865–1877," 46. Where black children were denied access to northern public schools—and even in some places where a public education was available—African Americans, often working through their churches, also founded private schools. Although frequently underfunded and limited to providing an elementary education, these schools were a source of pride and respect within the black community. See Carlson, "The Black Community in the Rural North," 92; Swift, *Black Prophets of Justice,* 280; Thornbrough, *The Negro in Indiana,* 167, 170, 181; Rael, *Black Identity and Protest in the Antebellum North,* 210–36; Reed, *Platform for Change,* 163–75, 198–201; Horton and Horton, *Free People of Color,* 17–25; and Pease and Pease, "Ends, Means, and Attitudes," 117–26. V. P. Franklin argues that these schools were rooted in black nationalist principles such as freedom, resistance, and self-determination. Franklin, *Black Self-Determination,* 99–101, 167, 170.

3. See, for example, Litwack, *North of Slavery,* 143–50; and Stanley K. Schultz, *The Culture Factory: The Boston Public Schools, 1789–1860* (New York, 1973), 205.

4. *Christian Recorder,* 27 January 1865; and *Elevator,* 9 June 1865.

5. On the deep-seated racism among northern whites, see Grossman, *The Democratic Party and the Negro,* 1–14; and Fredrickson, *The Black Image in the White Mind,* 165–97.

6. Finkleman, "Prelude to the Fourteenth Amendment," 463–64; Thornbrough, *The Negro in Indiana,* 481–82; and *Fourteenth Report of the Superintendent of Public Instruction for the State of Indiana* (Indianapolis, 1866), 49.

7. See Rusco, *"Good Time Coming?"* 29–34; Wollenberg, *All Deliberate Speed,* 13–15; Brown, *The Negro in Pennsylvania History,* 52; and Edward T. Price Jr., "School Segregation in Nineteenth-Century Pennsylvania," *Pennsylvania History* 43 (1976), 124–25.

8. McCaul, *The Black Struggle for Public Schooling in Nineteenth-Century Illinois,* 44–46; *Chicago Tribune,* 6 October 1864; *Sixth Biennial Report of the Superintendent of Public Instruction of the State of Illinois. 1865–1866* (Springfield, 1866), 28–29; and Philip T. K. Daniel, "A History of the Segregation-Discrimination Dilemma: The Chicago Experience," *Phylon* 41 (June 1980): 127.

9. Clark Waggoner, *History of the City of Toledo and Lucas County* (Toledo, Ohio, 1888), 628; Gerber, "Education, Expediency, and Ideology," 3; and Kusmer, *A Ghetto Takes Shape,* 16–17.

10. On the patterns in New Jersey, see Marion M. Thompson Wright, *The Education of Negroes in New Jersey* (New York, 1941), 151; and Herbert James Foster, "The Urban Experience of Blacks in Atlantic City: 1850–1915" (Ph.D. diss., Rutgers University, 1981), 214–16.

11. On Michigan, Connecticut, and Rhode Island, see Leslie H. Fishel Jr., "The North and the Negro, 1865–1900: A Study in Race Discrimination" (Ph.D. diss., Harvard University, 1953), 179; McPherson, *The Struggle for Equality,* 228; and *Liberator,* 24 March 1865. On New York, see Farley, "The Issue of Black Equality in New York State, 1865–1873," 152, 162; and *Thirteenth Annual Report of the Superintendent of Public Instruction of the State of New York* (Albany, N.Y., 1867), 196.

12. On African Americans' defense of all-black schools during the antebellum era, see Levesque, "Before Integration," 115–20; Cottrol, *The Afro-Yankees,* 99–101; Robert Austin Warner, *New Haven Negroes: A Social History* (New Haven, Conn., 1940), 77; Swift, *Black Prophets of Justice,* 280; Douglas, *Jim Crow Moves North,* 48–50; Pease and Pease, "Negro Conventions and the Problem of Black Leadership," 35–36; and Bell, ed., *Minutes of the Proceedings of the National Negro Conventions, 1830–1864,* 22–23.

13. Harold X. Connolly, *A Ghetto Grows in Brooklyn* (New York, 1977), 27; *Twenty-Eighth Annual Report of the Board of Education of the City of Detroit, for the Year Ending December 31, 1870* (Detroit, 1871), 12; Leonard Ernest Erickson, "The Color Line in Ohio Public Schools, 1829–1890" (Ph.D. diss., Ohio State University, 1959), 254; and *Daily Ohio State Journal,* 18 February 1878.

14. See David P. Thelan and Leslie H. Fishel Jr., "Reconstruction in the North: The World Looks at New York Negroes, March 16, 1867," *New York History* 49 (October 1968): 407; Rose Juanita Jackson, "The Black Educational Experience in a Northern City: Albany, New York, 1830–1870" (Ph.D. diss., Northwestern University, 1976), 53–54; Gerber, "Education, Expediency, and Ideology," 12; and Spencer R. Crew, *Black Life in Secondary Cities: A Comparative Analysis of the Black Communities of Camden and Elizabeth, New Jersey, 1860–1920* (New York, 1993), 130.

15. Harold N. Rabinowitz notes that southern blacks made similar demands during and after the Reconstruction era. *Race Relations in the Urban South, 1865–1890* (Athens, Ga., 1996), 172–75.

16. See Mabee, *Black Education in New York State,* 100–101; and Seth M. Scheiner, *Negro Mecca: A History of the Negro in New York City, 1865–1920* (New York, 1965), 160–61; see also Carlson, "The Black Community in the Rural North," 95, 100–101; and Jackson, "The Black Educational Experience in a Northern City," 48–52.

17. *Elevator,* 9 June 1865; and Reid, "Race, Class, Gender, and the Teaching Profession," 82.

18. *Proceedings of the State Equal Rights Convention of the Colored People of Pennsylvania, Held in the City of Harrisburg, February 8th, 9th, and 10th, 1865,* 19–20.

19. See ibid., 21; and *Liberator,* 3 March 1865; see also Shirley Turpin-Parham, "A History of Black Public Education in Philadelphia, Pennsylvania, 1864–1914" (Ed.D. diss., Temple University, 1986), 47–48.

20. *Proceedings of the State Equal Rights Convention of the Colored People of Pennsylvania, Held in the City of Harrisburg, February 8th, 9th, and 10th, 1865...,* 21.

21. See, for example, Harry C. Silcox, "Nineteenth Century Philadelphia Black Militant: Octavius V. Catto (1839–1871)," *Pennsylvania History* 44 (January 1977): 64; and Parham, "A History of Black Public Education in Philadelphia, Pennsylvania, 1864–1914," 48.

22. Carlson, "The Black Community in the Rural North," 103–6; Reid, "Race, Class, Gender and the Teaching Profession," 67; and Spencer R. Crew, *Black Life in Secondary Cities: A Comparative Analysis of the Black Communities of Camden and Elizabeth, New Jersey, 1860–1920* (New York, 1993), 130–31; see also Jackson, "The Black Educational Experience in a Northern City," 53–54; and Ann Greenwood Wilmoth, "Pittsburgh and the Blacks: A Short History, 1780–1875" (Ph.D. diss., Pennsylvania State University, 1975), 185.

23. *Elevator,* 2 December 1870; *Eighth Biennial Report of the Superintendent of Public Instruction of the State of Illinois, 1869–1870* (Springfield, 187), 27; and Jackson, "The Black Educational Experience in a Northern City," 53–54.

24. See Connolly, *A Ghetto Grows in Brooklyn,* 27.

25. See, for example, ibid.; Scheiner, *Negro Mecca,* 160–61; Jackson, "The Black Educational Experience in a Northern City," 48–52; Fishel, "The North and the Negro, 1865–1900," 207–8; Conner, "A Comparative Study of Black and White Public Education in New Brunswick, New Jersey," 271; Mabee, *Black Education in New York State,* 208, 212; John B. Reid, "Race, Class, Gender, and the Teaching Profession: African American Schoolteachers in the Urban Midwest, 1865–1950" (Ph.D. diss., Michigan State University, 1996), 67; Schwalm, *Emancipation's Diaspora,* 201–3; and Dabel, *A Respectable Woman,* 147.

26. Carlson, "The Black Community in the Rural North," 97; Robert S. Dixon, "The Education of the Negro in the City of New York, 1853 to 1900" (Master's thesis, College of the City of New York, 1935), 51–52; Roger Lane, *The Roots of Violence in Black Philadelphia, 1860–1900* (Cambridge, Mass., 1986), 55; and Schwalm, *Emancipation's Diaspora,* 201–2. Black teachers generally were paid less than their white counterparts, and black men earned more than black women in the teaching profession. Reid, "Race, Class, Gender, and the Teaching Profession," 69–70.

27. Mabee, *Black Education in New York State,* 210.

28. *Daily Ohio State Journal,* 9 February 1878.

29. Ibid., 11, 14 February 1878; also 18, 20 February 1878.

30. *Elevator,* 9 June 1865, 2 December 1870.

31. See David A. Gerber, "Peter Humphries Clark: The Dialogue of Hope and Despair," in *Black Leaders of the Nineteenth Century,* ed. Litwack and Meier, 179; Calkins, "Black Education and the Nineteenth-Century City," 164–65; Samuel Matthews, "The Black Educational Experience in Nineteenth-Century Cincinnati, 1817–1874" (Ed.D. diss., University of Cincinnati, 1985), viii, 98–100; and John B. Shotwell, *A History of the Schools of Cincinnati* (Cincinnati, 1902), 458. The situation in Camden, New Jersey, was similar to that in Cincinnati after 1856. Crew, *Black Life in Secondary Cities,* 130.

32. Calkins, "Black Education and the Nineteenth-Century City," 165.

33. Matthews, "The Black Educational Experience in Nineteenth-Century Cincinnati, 1817–1874," viii–ix, 60, 109–13; and Calkins, "Black Education and the Nineteenth-Century City," 165.

34. Matthews, "The Black Educational Experience in Nineteenth-Century Cincinnati, 1817–1874," 58, 75, 95–96; Gerber, "Peter Humphries Clark," 179; Lawrence Grossman, "In His Veins Coursed No Bootlicking Blood: The Career of Peter H. Clark," *Ohio History* 86 (Spring 1977): 82; and Gerber, "Education, Expediency, and Ideology," 4.

35. *Journal of the Senate of the State of Ohio, for the Regular Session of the Fifty-Eighth General Assembly, Commencing November 23, 1868. Vol. LXV* (Columbus, 1869), 94, 107, 183, 185, 207, 254, 267.

36. *Indianapolis Daily Journal,* 9 November 1866.

37. Matthews, "The Black Educational Experience in Nineteenth-Century Cincinnati, 1817–1874," 75, 98–99, 108, 124–32.

38. Ibid., 133–39; and Gerber, "Education, Expediency, and Ideology," 4–5.

39. Matthews, "The Black Educational Experience in Nineteenth-Century Cincinnati, 1817–1874," 125, 129–32; Gerber, "Peter Humphries Clark," 180–81; and *Daily Ohio State Journal,* 11 February 1878.

40. *Christian Recorder,* 9 April 1870.

41. *Pacific Appeal,* 20 June 1874; and *Christian Recorder,* 9 July 1870. Frederick Douglass made much the same point. Foner, *Frederick Douglass,* IV:288.

42. See, for example, *Pacific Appeal,* 25 November 1871; see also Memorial to Congress, 12 February 1866, Records of the Pennsylvania State Equal Rights League, 1–3, Leon Gardiner Collection on Negro History; and *Elevator,* 29 December 1871, 27 April 1872, 26 July 1873.

43. See *Proceedings of the Illinois Convention of Colored Men, Assembled at Galesburg, October 16th, 17th, and 18th* (Chicago, 1867), 6; *Christian Recorder,* 5 January 1867, 5 May 1870; Gerber, "Education, Expediency, and Ideology," 8–9; *Pacific Appeal,* 25 November 1871; and *Elevator,* 9 June 1865.

44. *Pacific Appeal,* 25 November 1871.

45. *Elevator,* 16 February 1866.

46. *Indianapolis Daily Journal,* 8, 9 November 1866, 8 October 1867.

47. *Indianapolis Daily Journal,* 8 October 1867. There is no evidence that this plan was ever implemented.

48. *Pacific Appeal,* 20 January 1872; also 17 April 1875; Arthur O. White, "The Black Movement against Jim Crow Education in Lockport, New York, 1835–1876," *New York History* 50 (July 1969): 282.

49. *Tenth Biennial Report of the Superintendent of Public Instruction of the State of Illinois. 1873–1874* (Springfield, 1875), 46–47. Indeed, four white men in Illinois sued to prevent a local school board from erecting a building and hiring a teacher to educate two black students. In *Chase v. Stephenson,* the Illinois Supreme Court declared in 1874 that the white school directors could not maintain a separate school for a few black children when they could, at a much lower cost, be accommodated at a white school. Had the school board "in good faith" provided a separate room for each race where facilities were "entirely equal," it would have been acceptable. But, in a ruling that sought above all to protect whites' economic interests and in no way challenged the state's policy mandating separate schools, the court declared that the school board's conduct "can only be regarded as a fraud upon the tax-payers of the district," who had the right to prevent public funds from being "squandered in such a reckless, unauthorized manner." *Chase v. Stephenson,* 71 Ill. 383 (1874).

50. See Katzman, *Before the Ghetto,* 85; Wollenberg, *All Deliberate Speed,* 16–17; Gerber, "Education, Expediency, and Ideology," 4–5; and Turpin-Parham, "A History of Black Public Education in Philadelphia, Pennsylvania, 1864–1914," 57–58.

51. Voegeli, *Free But Not Equal,* 172–73; Erickson, "The Color Line in the Ohio Public Schools, 1829–1890," 225–27, 235–40; Johnsen, "Equal Rights and the 'Heathen Chinee,'" 64; and Wollenberg, *All Deliberate Speed,* 16–17.

52. See Horace Mann Bond, *The Education of the Negro in the American Social Order* (New York, 1934), 384–85; and Charles A. Lofgren, *The Plessy Case: A Legal Historical Interpretation* (New York, 1987).

53. Turpin-Parham, "A History of Black Public Education in Philadelphia, Pennsylvania, 1864–1914," 244; Erickson, "The Color Line in Ohio Public Schools, 1829–1890," 235; and *Toledo Daily Commercial,* 21 January 1870.

54. Jackson, "The Black Educational Experience in a Northern City," 46–47; Conner, "A Comparative Study of Black and White Education in New Brunswick, New Jersey," 164–90, 214–21; and White, "The Black Movement against Jim Crow Education in Lockport, New York, 1835–1876," 272–76.

55. *Pacific Appeal,* 10 February 1872; *Elevator,* 9 June, 24 November 1865, 4 May 1872; and *Christian Recorder,* 27 February 1869.

56. See *Detroit Advertiser and Tribune,* 3 September 1867; *Journal of the Senate of the State of Ohio, for the Regular Session of the Fifty-Eighth General Assembly, Commencing on November 23, 1868, Vol. LXV,* 94, 107; *Christian Recorder,* 27 January 1865, 21 July 1866; *Toledo Daily Commercial,* 15 February 1870; *Liberator,* 11, 18 March 1864; *Journal of the House of Representatives of the Twenty-Fifth General Assembly of the State of Illinois.* Vol. II (Springfield, 1867), 231; and *Pacific Appeal,* 25 November 1871, 20 January 1872.

57. See *Detroit Advertiser and Tribune,* 11 January 1869; *Chicago Tribune,* 6 October 1864; *Indianapolis Daily Journal,* 8 January 1869; and *Pacific Appeal,* 31 September 1870, 7 January, 18 November, 16 December 1871, 4, 11 May 1872.

58. See, for example, *Detroit Advertiser and Tribune,* 2 February 1869; Arthur O. White, "The Black Movement against Jim Crow Education in Buffalo, New York, 1860–1900," *Phylon* 30 (1969): 385, and "The Black Movement against Jim Crow Education in Lockport, New York, 1835–1876," 279–80; *Illinois State Register,* 31 March 1871; Wollenberg, *All Deliberate Speed,* 16; Warner, *New Haven Negroes,* 117–19; Price, "School Segregation in Nineteenth-Century Pennsylvania," 126–27; Harmon Mothershead, "Negro Rights in the Colorado Territory (1859–1867)," *Colorado Magazine* 40 (July 1963): 59; Daniel, "A History of the Segregation Discrimination Dilemma," 127; Squibb, "Roads to Plessy," 138–39; and Berwanger, "Hardin and Langston," 105.

59. J. Morgan Kousser, *Dead End: The Development of Nineteenth-Century Litigation on Racial Discrimination in Schools* (Oxford, 1986), 14–15, 18–19.

60. Ibid., 16–17; and Schwalm, *Emancipation's Diaspora,* 197–98.

61. Finkleman, "Prelude to the Fourteenth Amendment," 464; Jonathan Lurie, "The Fourteenth Amendment: Use and Application in Selected State Court Civil Liberty Cases, 1870–1890—A Preliminary Assessment," *American Journal of Legal History* 28 (October 1984): 304; and Robert R. Dykstra, *Bright Radical Star: Black Freedom on the Hawkeye Frontier* (Cambridge, Mass., 1993), 229.

62. *Detroit Free Press,* 27 January 1865, 3 January 1867.

63. *Detroit Advertiser and Tribune,* 3 January, 3 September 1867 (quotation); also Kousser, *Dead End,* 18; and William Stephenson, "Integration of the Detroit Public School System during the Period 1839–1869," *Negro History Bulletin* 26 (October 1962): 27.

64. *Detroit Advertiser and Tribune,* 17 December 1867. For a discussion of the Detroit school issue between 1867–1869, see Katzman, *Before the Ghetto,* 85–87.

65. Robin S. Peebles, "Fanny Richards and the Integration of the Detroit Public Schools," *Michigan History* 65 (January/February 1981): 31.

66. On Workman's lawsuit, see Paludan, *A Covenant with Death,* 266; and Stephenson, "Integration of the Detroit Public School System during the Period 1839–1869," 27.

67. *Detroit Advertiser and Tribune,* 11 January 1869. Among those who helped to finance Workman's lawsuit were Fanny Richards, a black teacher, and members of the Second Baptist Church, where Richards taught Sunday School, as well as John Bagley, a wealthy Republican, tobacco manufacturer, and member of the Detroit Board of Education, who later was elected governor of Michigan. Peebles, "Fanny Richards and the Integration of the Detroit Public Schools," 30–31.

68. *Detroit Advertiser and Tribune,* 2 February, 6 April 1869; *Thirty-Third Annual Report of the Superintendent of Public Instruction of the State of Michigan, with Accompanying Documents, for the Year 1869* (Lansing, Mich., 1869), 23.

69. *Thirty-Third Annual Report of the Superintendant of Public Instruction of the State of Michigan, with Accompanying Documents, for the Year 1869,* 26–29; and Squibb, "Roads to Plessy," 119–21. Kousser has speculated that if Cooley had sought to apply the Fourteenth Amendment to the issue of segregated schools, he would have found that they violated the Constitution. Kousser, *Dead End,* 19. But Douglas and Squibb have contended that Cooley consciously cited Michigan

law and avoided any mention of federal questions. Douglas, *Jim Crow Moves North,* 114; and Squibb, "Roads to Plessy," 121–22.

70. *Detroit Advertiser and Tribune,* 12 October 1869. The Democratic *Detroit Free Press* echoed these sentiments, 13 October 1869.

71. See *Twenty-Eighth Annual Report of the Board of Education of the City of Detroit, for the Year Ending December 31, 1870* (Detroit, 1871), 12; and *Detroit Advertiser and Tribune,* 14 July 1871.

72. *Detroit Advertiser and Tribune,* 12 November 1872; and Katzman, *Before the Ghetto,* 87–88.

73. On school integration in Rhode Island, see Lawrence Grossman, "George T. Downing and the Desegregation of the Rhode Island Public Schools, 1855–1866," *Rhode Island History* 36 (November 1977): 104–5; and Charles Carroll, *Public Education in Rhode Island* (Providence, 1918), 158; on Connecticut, see Warner, *New Haven Negroes,* 118–19; in Minnesota, see William D. Green, "'Critical is Fifteen Coloreds!': De Facto and De Jure Policies of Racial Isolation in St. Paul's Schools and Housing Patterns during the Nineteenth Century, and Beyond," *Journal of Public Law and Policy* 17 (1996): 313.

74. On the Iowa situation, see Douglas, *Jim Crow Moves North,* 77; Schwalm, *Emancipation's Diaspora,* 198–99; on Indiana, see Thornbrough, *The Negro in Indiana,* 323–25; on California, see *Elevator,* 10, 17 July, 6 November 1868; and Chandler, "Friends in Time of Need," 331–32; on Illinois, see Vincent P. Franklin, "The Persistence of School Segregation in the Urban North: An Historical Perspective," *Journal of Ethnic Studies* 1 (1974): 57; on Pennsylvania, see *Christian Recorder,* 21 July 1866; and Brown, *The Negro in Pennsylvania History,* 52–53.

75. See, for example, *Detroit Advertiser and Tribune,* 6 April 1869; *Toledo Daily Commercial,* 14 July 1869; Davis, "The Pennsylvania State Equal Rights League and the Northern Black Struggle for Legal Equality," 625–26; and *Indianapolis Daily Journal,* 9 November 1866.

76. See, for example, Price, "School Segregation in Nineteenth-Century Pennsylvania," 128–32; White, "The Black Movement against Jim Crow Education in Buffalo, New York, 1800–1900," 385–86; *Elevator,* 20 December 1867, 15 January 1869, 4 July 1873; and William Hanchett, "Yankee Law and the Negro in Nevada, 1861–1868," 246.

Chapter 4

1. Goldman, *Reconstruction and Black Suffrage,* 16; and Louis Hayden to Wendell Phillips, 28 February 1870, Crawford Blagden Papers, Houghton Library, Harvard University; see also *Daily Ohio State Journal,* 13 January 1870.

2. *Elevator,* 10 June 1870.

3. Davis, ed., *Contributions of Black Women to America,* II:67–68; and Terborg-Penn, *African American Women in the Struggle for the Vote, 1850–1920,* 36, 56.

4. Painter, "Voices of Suffrage," 52; and Terborg-Penn, *African American Women in the Struggle for the Vote, 1850–1920,* 34, 38–39, 48, 52. For an analysis of the AWSA-NWSA split, see DuBois, *Feminism and Suffrage,* 188–200. Harriet Purvis, a prominent Philadelphia activist for universal suffrage, was more active in the NWSA than Truth, becoming in 1876 the first black woman to be elected a vice president of the organization. Davis, ed., *Contributions of Black Women to America,* II:68.

5. Painter, "Voices of Suffrage," 52; and Terborg-Penn, *African American Women in the Struggle for the Vote, 1850–1920,* 47–48.

6. *New National Era,* 24 November 1870; and Frederick Douglass to Charles Sumner, 6 July 1872, Charles Sumner Papers (quotation). For an analysis of blacks' concerns regarding the lessons that many whites drew from hundreds of years of slavery, see Blight, *Race and Reunion,* 98–139. Leslie Fishel's claim that northern black men's "euphoria" in response to the ratification of the amendment made them especially vulnerable to despair and regret as the 1870s unfolded does not hold up under close scrutiny. See Fishel, "Repercussions of Reconstruction," 326.

7. *Daily Ohio State Journal,* 14 April 1870. An Ohio black convention held on the eve of ratification expressed similar concerns. *Daily Ohio State Journal,* 17 November 1869.

8. Charles Lenox Remond 1872 speech, Box 87-1, Folder 51, Ruffin Family Papers.

9. Senate Committee on the Judiciary, 9 April 1870 petition, 41st Cong., 2d Sess. (quotation); and *Daily Ohio State Journal,* 4 April 1870.

10. See Johnsen, "Equal Rights and the 'Heathen Chinee,'" 63; *New National Era,* 29 December 1870; Farley, "The Denial of Black Equality under the States Rights Dictum," 17; Katzman, *Before the Ghetto,* 101–2; and Moore, "Response to Reconstruction," 151.

11. *Newark Daily Journal,* 7 April 1870; and Thornbrough, *The Negro in Indiana,* 293.

12. *Christian Recorder,* 25 November 1871; Price, "Let the Law be Just," 189–95; Harry C. Silcox, "The Black 'Better Class' Political Dilemma: Philadelphia Prototype Isaiah C. Wears," *Pennsylvania Magazine of History and Biography* 113 (January 1989): 49; and Silcox, "Nineteenth Century Philadelphia Black Militant," 75–76.

13. Wright, "Negro Suffrage in New Jersey, 1776–1875," 219–20; also *Cincinnati Commercial,* 20 February 1870. The evidence does not support claims by Edward J. Price, Leslie H. Fishel Jr., and Roger Lane that, once the Fifteenth Amendment was ratified, naive northern blacks, unschooled in the intricacies of the political process, blindly supported the Republican Party as the result of empty rhetoric and token gestures by the party's leadership. See Price, "Let the Law be Just," 201–2; Fishel, "Repercussions of Reconstruction," 326; and Lane, *Roots of Violence in Black Philadelphia, 1860–1900,* 124–30.

14. *Pacific Appeal,* 13 July 1872.

15. See, for example, *Christian Recorder,* 12, 19 November 1870; and Silcox, "The Black 'Better Class' Political Dilemma," 58.

16. *Christian Recorder,* 5 November 1870; and 1872 speech, John Jones Collection; see also *Pacific Appeal,* 22 July 1871.

17. Rusco, *"Good Time Coming?"* 92–93; and *New National Era,* 16 February 1872. For similar sentiments, see *New National Era,* 21 July 1870, 23 March 1871; *Christian Recorder,* 4 May, 5 October 1872; *Newark Daily Journal,* 7 April 1870; John Hope Franklin, *George Washington Williams: A Biography* (Chicago, 1985), 18; and *Pacific Appeal,* 23 January 1875.

18. See, for example, Blight, *Frederick Douglass' Civil War,* 212; and Martin, *The Mind of Frederick Douglass,* 86.

19. *Christian Recorder,* 31 August 1872; and Frederick Douglass to Cassius Clay, 26 July 1871, Frederick Douglass Papers; see also *Elevator,* 1, 15 June, 14 September 1872; *Pacific Appeal,* 25 May, 15 June 1872; *New Brunswick Daily Times,* 4 June 1872; and *New National Era,* 10, 31 August 1871, 23 May, 10, 24 October 1872.

20. Richardson, *The Death of Reconstruction,* 124–25; Ronald B. Jager, "Charles Sumner, the Constitution, and the Civil Rights Act of 1875," *New England Quarterly* 42 (1969): 359, 366; James M. McPherson, "The Abolitionists and the Civil Rights Act of 1875," *Journal of American History* 52 (December 1965): 500–506; and Alfred H. Kelley, "The Congressional Controversy over School Segregation, 1867–1875," *American Historical Review* 64 (April 1959): 537, 546.

21. See Joseph C. Bustill to Charles Sumner, 10 January 1872, Charles Sumner Papers; see also Frederick Douglass to Charles Sumner, 19 July 1872, Henry Highland Garnet to Charles Sumner, 23 December 1871, William Nesbit to Charles Sumner, 19 January 1872, George T. Downing to Charles Sumner, 20 January, 12 December 1871, 1 August 1873, William D. Forten to Charles Sumner, 18 January 1872, Charles Sumner Papers; Frederick Douglass to Theodore Freylinghuysen, 23 May 1874, Frederick Douglass Papers; *Journal of the Senate of the United States of America,* 42nd Cong., 2d Sess., 1872, 104, 105, 120, 305; Senate Committee on the Judiciary, 4 April 1870 petition, 41st Cong., 2d Sess., 30; and *Pacific Appeal,* 27 March 1875.

22. See, for example, *Pacific Appeal,* 13, 20, 27 April 1872; U.S. House, *Memorial of Colored Citizens.* 42nd Cong., 3d Sess., 1873, H. Misc. Doc. 58, 1–2. On the 1873 national convention, see

Elevator, 22 November, 27 December 1873; *Pacific Appeal*, 3 January 1874; and *Memorial of the National Convention of Colored Persons, Praying to be Protected in their Civil Rights*, 1–5. On the 1875 national convention, see *Washington National Republican*, 27 January 1875; *Pacific Appeal*, 6 February 1875; and *Christian Recorder*, 4 February 1875.

23. *Pacific Appeal*, 12 September 1874 (quotation); see also *Christian Recorder*, 16 October 1874; *Pacific Appeal*, 26 July 1873, 20 February 1875; *Our National Progress*, 11 October 1873; and *Inter-Ocean*, 2 April 1872.

24. On the opposition to Sumner's bill, see Richardson, *The Death of Reconstruction*, 124–26, 131–40.

25. See ibid., 138–39; *Annual Report of the Board of Education of the State of Connecticut, Presented to the General Assembly, May Session, 1874* (New Haven, 1874), 70; Bertram Wyatt-Brown, "The Civil Rights Act of 1875," *Western Political Quarterly* 18 (December 1965): 765–66; William Preston Vaughn, *Schools for All: The Blacks and Public Education in the South, 1865–1877* (Lexington, Ky., 1974), 123–38; and *Nation*, 17 September 1874.

26. *Elevator*, 3 October 1874; U.S. Senate, *Resolutions Adopted at a Public Meeting*, 42nd Cong., 2d Sess., 1872 S. Misc. Doc. 29, 3. For similar sentiments, see *Daily Ohio State Journal*, 25 February 1875; and *Pacific Appeal*, 8 March 1873.

27. Heather Cox Richardson, Leslie H. Fishel Jr., and David A. Gerber argue that northern black protest leaders were driven to agitate for equal rights primarily by considerations of what would best serve their class interests. The evidence, however, does not support this assertion. See Richardson, *The Death of Reconstruction*, 133–34; Gerber, *Black Ohio and the Color Line, 1860–1915*, 186–87; and Fishel, *Repercussions of Reconstruction*, 336–38.

28. U.S. Senate, *Resolutions Adopted at a Public Meeting*. 42nd Cong., 2d Sess., 1872, S. Misc. Doc. 29, 1–2; *Pacific Appeal*, 15 February 1873; and *Daily Ohio State* Journal, 25 February 1873.

29. See *Pacific Appeal*, 18 July 1874; and *Inter-Ocean*, 2 April 1872. For similar sentiments, see U.S. House, *Memorial of Colored Citizens*. 42nd Cong., 3d Sess., 1873, H. Misc. Doc. 58; *Elevator*, 22 November 1873; and *Pacific Appeal*, 18 October 1873. Bess Beatty criticizes Nell Irvin Painter, in her *Exodusters*, for exaggerating class divisions among southern blacks. Beatty, *A Revolution Gone Backward: The Black Response to National Politics, 1876–1896* (Westport, Conn., 1987), x–xi.

30. U.S. Senate, *Resolutions Adopted at a Public Meeting*. 42nd Cong., 2d Sess., 1872, S. Misc. Doc. 29, 1–2 (quotation); U.S. House, *Memorial of National Convention of Colored Persons*. 43rd Cong., 1st Sess., 1873 H. Misc. Doc. 44, 1; and *Pacific Appeal*, 18 October 1874 (quotation).

31. *Pacific Appeal*, 18 October 1874; U.S. House, *Memorial of National Convention of Colored Persons*. 43rd Cong., 1st Sess., 1873, H. Misc. Doc. 44, 4; and U.S. Senate, *Petition of the National Executive Committee of the Colored People*. 41st Cong., 2d Sess., 1870. S. Misc. Doc. 130, 1.

32. U.S. Senate, *Resolutions Adopted at a Public Meeting*. 42nd Cong., 2d Sess., 1872, S. Misc. Doc. 29, 2; and U.S. House, *Memorial of National Convention of Colored Persons*. 43rd Cong., 1st Sess., 1873, H. Misc. Doc. 44, 2. Their belief that school integration must be national in scope led them to dismiss the dire prediction that such a policy would destroy the southern public schools. If that occurred, a Massachusetts black wrote in the *Pacific Appeal*, "so be it." *Pacific Appeal*, 20 June 1874. Southern blacks gave some support for the school clause in Sumner's bill, but it appears that much of the lobbying was done by northern blacks. William Preston Vaughn argues that many southern blacks were more interested in equal educational opportunities than in encouraging integration, especially on the elementary level. Those who espoused racially integrated public schools encountered formidable white opposition, and a final reckoning on the issue was often avoided through legislative maneuvers. Most of the southern state constitutional convention delegates were whites who rejected school integration. Vaughn agrees with the critics of Sumner's proposal that, if the public schools had been integrated, funding for education for blacks probably would have been impossible in most southern states. Moreover, even many southern white Radicals sanctioned racially segregated public schools. *Schools for All*, 56–57, 77.

33. *Pacific Appeal,* 15 March 1873.
34. *New National Era,* 24 February 1870; and *Pacific Appeal,* 27 May 1871.
35. See William Seraile, "The Civil War's Impact on Race Relations in New York State, 1865–1875," *Afro-Americans in New York Life and History* 25 (January 2001): 70; Mabee, *Black Education in New York State,* 205; Jackson, "The Black Educational Experience in a Northern City," 72; and Dixon, "Education of the Negro in the City of New York, 1853 to 1900," 56–57.
36. *Toledo Daily Commercial,* 6 July 1869 (quotation), 21 January, 15 February 1870; and Leonard Ernest Erickson, "Toledo Desegregates, 1871," *Northwest Ohio Quarterly* 41 (Winter 1968–1969): 5–7. The *Christian Recorder* lauded the city for doing "the handsome thing in abolishing her negative Ku-Kluxism," 29 July 1871.
37. See Wilmoth, "Pittsburgh and the Blacks," 169–70, 180–81; and Warner, *New Haven Negroes,* 119, 174.
38. *Eighth Biennial Report of the Superintendent of Public Instruction of the State of Illinois. 1871–1872* (Springfield, 1873), 115–16.
39. See, for example, *Elevator,* 10 June 1870; Moore, "Response to Reconstruction," 158; Squibb, "Roads to Plessy," 85; Sanelli, "The Struggle for Black Suffrage in Pennsylvania, 1838–1870," 310–11; Wright, "Negro Suffrage in New Jersey, 1776–1875," 220–22; William Gillette, *Jersey Blue: Civil War Politics in New Jersey, 1854–1865* (New Brunswick, N.J., 1995), 8; Dykstra, *Bright Radical Star,* 230–37; and Thornbrough, *The Negro in Indiana,* 249–50.
40. *Pacific Appeal,* 15, 29 March 1873; and *New York Times,* 6 March 1873.
41. *New National Era,* 24 February 1870.
42. In his study on the Fifteenth Amendment, William Gillette has argued that the northern black vote during the 1870s had an impact on elections that was out of proportion to its numbers. Several historians have charged that Gillette exaggerated the significance of the northern African American vote. But even David Gerber and LaWanda and John H. Cox, who have vigorously challenged his claim, acknowledge that, especially in some urban centers, blacks were able to affect the outcome of elections. For this debate, see Gillette, *The Right to Vote,* 182–84. Among those who have challenged his assertion are Grossman, *The Democratic Party and the Negro,* 99–100; Farley, "The Issue of Black Equality in New York State, 1865–1873," 85–87; Crew, *Black Life in Secondary Cities,* 169–70; Gerber, "A Politics of Limited Options," 237–40; and Cox and Cox, "Negro Suffrage and Republican Politics," 321–30.
43. *Pacific Appeal,* 10 September 1870, 9 November 1872; and Gerald G. Eggert, "'Two Steps Forward, A Step and a Half Back': Harrisburg's African American Community in the Nineteenth Century," in *African Americans in Pennsylvania: Shifting Historical Perspectives,* ed. Joe William Trotter Jr. and Eric Ledell Smith (University Park, Pa., 1997), 236, 244.
44. Mittrick, "A History of Negro Voting in Pennsylvania during the Nineteenth Century," 81, 90, 93–95, 100; and Frank B. Evans, *Pennsylvania Politics, 1872–1877: A Study in Political Leadership* (Harrisburg, Pa., 1966), 198–99.
45. On the black vote's impact in New Jersey elections, see Moore, "Response to Reconstruction," 151–53; and Crew, *Black Life in Secondary Cities,* 170–71; in Connecticut, see Gillette, *The Right to Vote,* 130, 182; in Ohio, see Gerber, "Education, Expediency, and Ideology," 17; in Cairo, Illinois, see Christopher K. Hays, "The African American Struggle for Equality and Justice in Cairo, Illinois, 1865–1900," *Illinois Historical Journal* 90 (Winter 1997): 274–75. Hays also shows that black voters enabled Chicago Republicans to win a number of races by small margins during the 1870s, p. 75. Although most African American voters resided in the South, Peter Anderson pointedly reminded white Republicans that, while Grant won the presidency in 1872 by 700,000 votes, the national black vote totaled 880,000 in that election. *Pacific Appeal,* 9, 16 November 1872.
46. *National Anti-Slavery Standard,* 25 September 1869. Several delegates at an Ohio convention in 1871 expressed similar reservations about disbanding black rights organizations. *Daily Ohio State Journal,* 19 January 1871.

47. *National Anti-Slavery Standard,* 25 September 1869; and *Christian Recorder,* 5 May 1870, 31 August 1872.

48. *New York Times,* 25 July 1873 (quotation); and *Daily Ohio State Journal,* 19 January 1871 (quotation). For further evidence of such separate black Republican clubs, see Carlson, "The Black Community in the Rural North," 117–18; Katzman, *Before the Ghetto,* 178; and Gerber, *Black Ohio and the Color Line,* 213–15.

49. *Elevator,* 6 December 1873; and *New York Sun,* 29 September 1873.

50. Davis, *Black Americans in Cleveland from George Peake to Carl B. Stokes, 1796–1969,* 89, 92; and Grossman, "In His Veins Coursed No Bootlicking Blood," 87–88.

51. Hays, "The African American Struggle for Equality and Justice in Cairo, Illinois, 1865–1900," 275; Carlson, "The Black Community in the Rural North," 117–18, 123–26; *Illinois Times,* 20–26 January 2000; Bridges, "Equality Deferred," 98–99; and John H. Keiser, *Building for the Centuries: Illinois, 1865 to 1898* (Urbana, Ill., 1977), 15–44.

52. Katzman, *Before the Ghetto,* 178–80; and June Babar Woodson, "A Century with the Negroes of Detroit, 1830–1930" (Master's thesis, Wayne State University, 1949), 54.

53. See, for example, Charles A. Porter to Jacob C. White Jr., 5 October 1870, Jacob C. White Papers; *Christian Recorder,* 31 August 1872, 1 April 1875; Crew, *Black Life in Secondary Cities,* 172–73; and Warner, *New Haven Negroes,* 178.

54. See Gerber, "A Politics of Limited Options," 237–38.

55. See *Elevator,* 28 June 1873; *New National Era,* 24 November 1870; and *Cincinnati Commercial,* 23 August 1873.

56. *Philadelphia Press,* 3 February 1870; and *New National Era,* 24 November 1870. For similar sentiments, see *Pacific Appeal,* 30 September 1871, 13 April 1872, 1 February, 1 March 1873; *Elevator,* 21 February 1874; and *Detroit Free Press,* 19 August 1876. Martin E. Dann notes that southern blacks, including the freed people, likewise demanded equal treatment within the party. Dann, ed., *The Black Press, 1827–1900: The Quest for National Identity* (New York, 1971), 52; see also Foner, *Reconstruction,* 137, 142, 150–51.

57. *Elevator,* 21 February 1874; and *Pacific Appeal,* 12 August 1871.

58. *Cincinnati Commercial,* 23 August 1873.

59. See, for example, Foner, *Reconstruction,* 122–62; and Franklin, *Reconstruction after the Civil War,* 104–16, 154–63.

60. See, for example, Foner, *Reconstruction,* 180–84, 232–50; and Allen W. Trelease, *White Terror: The KKK Conspiracy and Southern Reconstruction* (Westport, Conn., 1971). On the Colfax massacre, see Charles Lane, *The Day Freedom Died: The Colfax Massacre, the Supreme Court, and the Betrayal of Reconstruction* (New York, 2008); and Lee Anna Keith, *The Colfax Massacre: The Untold Story of Black Power, White Terror, and the Death of Reconstruction* (New York, 2008). On the southern Democrats' rise to power, see Michael Perman, *The Road to Redemption: Southern Politics, 1869–1879* (Chapel Hill, N.C., 1984).

61. On Grant's Reconstruction policy, see William S. McFeely, *Grant: A Biography* (New York, 1980), 416–25; and Brooks Simpson, *The Reconstruction Presidents* (Lawrence, Kans., 1983), 133–96.

62. *Christian Recorder,* 1 April 1871; and *Indianapolis Daily Journal,* 22 September 1875.

63. *Christian Recorder,* 21 August 1873.

64. *Christian Recorder,* 29 June, 19 October 1876. For similar sentiments, see *Pacific Appeal,* 13, 27 May, 10 June 1873, 18 September 1875; *Christian Recorder,* 21 August 1873; and *Elevator,* 10 October 1874.

65. On the slow pace of removing restrictive suffrage clauses from many state constitutions, see *New National Era,* 7 July 1870; Sanelli, "The Struggle for Black Suffrage in Pennsylvania, 1838–1870," 310–11; Wright, "Negro Suffrage in New Jersey, 1776–1875," 220–22; Dykstra, *Bright Radical Star,* 230–37; and Thornbrough, *The Negro in Indiana,* 249–50.

66. See *New National Era,* 1, 22 May 1873; Farley, "The Issue of Black Equality in New York State, 1865–1873," 258, 260–61; and Mabee, *Black Education in New York State,* 203.

67. Brown, *The Negro in Pennsylvania History,* 52; Thomas C. Cox, *Blacks in Topeka, Kansas, 1865–1915: A Social History* (Baton Rouge, La., 1982), 28–29; and K. Keith Richard, "Unwelcome Settlers: Black and Mulatto Oregon Pioneers," *Oregon Historical Quarterly* 85 (Spring 1983): 29–55.

68. Crew, *Black Life in Secondary Cities,* 133–34.

69. On the Illinois situation, see *Ninth Biennial Report of the Superintendent of Public Instruction of the State of Illinois. 1871–1872,* 115–16; and *Tenth Biennial Report of the Superintendent of Public Instruction of the State of Illinois. 1873–1874,* 49–50; on California, see *Elevator,* 4 May 1872; on Indiana, see Heller, "Negro Education in Indiana From 1816 to 1869," 111–12, 117; and *Twenty-third Annual Report of the Superintendent of Public Instruction for the State of Indiana* (Indianapolis, 1875), 23–24.

70. See, for example, Nelson, *The Fourteenth Amendment,* 195–96; and Squibb, "Roads to Plessy," 24–25. J. Morgan Kousser has challenged those historians who question the efficacy of legal action and blacks' faith in, and use of, the courts, pointing out that these efforts proved worthwhile more often than not. Yet Kousser focuses especially on the post-1880 record and acknowledges that black plaintiffs were generally unsuccessful when they based their claims on the Fourteenth Amendment. *Dead End,* 15–16, 30.

71. See Squibb, "Roads to Plessy," 158–62; and Erickson, "The Color Line in Ohio Public Schools, 1829–1890," 241–42.

72. Austin Abbott, *Reports of Practice Cases Determined in the Courts of the State of New-York,* new series, vol. 13 (New York, 1886), 160–65.

73. Lurie, "The Fourteenth Amendment," 305; and Rusco, *"Good Time Coming?"* 89 (quotation).

74. *Pacific Appeal,* 7 October 1871; and *Elevator,* 29 December 1871.

75. John W. Dwinelle, *Argument of John W. Dwinelle on the Right of Colored Children to be Admitted to the Public Schools,* 1–6, 15–16; and Wollenberg, *All Deliberate Speed,* 21–22.

76. *Elevator,* 23 November 1872.

77. Wollenberg, *All Deliberate Speed,* 23; and Kaczorowski, *The Politics of Judicial Interpretation,* 191–92.

78. *Elevator,* 28 February, 7 March 1874; and *Pacific Appeal,* 28 February 1874.

79. *Reports of Cases Argued and Determined in the Supreme Judicature of the State of Indiana* (Indianapolis, 1875), vol. 48, 328–30, 349–50, 362–63.

80. *Cleveland Leader,* 15 December 1874; and Kousser, *Dead End,* 21.

81. *Tenth Biennial Report of the Superintendent of Public Instruction of the State of Illinois. 1873–1874,* 45–46. For a treatment of Republican and Democratic judges on the school issue, see Kousser, *Dead End,* 14–15.

82. For analyses of this retreat, see Gillette, *Retreat from Reconstruction, 1869–1879,* 367–71; Blight, *Race and Reunion,* 105–7; and Adam I. P. Smith and Peter J. Parish, "A Contested Legacy: The Civil War and Party Politics in the North," in *Legacy of Disunion,* ed. Grant and Parish, 92–93.

83. *Cleveland Leader,* 28 August 1873. On the role of sympathetic whites in the equal rights cause during the 1870s, see McPherson, *The Struggle for Equality,* 428–32.

84. *Pacific Appeal,* 20 June 1874, 6 April 1872.

85. George T. Downing to Charles Sumner, 7 July 1871, Charles Sumner Papers; and *New National Era,* 8 July 1871.

86. Grossman, "In His Veins Coursed No Bootlicking Blood," 85–86; *The Democratic Party and the Negro,* 38 (quotation); and *Cleveland Leader,* 23 August 1873.

87. Grossman, *The Democratic Party and the Negro*, 72–73; Silcox, "The Black 'Better Class' Political Dilemma," 52; and Bacon, *But One Race*, 177–78. For Still's remarks, see William Still, *An Address on Voting and Laboring, Delivered at Concert Hall, Tuesday Evening, March 10th, 1874* (Philadelphia, 1874), 6.

88. 10 March 1874 speech, William Still Papers, Leon Gardiner Collection on Negro History, Historical Society of Pennsylvania; *Daily Ohio State Journal*, 5 August 1873; and *Pacific Appeal*, 6, 20 April 1872.

89. *New Brunswick Daily Times*, 4 June 1873; and *Pacific Appeal*, 13 April 1872.

90. On efforts by "New Departure" Democrats to appeal to black voters, see *Cincinnati Commercial*, 1 April 1870; Moore, "Response to Reconstruction," 141–42; Katzman, *Before the Ghetto*, 181–83; and Grossman, *The Democratic Party and the Negro*, 63–64.

91. *New York Sun*, 8 July, 29 September 1873; and Block, *The Circle of Discrimination*, 187–88.

92. See Katzman, *Before the Ghetto*, 183; *Cleveland Leader*, 31 March 1871; *Pacific Appeal*, 4 November 1871; Farley, "The Issue of Black Equality in New York State," 252n39; Davis, *Black Americans in Cleveland from George Peake to Carl B. Stokes, 1796–1969*, 94; John Daniels, *In Freedom's Birthplace: A Study of the Boston Negroes* (Boston, 1914), 98; and *Elevator*, 19 October 1872. A small minority of southern blacks voted Democratic. Beatty, *A Revolution Gone Backward*, 7.

93. *Pacific Appeal*, 26 July 1873; see also Scheiner, *Negro Mecca*, 174; *Cleveland Leader*, 31 March, 25 August 1873; *Cincinnati Commercial*, 23 August 1873; and *Christian Recorder*, 31 December 1874.

94. Foner, *Frederick Douglass*, 27; Silcox, "The Black 'Better Class' Political Dilemma," 49–50; and *New National Era*, 3 November 1870 (quotation).

95. *New National Era*, 8 July 1871.

96. *Pacific Appeal*, 20 December 1873; *Elevator*, 8 July 1874; and Fisher, "A History of the Political and Social Development of the Black Community in California, 1850–1950," 140–41.

97. *Washington National Republican*, 24 January 1874. See also Richardson, *The Death of Reconstruction*, 134–36; and Vaughn, *Schools for All*, 56–70, 77.

98. *Daily Ohio State Journal*, 25 February 1875; and *Pacific Appeal*, 27 February 1875.

99. *Christian Recorder*, 21 May 1874; and *Pacific Appeal*, 6, 20 February 1874.

100. George T. Downing to Philip B. and Peter John Downing, 10 March 1875, DeGrasse-Howard Papers; and *Christian Recorder*, 11 March 1875.

101. *Pacific Appeal*, 27 March, 24 April 1875.

Chapter 5

1. *New York Times*, 6 February 1875.

2. Ibid. For Northern blacks' lawsuits filed under the provisions of the civil rights law, see, for example, *The Nation*, 8 August 1875; *Indianapolis Daily Journal*, 1, 3 September 1877; and Stephen J. Riegel, "The Persistent Career of Jim Crow: Lower Federal Courts and the 'Separate but Equal' Doctrine, 1865–1896," *American Journal of Legal History* 28 (January 1984): 23, 29. Gillette incorrectly claims that blacks did not demand that the law's provisions be strictly enforced. *Retreat from Reconstruction, 1869–1879*, 277.

3. See Gerber, *Black Ohio and the Color Line, 1869–1915*, 48–49; Valeria Weaver, "The Failure of Civil Rights, 1875–1883, and Its Repercussions," *Journal of Negro History* 54 (October 1969): 368–69; and Franklin, "The Enforcement of the Civil Rights Act of 1875," 230.

4. Kaczorowski, *The Politics of Judicial Interpretation*, 191–93.

5. Weaver, "The Failure of Civil Rights, 1875–1883, and Its Repercussions," 368; *Pacific Appeal*, 3 June 1876; and Riegel, "The Persistent Career of Jim Crow," 35–37.

6. Alessandra Lorini, *Rituals of Race: American Public Culture and the Search for Racial Democracy* (Charlottesville, Va., 1999), 30.

7. See, for example, *New York Times*, 3 November 1876 (quotation); and *Detroit Free Press*, 16, 29 August 1876 (quotation); also *Detroit Free Press*, 19 September 1876.

8. On the Nashville Convention, see *Pacific Appeal*, 15 April, 20 May 1876 (quotation).

9. *Boston Journal*, 16 October 1876; and *Christian Recorder*, 11 November 1875. For views similar to those expressed by the *Christian Recorder*, see *New York Times*, 22 October 1876; *Colored Radical*, 24 August 1876; and Franklin, *George Washington Williams*, 43–44.

10. Beatty, *A Revolution Gone Backward*, 10; and Rutherford B. Hayes to Peter H. Clark, 30 March 1876, Rutherford B. Hayes Papers, Hayes Historical Library.

11. Beatty, *A Revolution Gone Backward*, 10; and Foner, *Reconstruction*, 558, 567.

12. John D. Bagwell to Rutherford B. Hayes, 2 July 1876, Rutherford B. Hayes Papers.

13. *Christian Recorder*, 26 October 1876; Merline Pitre, "Frederick Douglass: Party Loyalist, 1870–1895" (Ph.D. diss., Temple University, 1976), 55; and John Mercer Langston to Rutherford B. Hayes, 19 June 1876, Rutherford B. Hayes Papers.

14. Keith Ian Polakoff effectively challenges C. Vann Woodward's contention that economic issues were at the heart of the 1877 bargain and that a nearly secret deal was struck by which southern Democrats of "Old Whig" antecedents agreed to support Hayes in the electoral crisis in return for various economic and political concessions by the Hayes administration. Polakoff counters that there was in fact no grand compromise, for the parties provided little central direction in the crisis and Samuel J. Tilden, the Democratic candidate, quickly conceded defeat. Keith Ian Polakoff, *The Politics of Inertia: The Election of 1876 and the End of Reconstruction* (Baton Rouge, La., 1973), ix–xi, 313, 314n.

15. Meeting with African Methodist Episcopal Church delegation, 23 March 1877, Rutherford B. Hayes Papers. For similar assurances by Hayes, see speech at Jeffersonville, Indiana, 18 September 1877, Rutherford B. Hayes Papers.

16. Diary entry for 18 February 1877, Rutherford B. Hayes Papers; McPherson, *The Abolitionist Legacy*, 92; Frederick Douglass to John Sherman, 13 March 1877, Frederick Douglass to F. S. Stebbins, 26 March 1877 (quotation), Rutherford B. Hayes Papers; *Pacific Appeal*, 17 March 1877; Pitre, "Frederick Douglass," 79–80; and Beatty, *A Revolution Gone Backward*, 23–24.

17. *Pacific Appeal*, 16 June 1877; and L. C. Mitchell to Rutherford B. Hayes, 8 March 1877, Rutherford B. Hayes Papers. In 1878, Downing complained bitterly to Hayes that other "persons who, as it has been known, are in all respects far less worthy than me," had received appointments while he had not. George T. Downing to Rutherford B. Hayes, 1 July 1878, Rutherford B. Hayes Papers. In a self-serving letter to Carl Schurz, Hayes's secretary of the interior, Downing requested that he be considered for a government position on the grounds of "national reputation and of merit" as well as the fact that, unlike many other equal rights activists, he had labored in the cause without compensation and against the wishes of many of his white clients. As a consequence of his agitation for equal rights he confessed to John Jay, his business interests had suffered, and he was saddled with enormous debts. Thus, he desperately needed a loan and a government job. See George T. Downing to Carl Schurz, 14 April 1877, Rutherford B. Hayes Papers; and George T. Downing to John Jay, 5 March 1877, Jay Family Papers, Butler Library, Columbia University.

18. Nashville speech, 19 September 1877, Rutherford B. Hayes Papers.

19. Kenneth E. Davison, *The Presidency of Rutherford B. Hayes* (Westport, Conn., 1972), 138, 140–42; also Ari Hoogenboom, *Rutherford B. Hayes: Warrior and President* (Lawrence, Kans., 1995), 304–8, 314–18, 375–76.

20. See Foner, *Reconstruction*, 247–53; Franklin, *Reconstruction after the Civil War*, 219–27; Gillette, *Retreat from Reconstruction*, 300–345; and J. Morgan Kousser, *The Shaping of Southern Politics: Suffrage Restriction and the Establishment of the One-Party South, 1880–1910* (New Haven, Conn., 1974), 11–14.

21. Gillette, *Retreat from Reconstruction,* 335–62; and Simpson, *The Reconstruction Presidents,* 199–228.

22. George T. Downing to Frederick Douglass, 19 March 1877, Frederick Douglass Papers; and *Christian Recorder,* 8 March 1877.

23. See *New York Times,* 23 August 1877; *Christian Recorder,* 5, 19 April, 9 August 1877; Erickson, "The Color Line in Ohio Public Schools, 1829–1890," 348; and John Mercer Langston to Rutherford B. Hayes, 9 November 1876, Rutherford B. Hayes Papers. For similar condemnation of Republicans for betraying African Americans that included threats of leaving the party, see *Christian Recorder,* 1 March, 9 August 1877.

24. George T. Downing, Rev. M. Van-horn, Rev. Jonathan Yeiser, Rev. J. N. Jeter, and Benjamin Burton to William Lloyd Garrison, 5 December 1876, Antislavery Papers, Boston Public Library.

25. George T. Downing to Frederick Douglass, 19 March 1877, Frederick Douglass Papers.

26. Sanelli, "The Struggle for Black Suffrage in Pennsylvania, 1838–1870," 305; also *Philadelphia Press,* 16 February 1877.

27. Silcox, "The Black 'Better Class' Political Dilemma," 56; and Grossman, *The Democratic Party and the Negro,* 76–77.

28. Lortie, "San Francisco's Black Community, 1870–1890," 15; and Fisher, "A History of the Social and Political Development of the Black Community in California, 1850–1950," 132–34.

29. Irving G. Hendrick, "Approaching Equality of Educational Opportunity in California: The Successful Struggle of Black Citizens, 1880–1920," *Pacific Historian* 25 (Winter 1981): 25.

30. Fisher, "A History of the Social and Political Development of the Black Community in California, 1850–1950," 134–35.

31. Erickson, "The Color Line in Ohio Public Schools, 1829–1890," 350; Douglas, *Jim Crow Moves North,* 89; and *Colored Radical,* 24 August 1876.

32. See Franklin, "The Persistence of School Segregation in the Urban North," 57; Weinberg, *A Chance to Learn,* 75; and Douglas, *Jim Crow Moves North,* 94–95. Indiana did not desegregate its public schools until 1949. Thornbrough, *Indiana in the Civil War Ear,* 482–83.

33. See Brown, "Pennsylvania and the Rights of the Negro, 1865–1877," 54–55; and Price, "School Segregation in Nineteenth-Century Pennsylvania," 132.

34. Brown, *The Negro in Pennsylvania History,* 53–54; and Price, "School Segregation in Nineteenth-Century Pennsylvania," 133–35.

35. See Douglas, *Jim Crow Moves North,* 83n38.

36. Erickson, "The Color Line in Ohio Public Schools, 1829–1890," 339–53; Squibb, "Roads to Plessy," 173–75; and Gerber, *Black Ohio and the Color Line, 1860–1915,* 234–44.

37. Martin, *The Mind of Frederick Douglass,* 84–85.

38. See Weaver, "The Failure of Civil Rights, 1875–1883, and Its Repercussions," 373–80; Katzman, *Before the Ghetto,* 90–91; Kirt H. Wilson, *The Reconstruction Desegregation Debate: The Politics of Equality and the Rhetoric of Place, 1870–1875* (East Lansing, Mich., 2002), 43; Gerber, *Black Ohio and the Color Line, 1860–1915,* 234–36; Schwalm, *Emancipation's Diaspora,* 207; and Douglas, *Jim Crow Moves North,* 94–95.

39. See, for example, Marsha Hurst, "Integration, Freedom of Choice, and Community Control in Nineteenth Century Brooklyn," *Journal of Ethnic Studies* 3 (Fall 1975): 33–34, 39–40, 47–48; and Douglas, *Jim Crow Moves North,* 107–8.

40. For a treatment of the Ohio law, see Erickson, "The Color Line in Ohio Public Schools, 1829–1890," 350. On the situation in Kansas, see *Colored Radical,* 24 August, 15 September 1876. For examples of gerrymandering and intimidation, see Douglas, *Jim Crow Moves North,* 100–105, 112–13.

41. See, for example, Weaver, "The Failure of Civil Rights, 1875–1883, and Its Repercussions," 375–81; Gerber, *Black Ohio and the Color Line, 1860–1915,* 236–37; Wilson, *The Reconstruction Desegregation Debate,* 43; Katzman, *Before the Ghetto,* 93; and Schwalm, *Emancipation's Diaspora,* 207, 324n143.

Epilogue

1. See, for example, August Meier, *Negro Thought in America, 1880–1915: Racial Ideologies in the Age of Booker T. Washington* (Ann Arbor, Mich., 1969), 29–34, 69–73, 128–30; Mary Frances Berry, *Black Resistance, White Law* (New York, 1971), 95–96; Charles F. Kellogg, *NAACP: A History of the National Association for the Advancement of Colored People* (Baltimore, 1967); and David Levering Lewis, *W. E. B. DuBois: Biography of a Race, 1868–1919* (New York, 1993).

2. On race relations during these decades, see Michael J. Klarman, *Unfinished Business: Racial Equality in American History* 309–30. On the *Plessy* decision, see Lofgren, *The Plessy Case,* 100–101, 174–75. On the rapid pace of racial ghettoization, see Stanley Liberson, *A Piece of the Pie: Blacks and White Immigrants since 1880* (Berkeley, Calif., 1980), 266–88; and Kuzmer, *A Ghetto Takes Shape,* 61–64, 175.

3. Philip A. Klinkner and Rogers M. Smith, *The Unsteady March: The Rise and Decline of Racial Equality in America* (Chicago, 1999), 105–8; McPherson, *The Abolitionist Legacy,* 386–90; and Meier, *Negro Thought in America, 1880–1915,* 164–66.

4. For treatments of the modern civil rights movement, see Sugrue, *Sweet Land of Liberty;* Self, *American Babylon;* Countryman, *Up South;* Sitkoff, *The Struggle for Black Equality, 1854–1992,* rev. ed. (New York, 1993); Taylor Branch, *Parting the Waters: America in the King Years, 1954–63* (New York, 1988), *Pillar of Fire, 1963–65: America in the King Years, 1963–65* (New York, 1998), and *At Canaan's Edge: America in the King Years, 1965–68* (New York, 2006).

Bibliography

Primary Sources

Manuscripts

Boston Public Library, Boston, Mass.
    Antislavery Papers
California State Archives, Sacramento, Calif.
    Petitions to the California Legislature, 1863–1866.
Chicago Historical Society, Chicago, Ill.
    John Jones Collection
Columbia University (Butler Library), New York, N.Y.
    Moncure Conway Collection
    Sydney Howard Gay Papers
    Jay Family Papers
    Kelley Family Papers
Connecticut Historical Society
    African Americans, 1821–1869, General Assembly Papers, RG002
Harvard University (Houghton Library), Cambridge, Mass.
    Crawford Blagden Papers
    Charles Sumner Papers

Hayes Historical Library, Fremont, Ohio
  Schuyler Colfax Papers
  Rutherford B. Hayes Papers
Historical Society of Pennsylvania, Philadelphia, Pa.
  Records of the Pennsylvania State Equal Rights League
  Records of the Social, Civil, and Statistical Association of the Colored People of Pennsylvania
  William Still Papers
  Isaiah C. Wears Papers
  Jacob C. White Jr. Papers
Howard University (Moorland-Spingarn Research Center), Washington, D.C.
  George T. Downing Papers
  John Mercer Langston Papers
  Ruffin Family Papers
Illinois State Archives, Springfield, Ill.
  Minutes of the Committee on Education of the House of Representatives, Twenty-ninth General Assembly, State of Illinois, 1875
  Illinois State Board of Education, Superintendent of Public Instruction, Outgoing Correspondence, 1863–1914, Record Series 106.000
Illinois State Historical Library, Springfield, Ill.
  Newton Bateman Papers
  Richard J. Oglesby Papers
  Yates Family Papers
Indiana State Library, Indianapolis, Indiana
  George W. Julian Papers
Library of Congress, Washington, D.C.
  Frederick Douglass Papers
  Thaddeus Stevens Papers
Massachusetts Historical Society, Boston, Mass.
  DeGrasse-Howard Papers
National Archives, Washington, D.C.
  U.S. Senate Committee on the Judiciary, "Petitions," 40th Cong., 1st Sess., RG46
  U.S. Senate Joint Committee on Reconstruction, "Petitions," 39th–41st Congress, RG 128
Syracuse University, Syracuse, N.Y.
  Gerrit Smith Miller Collection

Newspapers and Journals

Chicago Tribune, 1864, 1866–1867
Christian Recorder, 1864–1880
Christian Times and Witness, 25 October 1866
Cincinnati Colored Citizen, 1868
Cincinnati Commercial, 1867–1878
Cleveland Leader, 1866–1875

Colored Radical, 1876
Daily Ohio State Journal, 1867–1878
Detroit Advertiser and Tribune, 1867–1872
Detroit Free Press, 1865–1876
Elevator, 1865–1880
Illinois State Journal, 1865–1873, 1880
Illinois State Register, 1865–1873, 1880
Independent, 1867–1868
Indianapolis Daily Journal, 1865–1877
Inter-Ocean, 1872
Liberator, 1861–1862, 1864–1865
The Nation, 1865, 1874–1875
National Anti-Slavery Standard, 1864–1871
Newark Daily Journal, 7 April 1870
Newark Evening Courier, 13 August 1867
New Brunswick Daily Times, 4 June 1873
New Era, 19 October 1869
New National Era, 1870–1874
New York Sun, 1873
New York Times, 1866, 1873, 1875–1876
New York Tribune, 1865–1866
Ohio State Journal, 1875
Pacific Appeal, 1864–1880
Philadelphia Press, 1865–1866, 1870–1871, 1877
The Right Way, 1865–1867
Toledo Daily Commercial, 1869–1871
Washington National Republican, 1874–1875
Weekly Anglo-African, 1861–1865

Other Published Primary Sources

Abbott, Austin. *Reports of Practice Cases Determined in the Courts of the State of New-York.* New series, Vol. 13. New York, 1886.
Annual Report of the Board of Education of the State of Connecticut, Presented to the General Assembly, May Session, 1874. New Haven, 1874.
Bell, Howard Holman, ed. *Minutes of the Proceedings of the National Negro Conventions, 1830–1864.* Reprint, New York, 1969.
Berlin, Ira, et al., eds. *Freedom: A Documentary History of Emancipation, 1861–1867,* vol. 2, *The Black Military Experience.* Cambridge, Eng., 1982.
Dwinelle, John Whipple. *Argument of Mr. John W. Dwinelle on the Right of Colored Children to be Admitted to the Public Schools.* San Francisco, 1870.
Eighth Biennial Report of the Superintendent of Public Instruction of the State of Illinois. 1869–1870. Springfield, Ill., 1871.
The Equality of all Men before the Law, Claimed and Defended: In Speeches by Hon. William D. Kelley, Wendell Phillips, and Frederick Douglass, and Letters from Elizur Wright and William Heighton. Boston, 1865.

First Annual Meeting of the National Equal Rights League, Held in Cleveland, Ohio, October 19th, 20th, and 21st. Philadelphia, 1865.

Foner, Philip S., and George E. Walker, eds. *Proceedings of the Black State Conventions, 1840–1865. Volume I: New York, Pennsylvania, Michigan, Ohio.* Philadelphia, 1979.

Fourteenth Report of the Superintendent of Public Instruction for the State of Indiana. Indianapolis, 1866.

Fourth Biennial Report of the Superintendent of Public Instruction of the State of California for the School Years 1874 and 1875. Sacramento, Calif., 1875.

Hahn, Steven, et al., eds. *Land and Labor, 1865,* 3d ser., vol. 1 of *Freedom: A Documentary History of Emancipation, 1861–1867.* Chapel Hill, 2008.

Gellman, David N., and David Quigley, eds. *Jim Crow New York: A Documentary History of Race and Citizenship, 1777–1877.* New York, 2003.

Green, John P. *Fact Stranger than Fiction: Seventy-five Years of a Busy Life, with Reminiscences of Many Great and Good Men and Women.* Cleveland, 1920.

Journal of the Assembly of the State of New York: At Their Eighty-seventh Session. Albany, 1864.

Journal of the Assembly of the State of New York: At Their Ninety-sixth Session. Vol. I. Albany, 1873.

Journal of the Convention of the State of New York. Albany, 1867.

Journal of the House of Representatives of the State of Connecticut, May Session, 1865. Hartford, Conn., 1867.

Journal of the House of Representatives of the State of Indiana, during the Forty-sixth Regular Session of the General Assembly. Indianapolis, 1869.

Journal of the House of Representatives of the State of Indiana, during the Special Session of the General Assembly. Indianapolis, 1869.

Journal of the House of Representatives of the State of Michigan. 1865. Lansing, Mich., 1865.

Journal of the House of Representatives of the State of Ohio, For the Regular Session of the Fifty-seventh General Assembly, Commencing on Monday, January 1, 1866. Vol. LXII. Columbus, Ohio, 1866.

Journal of the House of Representatives of the State of Ohio for the Adjourned Session of the Fifty-seventh General Assembly, Commencing January 2, 1867. Vol. LXIII. Columbus, 1867.

Journal of the House of Representatives of the Twenty-fifth General Assembly of the State of Illinois. Vol. I. Springfield, Ill., 1867.

Journal of the Senate, during the Sixteenth Session of the Legislature of the State of California, 1865–6. Sacramento, Calif., 1866.

Journal of the Senate of the State of Connecticut, May Session, 1864. New Haven, 1864.

Journal of the Senate of the State of Connecticut, May Session, 1865. Hartford, 1865.

Journal of the Senate of the State of Ohio, for the Regular Session of the Fifty-eighth General Assembly, Commencing on January 2, 1867. Vol. LXIII. Columbus, Ohio, 1867.

Journal of the Senate of the State of Ohio, for the Regular Session of the Fifty-eighth General Assembly, Commencing on November 23, 1868. Vol. LXV. Columbus, Ohio, 1869.

Journal of the Senate of the Twenty-fourth General Assembly of the State of Illinois. Springfield, Ill., 1865.

Journal of the Senate of the Twenty-fifth General Assembly of the State of Illinois. Springfield, Ill., 1867.

Journal of the Twenty-second Senate of the State of New Jersey, Being the Ninetieth Session of the Legislature. Salem, N.J., 1866.
Journal of the Twenty-third Senate of the State of New Jersey, Being the Ninety-first Session of the Legislature. Newark, 1867.
Julian, George W. *Political Recollections, 1840 to 1872.* Chicago, 1884.
Kelley, William D. *Why Colored People in Philadelphia Are Excluded from the Street Cars.* Philadelphia, 1866.
Langston, John Mercer. *From the Virginia Plantation to the National Capitol: An Autobiography.* Reprint, New York, 1969.
Lerner, Gerda. *Black Women in White America: A Documentary History.* New York, 1972.
Minutes of Votes and Proceedings of the Ninetieth General Assembly of the State of New Jersey. Convened at Trenton, January 9th, 1866. Woodbury, N.J., 1866.
Minutes and Proceedings of the Ninety-first General Assembly of the State of New Jersey. Convened at Trenton, January 10th, 1867. Camden, N.J., 1887
Ninth Biennial Report of the Superintendent of Public Instruction of the State of Illinois. 1871–1872. Springfield, Ill., 1873.
Proceedings of a Convention of Colored Citizens, Held in the City of Lawrence, October 17, 1866. Leavenworth, Kans., 1866.
Proceedings of the Colored Men's Convention of the State of Michigan, Held in the City of Detroit, Tuesday and Wednesday, September 12th and 13th, '65. Adrian, Mich., 1865.
Proceedings of the Convention of Colored Newspaper Men. Cincinnati, 1875.
Proceedings of the Illinois State Convention of Colored Men, Assembled at Galesburg, October 16th, 17th, and 18th, Containing the State and National Addresses Promulgated by It, With a List of Delegates Composing It. Chicago, 1867.
Proceedings of the National Convention of Colored Men, Held in the City of Syracuse, October 4, 5, 6, and 7, 1864; With the Bill of Wrongs and Rights, and the Address to the American People. 1864.
Proceedings of the State Convention of Colored Men of the State of New Jersey, Held in the City of Trenton, New Jersey, July 13th and 14th, 1865. With a Short Address to the Loyal People of New Jersey. Bridgeton, N.J., 1865.
Proceedings of the State Equal Rights Convention of the Colored People of Pennsylvania, Held in the City of Harrisburg, February 8th, 9th, and 10th, 1865. Philadelphia, 1865.
Purvis, Robert. *Speeches and Letters.* 1898.
Putnam, Lewis H. *The Review of the Revolutionary Elements of the Rebellion, and of the Aspect of Reconstruction; With a Plan to Restore Harmony between the Two Races in the Southern States.* Brooklyn, N.Y., 1868.
Ray, Florence. *Sketch of the Life of Reverend Charles B. Ray.* New York, 1887.
Reports of Cases Argued and Determined in the Supreme Judicature of the State of Indiana. Vol. XLVIII. Indianapolis, 1875.
Ripley, C. Peter, et al., eds. *The Black Abolitionist Papers. Vol. V. The United States, 1859–1865.* Chapel Hill, N.C., 1992.
Sixth Biennial Report of the Superintendent of Public Instruction of the State of California for the School Years 1874 and 1875. Sacramento, Calif., 1875.
Stanton, Elizabeth Cady, Susan B. Anthony, and Matilda Joslyn Gage, eds. *History of Women Suffrage, Vol. 2, 1861–1876.* New York, 1882.

Still, William. *An Address on Voting and Laboring, Delivered at Concert Hall, Tuesday Evening, March 10th, 1874.* Philadelphia, 1874.

———. *A Brief Narrative of the Struggle for the Rights of the Colored People of Philadelphia in the City Railway Cars; and a Defence of William Still, Relating to His Agency Touching the Passage of the Late Bill, etc. Read Before a Large Public Meeting in Liberty Hall, April 8th, 1867.* Reprint, New York, 1969.

Tenth Biennial Report of the Superintendent of Public Instruction of the State of Illinois. 1873–1874. Springfield, Ill., 1875.

Thirteenth Annual Report of the Superintendent of Public Instruction of the State of New York. Albany, N.Y., 1867.

Thirty-third Annual Report of the Superintendent of Public Instruction of the State of Michigan, with Accompanying Documents, for the Year 1869. Lansing, Mich., 1869.

Twenty-eighth Annual Report of the Board of Education of the City of Detroit, for the Year Ending December 31, 1870. Detroit, 1871.

Twenty-sixth Annual Report of the Board of Education of the City of Detroit, for the Year Ending December 31, 1868. Detroit, 1869.

Twenty-third Annual Report of the Superintendent of Public Instruction of the State of Indiana. Indianapolis, 1875.

U.S. Bureau of the Census. *The Negro Population 1870–1915.* Washington, D.C., 1918.

U.S. House of Representatives. *Address of the Colored Citizens of Chicago to the Congress of the United States.* 39th Cong., 1st Sess., H. Doc. 109, serial 1271.

———. *Memorial of Colored Citizens, praying appropriate legislation in accordance with the Constitution, and the interests of freedom; respect for civil and political rights as citizens of the United States.* 42nd Cong., 3d Sess., 1873, H. Doc. 58.

———. *Memorial of the National Convention of Colored Persons, praying to be protected in their civil rights.* 43d Cong., 1st Sess., 1873, H. Doc. 44.

U.S. Senate. *Journal of the Senate of the United States of America.* 42nd Cong., 2d Sess., Washington, D.C., 1872

———. *Memorial of a Delegation Representing the Colored People of the Several States, remonstrating against the passage of joint resolution, H.R. no. 51, proposing to amend the Constitution of the United States.* 39th Cong., 1st Sess., 1866, S. Doc. 56, serial 1239.

———. *Memorial of the Executive Committee of the Late National Convention of the Colored Men of the Country, praying the right of Suffrage be granted to all Citizens, without regard to race, color, or previous condition.* 40th Cong., 3d Sess., 1869, S. Doc. 44.

———. *Petition of the National Executive Committee of the Colored People, praying that public instruction in the District of Columbia may be given without proscription of any class on account of color.* 41st Cong., 2d Sess., 1870, S. Doc. 130, serial 1408.

The Works of Charles Sumner, Vol. XIV. Boston, 1883.

Secondary Sources

Books

Abbott, Richard H. *The Republican Party and the South, 1855–1877: The First Southern Strategy.* Chapel Hill, N.C., 1986.

Bacon, Margaret Hope. *But One Race: The Life of Robert Purvis.* Albany, N.Y., 2007.

Baker, Jean H., ed. *Votes for Women: The Struggle for Suffrage Revisited.* New York, 2002.
Bay, Mia. *The White Image in the Black Mind: African-American Ideas about White People, 1830–1925.* New York, 2000.
Beatty, Bess. *A Revolution Gone Backward: The Black Response to National Politics, 1876–1896.* Westport, Conn., 1987.
Bederman, Gail. *Manliness and Civilization: A Cultural History of Gender and Race in the United States, 1880–1917.* Chicago, 1995.
Belz, Herman. *A New Battle of Freedom: Freedmen's Rights, 1861–1866.* Westport, Conn., 1976.
Benedict, Michael Les. *A Compromise of Principle: Congressional Republicans and Reconstruction, 1863–1869.* New York, 1974.
Berry, Mary Frances. *Black Resistance, White Law.* New York, 1971.
Berwanger, Eugene H. *The West and Reconstruction.* Urbana, Ill., 1981.
Blight, David W. *Frederick Douglass' Civil War: Keeping Faith in Jubilee.* Baton Rouge, La., 1989.
———. *Race and Reunion: The Civil War in American Memory.* Cambridge, Mass., 2001.
Block, Herman D. *The Circle of Discrimination: An Economic and Social Study of the Black Man in New York.* New York, 1969.
Bonadio, Felice A. *North of Reconstruction: Ohio Politics, 1865–1870.* New York, 1970.
Bond, Horace Mann. *The Education of the Negro in the American Social Order.* New York, 1934.
Borritt, Gabor S., ed. *Why the Civil War?* New York, 1996.
Branch, Taylor. *At Canaan's Edge: America in the King Years, 1965–68.* New York, 2006.
———. *Parting the Waters: America in the King Years, 1954–63.* New York, 1988.
———. *Pillars of Fire: America in the King Years, 1963–65.* New York, 1998.
Brock, W. R. *An American Crisis.* New York, 1963.
Brown, Ira V. *The Negro in Pennsylvania History.* University Park, Pa., 1970.
Brown, Lois. *Pauline Elizabeth Hopkins: Black Daughter of the Revolution.* Chapel Hill, N.C., 2008.
Brown, Thomas J., ed. *Reconstructions: New Perspectives on the Postbellum United States.* New York, 2006.
Buzby, J. Harlan. *John Stewart Rock: Teacher, Healer, Counselor.* Salem, N.J., 2002.
Campbell, Stanley. *The Slavecatchers: The Enforcement of the Fugitive Slave Law.* Chapel Hill, N.C., 1970.
Carroll, Charles. *Public Education in Rhode Island.* Providence, 1918.
Cheek, William, and Aimee Lee. *John Mercer Langston and the Fight for Black Freedom, 1829–65.* Urbana, Ill., 1989.
Clinton, Catherine, and Nina Silber, eds. *Divided Houses: Gender and the Civil War.* New York, 1992.
Connolly, Harold X. *A Ghetto Grows in Brooklyn.* New York, 1977.
Cottrol, Robert J. *The Afro-Yankees: Providence's Black Community in the Antebellum Era.* Westport, Conn., 1982.
Countryman, Matthew J. *Up South: Civil Rights and Black Power in Philadelphia.* Philadelphia, 2006.
Cox, Thomas C. *Blacks in Topeka, Kansas, 1865–1915: A Social History.* Baton Rouge, La., 1982.

Crew, Spencer R. *Black Life in Secondary Cities: A Comparative Analysis of the Black Communities of Camden and Elizabeth, New Jersey, 1860–1920.* New York, 1993.

Cruden, Robert. *The Negro in Reconstruction.* Englewood Cliffs, N.J., 1969.

Current, Richard N. *The History of Wisconsin. Vol. II: The Civil War Era, 1848–1873.* Madison, Wisc., 1976.

Curry, Leonard P. *The Free Black in Urban America, 1800–1850: The Shadow of the Dream.* Chicago, 1981.

Dabel, Jane E. *A Respectable Woman: The Public Roles of African American Women in Nineteenth-Century New York.* New York, 2008.

Daniels, John. *In Freedom's Birthplace: A Study of the Boston Negroes.* Boston, 1914.

Dann, Martin E., ed. *The Black Press, 1827–1900: The Quest for National Identity.* New York, 1971.

Davis, Marianna W., ed. *Contributions of Black Women to America, Vol. II: Civil Rights, Politics and Government, Education, Medicine, Sciences.* Columbia, S.C., 1982.

Davis, Russell H. *Black Americans in Cleveland from George Peake to Carl B. Stokes, 1796–1969.* Washington, D.C., 1972.

Davison, Kenneth E. *The Presidency of Rutherford B. Hayes.* Westport, Conn., 1972.

Douglas, Davison M. *Jim Crow Moves North: The Battle over Northern School Segregation, 1865–1954.* Cambridge, Eng., 2005.

Drago, Edmund L. *Black Politicians and Reconstruction in Georgia: A Splendid Failure.* Baton Rouge, La., 1982.

Duberman, Martin B., ed. *The Antislavery Vanguard: New Essays on the Abolitionists.* Princeton, N.J., 1965.

DuBois, Ellen Carol. *Feminism and Suffrage: The Emergence of an Independent Women's Movement in America, 1848–1869.* Ithaca, N.Y., 1978.

———. *Woman Suffrage and Women's Rights.* New York, 1998.

DuBois, W. E. B. *Black Reconstruction in America: An Essay toward a History of the Part Which Black Folk Played in the Attempt to Reconstruct Democracy in America, 1860–1880.* New York, 1935.

Dunbar, Willis F. *Michigan: A History of the Wolverine State.* 3d ed. Grand Rapids, Mich., 1995.

Dykstra, Robert R. *Bright Radical Star: Black Freedom on the Hawkeye Frontier.* Cambridge, Mass., 1993.

Ehrlich, Walter. *They Have No Rights: Dred Scott's Struggle for Freedom.* Westport, Conn., 1979.

Elliott, Russell R. *Servant of Power: A Political Biography of William M. Stewart.* Reno, Nev., 1983.

Evans, Frank B. *Pennsylvania Politics, 1872–1877: A Study in Political Leadership.* Harrisburg, Pa., 1966.

Farrison, William Edward. *William Wells Brown: Author and Performer.* Chicago, 1969.

Fehrenbacher, Don E. *The South and Three Sectional Crises.* New York, 1980.

Ferrier, William Warren. *Ninety Years of Education in California, 1846–1936: A Presentation of Educational Movements and Their Outcome in Education Today.* Berkeley, Calif., 1937.

Field, Phyllis F. *The Politics of Race in New York: The Struggle for Black Suffrage in the Civil War Era*. Ithaca, N.Y., 1982.
Foner, Eric. *Forever Free: The Story of Emancipation and Reconstruction*. New York, 2005.
———. *Reconstruction: America's Unfinished Revolution, 1863–1877*. New York, 1988.
Foner, Philip S. *Frederick Douglass*. New York, 1964.
Forbes, Ella. *African American Women during the Civil War*. New York, 1988.
Franklin, John Hope. *George Washington Williams: A Biography*. Chicago, 1985.
———. *Reconstruction after the Civil War*. Chicago, 1961.
Franklin, Vincent P. *Black Self-Determination: A Cultural History of African American Resistance*. Brooklyn, N.Y., 1989.
———. *The Education of Black Philadelphia: The Social and Educational History of a Minority Community, 1900–1950*. Philadelphia, 1979.
Fredrickson, George M. *The Black Image in the White Mind: The Debate on Afro-American Character and Destiny, 1817–1914*. New York, 1971.
———. *Black Liberation: A Comparable History of Black Ideologies in the United States and South Africa*. New York, 1995.
Freehling, William W. *The Road to Disunion: Secessionists at Bay, 1776–1854*. New York, 1990.
Gates, Henry Louis, and Evelyn Brooks Higginbotham, eds. *African American National Biography*, 8 vols. New York, 2008.
Gerber, David A. *Black Ohio and the Color Line, 1860–1915*. Urbana, Ill., 1976.
Giddings, Paula. *When and Where I Enter: The Impact of Black Women on Race and Sex in America*. Toronto, 1984.
Gillette, William. *Jersey Blue: Civil War Politics in New Jersey, 1854–1865*. New Brunswick, N.J., 1995.
———. *Retreat from Reconstruction, 1869–1879*. Baton Rouge, La., 1979.
———. *The Right to Vote: Politics and the Passage of the Fifteenth Amendment*. Baltimore, 1969.
Ginzberg, Lori D. *Elizabeth Cady Stanton: An American Life*. New York, 2009.
———. *Untidy Origins: A Story of Woman's Rights in Antebellum New York*. Chapel Hill, N.C., 2005.
Gliozzo, Charles A. *John Jones and the Repeal of the Illinois Black Laws*. Duluth, Minn., 1975.
Goldman, Robert M. *Reconstruction and Black Suffrage: Losing the Vote in Reese and Cruikshank*. Lawrence, Kan., 2001.
Gordon, Ann D., et al., eds. *African American Women and the Vote, 1837–1965*. Amherst, Mass., 1997.
Grant, Susan-Mary, and Peter J. Parish, eds. *Legacy of Disunion: The Enduring Significance of the American Civil War*. Baton Rouge, La., 2003.
Grossman, Lawrence. *The Democratic Party and the Negro: Northern and National Politics, 1868–92*. Urbana, Ill., 1976.
Guelzo, Allen C. *Lincoln's Emancipation Proclamation: The End of Slavery in America*. New York, 2004.
Hahn, Steven. *A Nation under Our Feet: Black Political Struggles in the Rural South from Slavery to the Great Migration*. Cambridge, Mass., 2003.

Haller, John S. *Outcasts from Evolution: Scientific Attitudes of Racial Inferiority, 1859–1900.* Urbana, Ill., 1971.

Hamilton, Holman. *Prologue to Conflict: The Crisis and Compromise of 1850.* Lexington, Ky., 1964.

Harding, Vincent S. *There Is a River: The Black Struggle for Freedom in America.* New York, 1981.

Harris, William C. *With Charity for All: Lincoln and the Restoration of the Union.* Lexington, Ky., 1997.

Harrold, Stanley. *The Rise of Aggressive Abolitionism: Addresses to the Slaves.* Lexington, Ky., 2004

Hickok, Charles Thomas. *The Negro in Ohio, 1802–1870.* Cleveland, 1896.

Hine, Darlene Clark, ed. *Black Women in America,* 2d ed. 3 vols. New York, 2005.

———, ed. *Black Women in United States History.* Brooklyn, N.Y., 1990.

———, ed. *The State of Afro-American History: Past, Present, and Future.* Baton Rouge, La., 1986.

Holt, Michael F. *By One Vote: The Disputed Presidential Election of 1876.* New York, 2008.

Homel, Michael W. *Down from Equality: Black Chicagoans and the Public Schools, 1920–1941.* Urbana, Ill., 1984.

Hoogenboom, Ari. *Rutherford B. Hayes: Warrior and President.* Lawrence, Kans., 1995.

Horton, James Oliver. *Free People of Color: Inside the African American Community.* Washington, D.C., 1993.

Hunter, Tera W. *To 'Joy My Freedom: Southern Black Women's Lives and Labors after the Civil War.* Cambridge, Mass., 1997.

Hyman, Harold M. *A More Perfect Union: The Impact of the Civil War and Reconstruction on the Constitution.* New York, 1973.

Jacobs, Donald M., ed. *Courage and Conscience: Black and White Abolitionists in Boston.* Bloomington, Ind., 1993.

Johannsen, Robert W. *The Impending Crisis, 1848–1861.* New York, 1976.

Jones, Martha S. *All Bound Up Together: The Woman Question in African American Public Culture, 1830–1900.* Chapel Hill, N.C., 2007.

Kaczorowski, Robert J. *The Politics of Judicial Interpretation: The Federal Courts, the Department of Justice, and Civil Rights, 1866–1876.* New York, 1985.

Katzman, David M. *Before the Ghetto: Black Detroit in the Nineteenth Century.* Urbana, Ill., 1973.

Keiser, John H. *Building for the Centuries: Illinois, 1865–1898.* Urbana, Ill., 1977.

Keith, Lee Anna. *The Colfax Massacre: The Untold Story of Black Power, White Terror, and the Death of Reconstruction.* New York, 2008.

Kellogg, Charles F. *NAACP: A History of the National Association for the Advancement of Colored People.* Baltimore, 1967.

Keyssar, Alexander. *The Right to Vote: The Contested History of Democracy in the United States.* New York, 2000.

Klarman, Michael J. *Unfinished Business: Racial Equality in American History.* New York, 2007.

Klinker, Philip A., and Rogers M. Smith. *The Unsteady March: The Rise and Decline of Racial Equality in America.* Chicago, 1999.

Kousser, J. Morgan. *Dead End: The Development of Nineteenth-Century Litigation on Racial Discrimination in Schools.* Oxford, 1986.

Kummel, Michael. *Manhood in America: A Cultural History.* New York, 1996.

Kusmer, Kenneth L. *A Ghetto Takes Shape: Black Cleveland, 1870–1930.* Urbana, Ill., 1976.

Lane, Charles. *The Day Freedom Died: The Colfax Massacre, the Supreme Court, and the Betrayal of Reconstruction.* New York, 2008.

Lane, Roger. *The Roots of Violence in Black Philadelphia, 1860–1900.* Cambridge, Mass., 1986.

Levine, Michael L. *African Americans and Civil Rights: From 1619 to the Present.* Phoenix, 1996.

Lewis, David Levering. *W. E. B. DuBois: Biography of a Race, 1868–1919.* New York, 1993.

Lieberson, Stanley. *A Piece of the Pie: Blacks and White Immigrants since 1880.* Berkeley, Calif., 1980.

Litwack, Leon F. *North of Slavery: The Negro in the Free States, 1790–1860.* Chicago, 1961.

Litwack, Leon F., and August Meier, eds. *Black Leaders of the Nineteenth Century.* Urbana, Ill., 1988.

Lofgren, Charles A. *The Plessy Case: A Legal Historical Interpretation.* New York, 1987.

Lorini, Alessandra. *Rituals of Race: American Public Cultures and the Search for Racial Democracy.* Charlottesville, Va., 1999.

Mabee, Carlton. *Black Education in New York State: From Colonial to Modern Times.* Syracuse, N.Y., 1979.

———. *Black Freedom: The Nonviolent Abolitionists from 1830 through the Civil War.* New York, 1970.

Maltz, Earl M. *Civil Rights, the Constitution, and Congress, 1863–1869.* Lawrence, Kans., 1990.

Martin, Waldo. *The Mind of Frederick Douglass.* Chapel Hill, N.C., 1984.

McCaul, Robert L. *The Black Struggle for Public Schooling in Nineteenth-Century Illinois.* Carbondale, Ill., 1987.

McFeely, William S. *Grant: A Biography.* New York, 1980.

McKay, Ernest A. *The Civil War and New York City.* Syracuse, N.Y., 1990.

McPherson, James M. *The Abolitionist Legacy: From Reconstruction to the NAACP.* Princeton, N.J., 1975.

———. *The Negro's Civil War: How American Negroes Felt and Acted during the War for the Union.* New York, 1965.

———. *The Struggle for Equality: Abolitionists and the Negro in the Civil War and Reconstruction.* Princeton, N.J., 1964.

Meier, August. *Negro Thought in America, 1880–1915: Racial Ideologies in the Age of Booker T. Washington.* Ann Arbor, Mich., 1969.

Miller, Floyd J. *The Search for a Black Nationality: Black Emigration and Colonization, 1787–1863.* Urbana, Ill., 1975.

Mohr, James C. *The Radical Republicans and Reform in New York during Reconstruction.* Ithaca, N.Y., 1973.

———, ed. *Radical Republicans in the North*. Baltimore, 1976.
Mushkat, Jerome. *The Reconstruction of the New York Democracy, 1861–1874*. East Brunswick, N.J., 1981.
Nelson, William E. *The Fourteenth Amendment: From Political Principle to Judicial Doctrine*. Cambridge, Mass., 1988.
Ofari, Earl. *"Let Your Motto Be Resistance": The Life and Thought of Henry Highland Garnet*. Boston, 1972.
Packard, Jerrold M. *American Nightmare: The History of Jim Crow*. New York, 2002.
Painter, Nell Irvin. *Sojourner Truth: A Life, A Symbol*. New York, 1996.
Paludan, Philip S. *A Covenant with Death: The Constitution, Law, and Equality in the Civil War Era*. Urbana, Ill., 1975.
Patrick, Rembert W. *The Reconstruction of the Nation*. New York, 1967.
Pease, Jane H., and William H. Pease. *Bound with Them in Chains: A Biographical History of the Antislavery Movement*. Westport, Conn., 1972.
———. *They Who Would Be Free: Blacks' Search for Freedom, 1830–1861*. New York, 1974.
Perman, Michael. *The Road to Redemption: Southern Politics, 1869–1879*. Chapel Hill, N.C., 1984.
Polakoff, Keith Ian. *The Politics of Inertia: The Election of 1876 and the End of Reconstruction*. Baton Rouge, La., 1973.
Quarles, Benjamin. *The Negro in the Civil War*. New York, 1953.
Quigley, David. *Second Founding: New York City, Reconstruction, and the Making of American Democracy*. New York, 2004.
Rabinowitz, Harold N. *Race Relations in the Urban South, 1865–1890*. Athens, Ga., 1996.
———, ed. *Southern Black Leaders of the Reconstruction Era*. Urbana, Ill., 1982.
Rael, Patrick. *Black Identity and Black Protest in the Antebellum North*. Chapel Hill, N.C., 2002.
Rawley, James. *Race and Politics: "Bleeding Kansas" and the Coming of the Civil War*. Philadelphia, 1969.
Redkey, Edwin S., ed. *A Grand Army of Black Men: Letters from African-American Soldiers in the Union Army, 1861–1865*. Cambridge, Eng., 1992.
Reed, Harry. *Platform for Change: The Foundations of the Northern Free Black Community, 1775–1865*. East Lansing, Mich., 1994.
Regosin, Elizabeth. *Freedom's Promise: Ex-Slave Families and Citizenship in the Era of Emancipation*. Charlottesville, Va., 2002.
Richardson, Heather Cox. *The Death of Reconstruction: Race, Labor, and Politics in the Post-Civil War North, 1865–1901*. Cambridge, Mass., 2001.
Rusco, Elmer R. *"Good Time Coming?": Black Nevadans in the Nineteenth Century*. Westport, Conn., 1975.
Samito, Christian G. *Becoming American under Fire: Irish Americans, African Americans, and the Politics of Citizenship during the Civil War Era*. Ithaca, N.Y., 2009.
Sawrey, Robert D. *Dubious Victory: The Reconstruction Debate in Ohio*. Lexington, Ky., 1992.
Scheiner, Seth M. *Negro Mecca: A History of the Negro in New York City, 1865–1920*. New York, 1965

Schor, Joel. *Henry Highland Garnet: A Voice of Black Radicalism in the Nineteenth Century.* Westport, Conn., 1977.

Schultz, Stanley K. *The Culture Factory: The Boston Public Schools, 1789–1860.* New York, 1973.

Schwalm, Leslie A. *Emancipation's Diaspora: Race and Reconstruction in the Upper Midwest.* Chapel Hill, N.C., 2009.

Self, Robert O. *American Babylon: Race and the Struggle for Postwar Oakland.* Princeton, N.J., 2003.

Seraile, William. *Fire in His Heart: Bishop Benjamin Tucker Tanner and the A.M.E. Church.* Knoxville, Tenn., 1998.

Shaffer, Donald R. *After the Glory: The Struggles of Black Civil War Veterans.* Lawrence, Kans., 2004.

Sherman, Richard B. *The Republican Party and Black America: From McKinley to Hoover, 1896–1933.* Charlottesville, Va., 1973.

Simpson, Brooks. *Let Us Have Peace: Ulysses S. Grant and the Politics of Reconstruction, 1861–1868.* Chapel Hill, N.C., 1991.

———. *The Reconstruction Presidents.* Lawrence, Kans., 1998.

Sitkoff, Haravard. *The Struggle for Black Equality, 1954–1992.* Rev. ed. New York, 1993.

Spear, Allan H. *Black Chicago: The Making of a Negro Ghetto, 1890–1920.* Chicago, 1967.

Stampp, Kenneth M. *America in 1857: A Nation on the Brink.* New York, 1990.

Stauffer, John. *The Black Hearts of Men: Radical Abolitionists and the Transformation of Race.* Cambridge, Mass., 2002.

Stewart, James Brewer. *Holy Warriors: The Abolitionists and American Slavery.* 2d ed. New York, 1996.

Sugrue, Thomas J. *Sweet Land of Liberty: The Forgotten Struggle for Civil Rights in the North.* New York, 2008.

Sweet, Leonard I. *Black Images of America, 1784–1870.* New York, 1976.

Swift, David E. *Black Prophets of Justice: Activist Clergy before the Civil War.* Baton Rouge, La., 1989.

Taylor, Quintard. *In Search of the Racial Frontier: African Americans in the American West, 1528–1990.* New York, 1998.

Terborg-Penn, Rosalyn. *African American Women in the Struggle for the Vote, 1850–1920.* Bloomington, Ind., 1998.

Theoharis, Jeanne, and Kamozi Woodward, eds. *Freedom North: Black Freedom Struggles outside the South, 1940–1980.* New York, 2003.

Thornbrough, Emma Lou. *Indiana in the Civil War Era, 1850–1880.* Indianapolis, 1965.

———. *The Negro in Indiana.* Indianapolis, 1957.

Toll, William. *The Resurgence of Race: Black Social Theory from Reconstruction to the Pan-African Conferences.* Philadelphia, 1979.

Trefousse, Hans L. *Thaddeus Stevens: Nineteenth-Century Egalitarian.* Chapel Hill, N.C., 1997.

Trelease, Allen W. *Reconstruction: The Great Experiment.* New York, 1977.

———. *White Terror: The KKK Conspiracy and Southern Reconstruction.* Westport, Conn., 1971.
Trotter, Joe William, Jr., and Eric Ledell Smith, eds. *African Americans in Pennsylvania: Shifting Historical Perspectives.* University Park, Pa., 1997.
Valelly, Richard M. *The Two Reconstructions: The Struggle for Black Enfranchisement.* Chicago, 2004.
Vaughn, William Preston. *Schools for All: The Blacks and Public Education in the South, 1865–1877.* Lexington, Ky., 1974.
Voegeli, V. Jacque. *Free but Not Equal: The Midwest and the Negro during the Civil War.* Chicago, 1967.
Vorenberg, Michael. *Final Freedom: The Civil War, the Abolition of Slavery, and the Thirteenth Amendment.* Cambridge, Eng., 2001.
Waggoner, Clark. *The History of the City of Toledo and Lucas County.* Toledo, Ohio, 1888.
Walker, Clarence E. *Deromanticizing Black History: Critical Essays and Reappraisals.* Knoxville, Tenn., 1991.
———. *A Rock in a Weary Land: The African Methodist Episcopal Church during the Civil War and Reconstruction.* Baton Rouge, La., 1982.
Walther, Eric. *The Shattering of the Union: America in the 1850s.* Wilmington, N.C., 2004.
Wang, Xi. *The Trial of Democracy: Black Suffrage and Northern Republicans, 1860–1910.* Athens, Ga., 1997.
Warner, Robert Austin. *New Haven Negroes: A Social History.* New Haven, Conn., 1940.
Warner, Sam Bass. *The Private City: Philadelphia in Three Periods of Its Growth.* Philadelphia, 1968.
Weinberg, Meyer. *A Chance to Learn: The History of Race and Education in the United States.* Cambridge, Eng., 1977.
Welke, Barbara Young. *Recasting American Liberty: Gender, Race, Law, and the Railroad Revolution, 1865–1920.* Cambridge, Eng., 2001.
Williamson, Joel. *After Slavery: The Negro in South Carolina during Reconstruction.* Chapel Hill, N.C., 1965.
Wilson, Kirt H. *The Reconstruction Desegregation Debate: The Politics of Equality and the Rhetoric of Place, 1870–1875.* East Lansing, Mich., 2002.
Winch, Julie. *Philadelphia's Black Elite: Activism, Accommodation, and the Struggle for Autonomy, 1787–1848.* Philadelphia, 1988.
Wollenberg, Charles. *All Deliberate Speed: Segregation and Exclusion in California Schools, 1855–1975.* Berkeley, Calif., 1976.
Wood, Forrest G. *Black Scare: The Racist Response to Emancipation and Reconstruction.* Berkeley, Calif., 1968.

Articles

Bacon, Margaret Hope. "'One Great Bundle of Humanity': Frances Ellen Watkins Harper (1825–1911)." *Pennsylvania Magazine of History and Biography* 113 (January 1989): 21–43.
Belz, Herman. "Law, Politics, and Race in the Struggle for Equal Pay during the Civil War." *Civil War History* 22 (September 1976): 197–222.

Benedict, Michael Les. "Equality and Expediency in the Reconstruction Era: A Review Essay." *Civil War History* 23 (December 1977): 322–35.

———. "The Rout of Radicalism: Republicans and the Election of 1867." *Civil War History* 18 (December 1972): 334–44.

Berrier, G. Galin. "The Negro Suffrage Issue in Iowa—1865–1869." *Annals of Iowa* 39 (Spring 1968): 241–61.

Berwanger, Eugene H. "Hardin and Langston: Western Black Spokesmen of the Reconstruction Era." *Journal of Negro History* 64 (Spring 1979): 101–15.

———. "Reconstruction on the Frontier: The Equal Rights Struggle in Colorado, 1865–1867." *Pacific Historical Review* 44 (August 1975): 313–29.

———. "William J. Hardin: Colorado Spokesman for Racial Justice, 1863–1873." *Colorado Magazine* 52 (Winter 1975): 52–65.

Bigham, Darrel E. "The New History and Neglected Hoosiers: A Case Study of Blacks in Vanderburgh County, 1850–1880." *Indiana Academy of the Social Sciences Proceedings* (1977), Third Series, Vol. 12: 88–96.

Blight, David W. " 'For Something beyond the Battlefield': Frederick Douglass and the Struggle for the Memory of the Civil War." *Journal of American History* 75 (March 1989): 1156–78.

Bridges, Roger D. "Equality Deferred: Civil Rights for Illinois Blacks, 1865–1885." *Journal of the Illinois State Historical Society* 74 (Summer 1981): 82–108.

Brown, Ira V. "Pennsylvania and the Rights of the Negro, 1865–1887." *Pennsylvania History* 28 (January 1961): 45–57.

———. "William D. Kelley and Radical Reconstruction." *Pennsylvania Magazine of History and Biography* 85 (July 1961): 316–29.

Brownlow, Paul C. "The Pulpit and Black America: 1865–1877." *Quarterly Journal of Speech* 58 (December 1972): 431–40.

Butchart, Ronald E. " 'We Best Can Instruct Our Own People': New York African Americans in the Freedmen's Schools, 1861–1875." *Afro-Americans in New York Life and History* 12 (January 1988): 27–40.

Calkins, David L. "Black Education and the Nineteenth-Century City: An Institutional Analysis of Cincinnati's Colored Schools, 1850–1877." *Cincinnati Historical Society Bulletin* 33 (Fall 1975): 161–71.

Chandler, Robert J. "Friends in Time of Need: Republicans and Black Civil Rights in California during the Civil War Era." *Arizona and the West* 24 (Winter 1982): 319–40.

Cox, Lawanda, and John H. Cox. "Negro Suffrage and Republican Politics: The Problem of Motivation in Reconstruction Historiography." *Journal of Southern History* 33 (August 1967): 303–30.

Daniel, Philip T. K. "A History of the Segregation-Discrimination Dilemma: The Chicago Experience." *Phylon* 41 (June 1980): 126–36.

Davis, Hugh. "The Pennsylvania State Equal Rights League and the Northern Black Struggle for Legal Equality, 1864–1877." *Pennsylvania Magazine of History and Biography* 126 (October 2002): 611–34.

Diemer, Andrew. "Reconstruction Philadelphia: African Americans and Politics in the Post-Civil War North." *Pennsylvania Magazine of History and Biography* 133 (January 2009): 29–58.

Dunbar, Willis F., with William G. Shade. "The Black Man Gains the Vote: The Centennial of 'Impartial Suffrage' in Michigan." *Michigan History* 56 (Spring 1972): 42–57.

Dykstra, Robert R., and Harlan Hahn. "Northern Voters and Negro Suffrage: The Case of Iowa, 1868." *Public Opinion Quarterly* 32 (Summer 1968): 202–15.

Erickson, Leonard. "Toledo Desegregates, 1877." *Northwest Ohio Quarterly* 41 (Winter 1968–1969): 5–12.

Farley, Ena L. "The Denial of Black Equality Under the States Rights Dictum: New York, 1865–1877." *Afro-Americans in New York Life and History* 1 (January 1977): 9–23.

Farrison, W. Edward. "William Wells Brown, Social Reformer." *Journal of Negro Education* 18 (Winter 1949): 29–39.

Ficker, Douglas J. "From *Roberts* to *Plessy:* Educational Segregation and the 'Separate but Equal' Doctrine." *Journal of Negro History* 84 (Autumn 1999): 301–14.

Finkleman, Paul. "Prelude to the Fourteenth Amendment: Black Legal Rights in the Antebellum North." *Rutgers Law Journal* 17 (Spring and Summer 1986): 415–82.

Fishel, Leslie H. Jr. "Northern Prejudice and Negro Suffrage, 1865–1870." *Journal of Negro History* 39 (January 1954): 8–26.

———. "Repercussions of Reconstruction: The Northern Negro, 1870–1883." *Civil War History* 14 (December 1968): 325–45.

Fisher, James. "The Struggle for Negro Testimony in California, 1851–1863." *Southern California Quarterly* 51 (December 1969): 313–24.

Foner, Philip S. "The Battle to End Discrimination against Negroes on Philadelphia's Streetcars: (Part I) Background and the Beginning of the Battle." *Pennsylvania History* 40 (July 1973): 261–90.

———. "The Battle to End Discrimination against Negroes on Philadelphia's Streetcars: (Part II) The Victory." *Pennsylvania History* 40 (October 1973): 355–99.

Franklin, John Hope. "The Enforcement of the Civil Rights Act of 1875." *Prologue: Quarterly of the National Archives* 6 (1974): 225–35.

Franklin, Vincent P. "The Persistence of School Segregation in the Urban North: An Historical Perspective." *Journal of Ethnic Studies* 1 (Winter 1974): 51–68.

Gerber, David A. "Education, Expediency, and Ideology: Race and Politics in the Desegregation of Ohio Public Schools in the Late Nineteenth Century." *Journal of Ethnic Studies* 1 (Fall 1973): 1–31.

———. "A Politics of Limited Options: Northern Black Politics and the Problem of Change and Continuity in Race Relations Historiography." *Journal of Social History* 14 (Winter 1980): 235–55.

Gerichs, William C. "The Ratification of the Fifteenth Amendment in Indiana." *Indiana Magazine of History* 9 (September 1913): 131–66.

Green, William D. "'Critical Mass is Fifteen Coloreds!': De Facto and De Jure Policies of Racial Isolation in St. Paul's Schools and Housing Patterns during the Nineteenth Century, and Beyond." *Journal of Public Law and Policy* 17 (1996): 299–321.

———. "Minnesota's Long Road to Black Suffrage, 1849–1868." *Minnesota History* 56 (Summer 1998): 58–84.

Gregory, John Goadby. "Negro Suffrage in Wisconsin." *Transactions of the Wisconsin Academy of Sciences, Arts, and Letters* 11 (1896–97): 94–101.

Grossman, Lawrence. "George T. Downing and the Desegregation of the Rhode Island Public Schools, 1855–1866." *Rhode Island History* 36 (November 1977): 99–105.

——. "In His Veins Coursed No Bootlicking Blood: The Career of Peter H. Clark." *Ohio History* 86 (Spring 1977): 79–95.

Hanchett, Catherine M. "George Boyer Vashon, 1824–1878: Black Educator, Poet, Fighter for Equal Rights: Part Two." *Western Pennsylvania Historical Magazine* 68 (October 1985): 333–49.

Hanchett, William. "Yankee Law and the Negro in Nevada, 1861–1869." *Western Humanities Review* 10 (Summer 1956): 241–49.

Harding, Vincent. "Wrestling Toward the Dawn: The Afro-American Freedom Movement and the Changing Constitution." *Journal of American History* 74 (December 1987): 718–39.

Hays, Christopher K. "The African American Struggle for Equality and Justice in Cairo, Illinois, 1865–1900." *Illinois Historical Journal* 90 (Winter 1997): 265–84.

Hendrick, Irving G. "Approaching Equality of Educational Opportunity in California: The Successful Struggle of Black Citizens 1880–1920." *Pacific Historian* 25 (Winter 1981): 22–29.

Hurst, Marsha. "Integration, Freedom of Choice, and Community Control in Nineteenth Century Brooklyn." *Journal of Ethnic Studies* 3 (Fall 1975): 33–55.

"The Illinois Black Laws." *Chicago History* 8 (Spring 1967): 65–75.

Jackson, Debra. "A Cultural Stronghold: The *Anglo-African* Newspaper and the Black Community in New York." *New York History* 85 (Fall 2004): 331–57.

Jacobs, Donald M. "The Nineteenth-Century Struggle over Segregated Education in the Boston Schools." *Journal of Negro Education* 39 (Winter 1970): 76–85.

Jager, Ronald B. "Charles Sumner, the Constitution, and the Civil Rights Act of 1875." *New England Quarterly* 42 (1969): 350–72.

Johnsen, Leigh Dana. "Equal Rights and the 'Heathen Chinee': Black Activism in San Francisco." *Western Historical Quarterly* 11 (January 1980): 57–68.

Kaczorowski, Robert J. "Revolutionary Constitutionalism in the Era of the Civil War and Reconstruction." *New York University Law Review* 61 (November 1986): 863–940.

——. "To Begin the Nation Anew: Congress, Citizenship, and Civil Rights after the Civil War." *American Historical Review* 92 (February 1987): 45–68.

Kelley, Alfred H. "The Congressional Controversy over School Segregation, 1867–1875." *American Historical Review* 64 (April 1959): 537–63.

Levesque, George A. "Before Integration: The Forgotten Years of Jim Crow Education in Boston." *Journal of Negro Education* 48 (Spring 1979): 113–25.

Lowenberg, Ted. "The *Blade* and the Black Man: 1867." *Northwest Ohio Quarterly* 44 (Summer 1972): 40–50.

Lurie, Jonathan. "The Fourteenth Amendment: Use and Application in Selected State Court Civil Liberties Cases, 1870–1890—A Preliminary Assessment." *American Journal of Legal History* 28 (October 1984): 295–313.

MacMaster, Richard. "Henry Highland Garnet and the African Civilization Society." *Journal of Presbyterian Church History* 48 (Summer 1970): 90–112.

McAfee, Ward M. "Reconstruction Revisited: The Republican Public Education Crusade of the 1870s." *Civil War History* 42 (June 1996): 133–53.

McCormick, Richard P. "William Whipper: Moral Reformer." *Pennsylvania History* 43 (January 1976): 23–46.

McPherson, James M. "The Abolitionists and the Civil Rights Act of 1875." *Journal of American History* 52 (December 1965): 493–510.

Montgomery, David. "Radical Republicanism in Pennsylvania, 1866–1873." *Pennsylvania Magazine of History and Biography* 85 (October 1961): 439–57.

Mothershead, Harmon. "Negro Rights in Colorado Territory (1859–1867)." *Colorado Magazine* 40 (July 1963): 212–23.

Pease, Jane H., and William H. Pease. "Ends, Means, and Attitudes: Black-White Conflict in the Antislavery Movement." *Civil War History* 18 (June 1972): 117–28.

———. "Negro Conventions and the Problem of Black Leadership." *Journal of Black Studies* 2 (September 1972): 29–44.

Peebles, Robin S. "Fanny Richards and the Integration of the Detroit Public Schools." *Michigan History* 65 (January/February 1981): 30–31.

Price, Edward J. "School Segregation in Nineteenth-Century Pennsylvania." *Pennsylvania History* 43 (April 1976): 121–37.

Richard, K. Keith. "Unwelcome Settlers: Black and Mulatto Oregon Pioneers." *Oregon Historical Quarterly* 84 (Spring 1983): 29–55.

Riegel, Stephen J. "The Persistent Career of Jim Crow: The Lower Federal Courts and the 'Separate but Equal' Doctrine, 1856–1896." *American Journal of Legal History* 28 (January 1984): 17–40.

Saville, Julie. "Rites and Power: Reflections on Slavery, Freedom, and Political Ritual." *Slavery and Abolition* 20 (January 1999): 81–102.

Schor, Joel. "The Rivalry between Frederick Douglass and Henry Highland Garnet." *Journal of Negro History* 64 (Spring 1979): 101–15.

Seraile, William. "The Civil War's Impact on Race Relations in New York State, 1865–1875." *Afro-Americans in New York Life and History* 25 (January 2001): 57–89.

Silcox, Harry C. "The Black 'Better Class' Political Dilemma: Philadelphia Prototype Isaiah C. Wears." *Pennsylvania Magazine of History and Biography* 113 (January 1989): 45–66.

———. "Nineteenth-Century Philadelphia Black Militant: Octavius V. Catto (1839–1871)." *Pennsylvania History* 44 (January 1977): 53–76.

Snorgrass, J. William. "The Black Press in the San Francisco Bay Area, 1856–1900." *California History* 60 (Winter 1981/82): 306–17.

Stephenson, William "The Integration of the Detroit Public School System during the Period 1839–1869." *Negro History Bulletin* 26 (October 1962): 23–28.

Thelan, David P., and Leslie H. Fishel Jr. "Reconstruction in the North: The *World* Looks at New York's Negroes, March 16, 1867." *New York History* 49 (October 1968): 404–40.

Van Meter, Sondra. "Black Resistance to Segregation in the Wichita Public Schools, 1870–1912." *Midwest Quarterly* 20 (Autumn 1978): 64–77.

Weaver, Valeria W. "The Failure of Civil Rights, 1875–1883, and Its Repercussions." *Journal of Negro History* 54 (October 1969): 368–82.

White, Arthur O. "The Black Movement against Jim Crow Education in Buffalo, New York, 1800–1900." *Phylon* 30 (Winter 1969): 375–93.

———. "The Black Movement against Jim Crow Education in Lockport, New York, 1835–1876." *New York History* 50 (July 1969): 265–82.

Woodward, C. Vann. "Equality: America's Deferred Commitment." *American Scholar* 27 (Autumn 1958): 459–72.

Wright, Marion Thompson. "Negro Suffrage in New Jersey, 1776–1875." *Journal of Negro History* 33 (April 1948): 168–224.

Wubben, Hubert H. "The Uncertain Trumpet: Iowa Republicans and Black Suffrage, 1860–1868." *Annals of Iowa* 47 (Summer 1984): 409–29.

Wyatt-Brown, Bertram. "The Civil Rights Act of 1875." *Western Political Quarterly* 18 (December 1965): 763–75.

Dissertations

Caldwell, Martha Belle. "The Attitude of Kansas toward the Reconstruction of the South." Ph.D. diss., University of Kansas, 1933.

Carlson, Shirley Jean Motley. "The Black Community in the Rural North: Pulaski County, Illinois, 1860–1900." Ph.D. diss., Washington University, 1982.

Connor, Malcolm. "A Comparative Study of Black and White Public Education in New Brunswick, New Jersey." Ph.D. diss., Rutgers University, 1976.

Erickson, Leonard Ernest. "The Color Line in Ohio Public Schools, 1829–1890." Ph.D. diss., Ohio State University, 1959.

Farley, Ena Lunette. "The Issue of Black Equality in New York State, 1865–1873." Ph.D. diss., University of Wisconsin, 1973.

Fishel, Leslie H., Jr. "The North and the Negro, 1865–1900: A Study in Race Discrimination." Ph.D. diss., Harvard University, 1953.

Fisher, James Adolphus. "A History of the Political and Social Development of the Black Community in California, 1850–1950." Ph.D. diss., State University of New York at Stony Brook, 1971.

Foster, Herbert James. "The Urban Experience of Blacks in Atlantic City: 1850–1915." Ph.D. diss., Rutgers University, 1981.

Heller, Herbert Lynn. "Negro Education in Indiana from 1816 to 1869." Ph.D. diss., Indiana University, 1951.

Jackson, Rose J. "The Black Educational Experience in a Northern City: Albany, New York, 1830–1970." Ph.D. diss., Northwestern University, 1976.

Lewis, Janice Sumler. "The Fortens of Philadelphia: An Afro-American Family and Nineteenth-Century Reform." Ph.D. diss., Georgetown University, 1978.

Libman, Gary. "Minnesota and the Struggle for Black Suffrage: 1849–1870. A Study in Party Motivation." Ph.D. diss., University of Minnesota, 1972.

Matthews, Samuel. "The Black Educational Experience in Nineteenth-Century Cincinnati, 1817–1874." Ph.D. diss., University of Cincinnati, 1985.

Mittrick, Robert. "A History of Negro Voting in Pennsylvania during the Nineteenth Century." Ph.D. diss., Rutgers University, 1985.

Moore, Louis B. "The Response to Reconstruction: Change and Continuity in New Jersey Politics, 1866–1874." Ph.D. diss., Rutgers University, 1999.

Pitre, Merline. "Frederick Douglass: A Party Loyalist, 1870–1895." Ph.D. diss., Temple University, 1976.

Price, Edward J. "Let the Law be Just: The Quest for Racial Equality in Pennsylvania, 1780–1915." Ph.D. diss., Pennsylvania State University, 1973.

Reid, John B. "Race, Class, Gender and the Teaching Profession: African American Schoolteachers of the Urban Midwest, 1865–1950." Ph.D. diss., Michigan State University, 1996.

Sanelli, Thomas A. "The Struggle for Black Suffrage in Pennsylvania, 1838–1870." Ph.D. diss., Temple University, 1977.

Squibb, John Roy. "Roads to Plessy: Blacks and the Law in the Old Northwest: 1860–1896." Ph.D. diss., University of Wisconsin, 1992.

Terborg-Penn, Rosalyn M. "Afro-Americans in the Struggle for Woman Suffrage." Ph.D. diss., Howard University, 1977.

Turpin-Parham, Shirley. "A History of Black Public Education in Philadelphia, Pennsylvania, 1864 to 1914." Ph.D. diss., Temple University, 1986.

Ward, William E. "Charles Lenox Remond: Black Abolitionist, 1838–1873." Ph.D. diss., Clark University, 1977.

Williams, Gilbert Anthony. "The 'A.M.E. Christian Recorder': A Forum for the Social Ideas of Black Americans, 1854–1902." Ph.D. diss., University of Illinois, 1979.

Wilmoth, Ann Greenwood. "Pittsburgh and the Blacks: A Short History, 1780–1875." Ph.D. diss., Pennsylvania State University, 1975.

Master's Theses

Dixon, Robert S. "The Education of the Negro in the City of New York, 1853 to 1900." Master's thesis, College of the City of New York, 1935.

Emmer, Dorothy. "The Civil and Political Status of the Negro in Michigan and the Northwest before 1870." Master's thesis, Wayne State University, 1935.

Hamblin, Thomas Dean. "Drive the Last Nail: John M. Palmer and the Blacks in Illinois and Kentucky." Master's thesis, Southern Illinois University, 1976.

Holderried, Elsa. "The Public Life of Jacob Merritt Howard." Master's thesis, Wayne State University, 1950.

Marshall, Arthur R. "The Negro in Illinois Politics, 1865–1870: A Study of the Race Issue in Illinois during Reconstruction." Master's thesis, University of Maryland, 1977.

Woodson, June Babar. "A Century with the Negroes of Detroit, 1830–1930." Master's thesis, Wayne State University, 1949.

Index

abolitionists, 7–8
African Americans: and all-black organizations, 8, 36; and antebellum protest, 6–7; and black Civil War troops, 13–14; and Charles Sumner's Civil Rights Bill, 102–7, 130–31; and Civil Rights Act of 1875, 134; and Democratic Party, 127–28, 142; divisions among, 3, 12, 31–38, 111–12; elitism among, 105–6; and emancipation, 14; and emigration, 10–11; and Fifteenth Amendment, 63–66, 107, 120–25; and Fourteenth Amendment, 61; and the freed people, 42–43; and Fugitive Slave Law, 10; and Liberal Republicans, 102; and national black delegation, 56–58; and northern state courts, 120–24; and northern state elections, 54–55; political astuteness of, 4–5, 101–2; political violence against, 100–101, 116–17; and Republican Party, 4–5, 14, 38, 51–55, 58–66, 101–2, 109–18, 125–30, 135–43; and Rutherford B. Hayes, 137–39, 141; shared experience of, 3–4, 28–29, 105–6; and social equality, 42–43, 104–5; and southern Reconstruction, 115–18, 141–42; and state civil rights laws, 109, 118, 147; and teaching profession, 77–81; and testimony in court, 14–15; and Ulysses S. Grant, 117; and white abolitionists, 7–8; and white racism, 6, 31, 99, 106; and woman suffrage, 66–69

African American women: and American Equal Rights Association, 68–69; American Woman Suffrage Association, 98; and black community, 66; and citizenship rights, 98; female and black identity of, 69; and National Woman Suffrage Association, 98; and role in equal rights movement, xii, 15, 28–29, 67–69, 98; as teachers, 80; and urban railroads, 15; and woman suffrage, 66–69, 98

African Civilization Society: and Henry Highland Garnet, 10–11; opposition to, 10; and Syracuse Convention, 24–25

American Equal Rights Association, 68–69
American Woman Suffrage Association, 98
Anderson, Peter: and Charles Sumner's Civil Rights Bill, 105, 107; and Civil Rights Act of 1875, 131; middle-class values of, 64; and *Pacific Appeal*, 33; and Philip A. Bell, 33, 47, 129; and political astuteness of blacks, 101; and public school integration, 85; and Republican Party, 115, 125, 127, 129, 143; and southern blacks, 115
Anthony, Susan B., 68–69, 98

Bateman, Newton, 74, 79, 86–87, 109, 119, 124
Bell, Philip A.: and black manhood suffrage, 47–48, 64, 129; and Chinese Americans, 44; and *Elevator*, 33; and Fifteenth Amendment, 70, 98; and importance of education, 73, 107; middle-class values of, 64; and Peter Anderson, 33, 47, 129; and public school integration, 81, 122; and Republican Party, 112, 129; and separate black organizations, 112–13; and social equality, 105
Black Committee, 13
Black Laws, 16

Cairo, Illinois, 111, 113
California, 47–48, 100, 129–30, 143–41; and public school policy, 74, 95, 119–20, 143–44; state supreme court of, 122–23; and testimony law, 14–15
California State Equal Rights League, 47–48
Catto, Octavius V.: and black teachers in black schools, 78; and class bias among blacks, 32; and generational tension among blacks, 32–33; murder of, 101; and Pennsylvania State Equal Rights League, 27, 30, 78; and woman suffrage, 67
Centennial Exposition (1876), 135
Chillicothe, Ohio Convention (1873), 115, 126
Christian Recorder: and black Civil War troops, 11; and black manhood suffrage, 41, 44, 54, 62; and blacks' treatment of each other, 37; and Democratic Party, 52; and equal access to public schools, 84; and Fifteenth Amendment, 70; and interracial marriage, 42; and national black delegation, 55; as organ of African Methodist Episcopal Church, 11; and Philadelphia's streetcars, 30; and Republican Party, 118;

and southern Reconstruction, 117–18; and Syracuse Convention, 25–26
Cincinnati, Ohio, 15, 25, 81–83
Civil Rights Act of 1866, 30, 60, 124
Civil Rights Act of 1875, 131, 133, 143; declared unconstitutional, 146; limited enforcement of, 139, 143; and lawsuits by blacks, 134
Civil Rights Bill, Charles Sumner's, xiv, 4, 37, 97, 125, 132; blacks' support of, 102–7; contents of, 103, 135; opposition to, 104; school integration clause of, 104–7, 130–31, 175–32
Civil Rights Cases, 146
Clark, Peter H.: and Chillicothe Convention, 115, 126; and Cincinnati's black schools, 82–84; and independent political action, 126, 136; and public school integration, 82–84; and Republican Party, 115, 126; and Syracuse Convention, 20–21
Clark v. Board of Directors (Iowa), 90–91, 122
Cleveland, Ohio, 18, 25, 75, 111
Colorado Territory, 61
Colored Soldiers' and Sailors' League, 45
Congressional Republicans. *See* Republican Party
Connecticut, 9, 52, 105, 108; and black manhood suffrage, 51; and black vote, 110; and public school policy, 75, 95
Convention of Colored People of New England (1865), 55–56
Convention of the Pacific States and Territories (1870), 98
Cooley, Thomas, 93, 172–73n69
Cory et al. v. Carter (Indiana), 123–24
Countryman, Matthew J. x–xi

Daily Ohio State Journal, 80–81, 127
Day, Solomon, 80–81
Deimer, Andrew, x
Delany, Martin, 10–13, 24
Democratic Party, 4–5, 44, 47, 101–2, 110, 126; and black Civil War troops, 13; and black manhood suffrage, 42, 44, 52, 99–100, 118; black support for, 127–28, 136–37, 143; and Charles Sumner's Civil Rights Bill, 104; and equal access to public schools, 73, 75, 96; and Fifteenth Amendment, 4, 99–100; and "New Departure" strategy, 127; racism of, 31, 52, 99; resurgence of, 143; and social

equality, 42; and southern Reconstruction, 116–17, 140; and violence against blacks, 100–101
Detroit, 76, 87, 89, 94, 136; and black Democrats, 128; and public school integration, 91–94; and patronage for blacks, 113
Douglass, Frederick, 2, 8–9, 13, 43, 130; and American Anti-Slavery Society, 41; and American Equal Rights Association, 68; and Andrew Johnson, 56; and black manhood suffrage, 40–41, 59, 68; and black vote, 99, 109–10; and Centennial Exposition, 135; and *Civil Rights Cases*, 146; and Democratic Party, 102; and Emancipation Proclamation, 11–12; and emigration, 11; and Fifteenth Amendment, 63, 97, 99; and George T. Downing, 129; and impartial suffrage, 64; and Liberal Republicans, 102; and national black delegation, 56–58; and National Convention of Colored Men (1869), 63; and *New National Era*, 48, 102; and Republican Party, 59, 114–15, 128–29; and Rutherford B. Hayes, 138–39; and separate black institutions, 8; and Syracuse Convention, 2, 19–20, 22–23; and woman suffrage, 67
Downing, George T., 2, 13, 130; and American Equal Rights Association, 68; and Andrew Johnson, 56; and Black Committee, 13; and black manhood suffrage, 46, 64; and Charles Sumner's Civil Rights Bill, 103, 106, 131; and Civil Rights Act of 1875, 131; and Fifteenth Amendment, 64; and Frederick Douglass, 129; and Henry Highland Garnet, 23–26; and impartial suffrage, 64; and national black delegation, 55–58; and National Convention of Colored Men (1869), 63; and National Executive Committee of Colored Persons, 103; and public school integration, 106, 131; and Republican Party, 126–42; and Rutherford B. Hayes, 139, 141; and Syracuse Convention, 2, 19, 23–26; and Ulysses S. Grant, 103; and woman suffrage, 67–68
Dred Scott v. Sanford, 1, 10, 17

Elevator: and all-black organizations, 112; and black manhood suffrage, 47, 64; and Chinese Americans, 44; and equal access to public schools, 73, 122–23; and Fifteenth Amendment, 70; and *Pacific Appeal*, 47; and Republican Party, 114
Elizabeth, New Jersey, 119
Emancipation Proclamation, 1, 11–12, 16–17, 28, 49, 91
emigration, 9–11, 24, 53
Equal Rights League of Michigan, 33–34, 56

Fifteenth Amendment: and black vote, 109–11; blacks' response to, 47, 70–71; Democratic opposition to, 70; and equal access to public schools, 107–8; and northern state constitutions, 109, 118; ratification of, 70, 97
Fishel, Leslie H., xi
Foner, Eric, ix, 137
Forten, James D.: and Charles Sumner's Civil Rights Bill, 106; and divisions within equal rights movement, 32–33, 37; and Fifteenth Amendment, 65–66; and Republican Party, 53; and woman suffrage, 67
Fourteenth Amendment, 4, 30, 77, 98–107; and black manhood suffrage, 60–61, 68; and Charles Sumner's Civil Rights Bill, 103–4; and *Civil Rights Cases*, 146; and lawsuits for equal access to public schools, 120–24, 145
Franklin, John Hope, ix–x
Fugitive Slave Law, 9–10

Garnet, Henry Highland, 2, 8–9, 12, 59, 80–81; and African Civilization Society, 10, 12, 24–25; and Black Committee, 13; and black manhood suffrage, 59; and George T. Downing, 23–26; and National Equal Rights League, 26; and public school integration, 80; and Syracuse Convention, 17–20, 22–26
Garrisonians, 7–8
Garrison, William Lloyd, 7–8, 41, 54, 142
Grant, Ulysses S., 70, 102, 131; and Charles Sumner's Civil Rights Bill, 103; elected President, 62; and Fifteenth Amendment, 70, 97; and southern Reconstruction, 117, 133, 135

Hamilton, Robert, 11–14, 65
Harper, Frances Ellen Watkins: and American Equal Rights Association, 69; and American Woman Suffrage Association, 98; female and black identity of, 98; and Sojourner

Harper, Frances Ellen Watkins *(continued)*
Truth, 68–69, 98; and Syracuse Convention, 2, 20; and woman suffrage, 67–68
Harrisburg, Pennsylvania, 28–29, 110
Hayes, Rutherford B.: and African Americans, 137–39; election of, 138, 180n14; and Fifteenth Amendment, 137; and home rule for South, 137, 140; northern blacks' reaction to, 137–38; and southern Republicans, 139–40

Illinois, 47–48, 124; and Black Laws, 16; and public school policy, 74, 109, 119
Illinois Equal Rights League, 47–48, 103–4
Impartial Suffrage League, 54
Indiana, 83, 85–86; and public school policy, 77, 95, 120; state supreme court of, 123–24
Indiana Colored Equal Rights League, 86
Indiana Convention of Colored Men (1866), 83, 86
Institute for Colored Youth, 78
Iowa: and black manhood suffrage, 50–51, 99; and public school policy, 90–91, 95; state supreme court of, 90–91, 122

Johnson, Andrew, 56–58, 103
Jones, John: election as County Commissioner, 113; and Illinois Black Laws, 16; and Illinois Equal Rights League, 48; and Illinois State Central Suffrage Committee, 48; and national black delegation, 55–56; and Republican Party, 101
Julian, George W., 52

Kansas, 16, 119, 145
Kansas-Nebraska Act, 10
Kelley, William D., 30, 50
Ku Klux Klan, 116–17

Langston, John Mercer, 2, 56, 103, 106; and Andrew Johnson, 56–57; and black businessmen, 37; and Charles Sumner's Civil Rights Bill, 103, 105–7, 131; and Henry Highland Garnet, 18; and national black delegation, 56; and National Equal Rights League, 22, 34–36, 63; and National Executive Committee of Colored Persons, 103; and Pennsylvania State Equal Rights League, 26, 35; and Rutherford B. Hayes, 138–39, 141; and suffrage rights, 43, 46, 49, 64; and Syracuse Convention, 17–20, 24–25; and Ulysses S. Grant, 64
Liberal Republicans, 102, 125, 136
Lincoln, Abraham, 1, 11

Maine, 40, 74
Martin, J. Sella, 49
Massachusetts, 9, 40, 72, 74
Michigan, 16, 41, 44, 51, 91–92, 100; and public school policy, 75, 90–94; state supreme court of, 91–93
Michigan Equal Rights League, 33
Minnesota: and black manhood suffrage, 50–51, 99; and public school integration, 95
modern civil rights movement, x, 150

National Convention of Colored Citizens (1876), 136
National Convention of Colored Democrats (1872), 128
National Convention of Colored Men (1864). *See* Syracuse Convention
National Convention of Colored Men (1869), 63–64
National Convention of Colored Persons (1873), 103, 106–7
National Equal Rights League, xiii, 21–29, 33, 37, 62, 88; and all-black organizations, 36; and Andrew Johnson, 56; annual meetings of, 34–35, 59, 61; auxiliaries of, 26, 28, 88–89; and black manhood suffrage, 43, 59; and black non-elites, 28–29; constitution of, 21; disputes within, 33–35; formation of, 3, 22; functions of, 26; geographical scope of, 3; headquarters of, 25; and national black delegation, 43, 56; and National Executive Committee of Colored Persons, 63–64; officers of, 22, 43; and Pennsylvania State Equal Rights League, 26,35; and Republican Party, 59; structure of, 22
National Executive Committee of Colored Persons, 136, 143; and Charles Sumner's Civil Rights Bill, 103, 131; and federal protection of equal rights, 107; formation of, 63, 103; and National Equal Rights League, 63–64
National Negro Convention Movement, 7
National Woman Suffrage Association, 98
Nesbit, William: and blacks' treatment of each other, 37; and divisions within equal rights

movement, 38; and Fifteenth Amendment, 65; and John Mercer Langston, 35; and lobby in Washington, 58; and National Equal Rights League, 35; and Pennsylvania State Equal Rights League, 28–29, 58, 74; and Republican Party, 112

Nevada, 74, 85, 96, 121–22

New Hampshire, 40, 74

New Jersey, 51, 100; and public school policy, 75, 146; and Republican Party and black vote, 110

New Jersey Equal Rights League, 49–50

New York, 8, 15, 18, 40, 49, 51, 96, 100, 135; and public school policy, 75–76, 108; and state civil rights act, 109, 112, 118–19; state supreme court of, 121

New York Citizens' Civil Rights Committee, 109

New York City, 2, 11, 18, 76, 81, 128; and draft riot, 13; and Jim Crow railroads, 15

New York Equal Rights League, 49, 103–4

New York Times, 133–34

Ohio, 18, 51, 53, 100, 108, 137, 145; and public school policy, 75, 144, 146; and Republican Party and black vote, 110–11; state supreme court of, 120–21

Ohio Conference of Colored Men, 112

Ohio Equal Rights League, 81

Oregon, 119

Pacific Appeal: and black manhood suffrage, 47, 54, 65; and Charles Sumner's Civil Rights Bill, 131; and Civil Rights Act of 1875, 131, 135; and *Elevator*, 47; and equal access to public schools, 84–86, 122–23; and Republican Party, 125, 131; and Rutherford B. Hayes, 138–39, 141; and southern Reconstruction, 117–18; and Ulysses S. Grant, 117

Pennsylvania, 9, 16, 18, 27–3, 49, 95, 143; and public school policy, 74, 95, 119, 145–46; and Republican Party and black vote, 110

Pennsylvania State Equal Rights League: annual meetings of, 37, 37; auxiliaries of, 26, 28–29; and black manhood suffrage, 41, 49–50, 55; and blacks-only organizations, 36; and black teachers in black schools, 77–78; and blacks' treatment of each other, 36–37; as case study of equal rights cause, 27; and Charles Sumner's Civil Rights Bill, 103–4,

106; divisions within, 37, 31–33, 36–38, 111–12; and equal access to public schools, 112, 145; formation of, 26–27; importance of, 27, 29; and John Mercer Langston, 35; and Liberal Republicans, 102; and lobby in Washington, 58–59; membership of, 28–29; and National Equal Rights League, 25–26, 35; and New Jersey Equal Rights League, 49–50; and Republican Party, 111–12, 128, 143; and urban railroads, 29–31

People ex rel. Dietz v. Easton (New York), 121–23

The People ex rel. Joseph Workman v. the Board of Education of Detroit (Michigan), 91, 122

Philadelphia, xxi, 25–30, 71, 81, 100, 126–28, 143; as headquarters of National Equal Rights League, 25; and public school policy, 77–78; racial segregation in, 30; and Republican Party and black vote, 110

Pittsburgh, 27, 95, 108

Plessy v. Ferguson, 120, 150

Poindexter, James: and Charles Sumner's Civil Rights Bill, 105; and Civil Rights Act of 1875, 130–31; and Fifteenth Amendment, 99; and public school integration, 81; and Republican Party, 127; and Rutherford B. Hayes, 138

public schools, equal access to: black support for, 73, 81, 84–89, 91–93; black opposition to integration, 76–77, 79–81; and black schools and the black community, 77–79; and Charles Sumner's Civil Rights Bill, 104–7; and Cincinnati's black school system, 81–83; and black teachers in black schools, 77–81; and exclusion of blacks from public schools, 73–74, 85; and Fourteenth Amendment, 118–24; and importance in equal rights cause, 73, 84; and National Equal Rights League, 72–73, 88; and numerical requirements for creation of black schools, 74–75, 85; and persistence of segregation and exclusion of blacks, 73–74, 95, 119–20, 147; and progress of school integration, 94–95, 108–9, 143–45; and quality of black schools, 83, 87–88; and school integration and black teachers, 79–80; and state supreme court decisions, 90–94, 120–24; and suffrage issue, 73, 88; and tactics employed by northern blacks, 88–94; and racial prejudice of white teachers and students, 76–79; and taxation issue, 85–86

Purvis, Harriet, 67, 178n4
Purvis, Robert, 16–17, 67, 126–27

Quigley, David, x–xi

Radical Republicans. *See* Republican Party
railroads, urban, 15, 29–31
Ray, Charles Bennett, 12, 70
Reconstruction, southern: collapse of, 117, 139; and northern blacks, 115–18, 138–42; and Reconstruction governments, 116–17; and southern blacks, 139–40; and southern Republican Party, 116–17
Remond, Charles Lenox, 18, 54, 99
Republican Party, 4–5, 14, 17, 38, 51–52, 75, 91; and Andrew Johnson, 58; and black Civil War troops, 13; and black manhood suffrage, 52, 51–55., 63, 68–70; black pressure on, 40, 58–66, 103, 130–31, 142–44; and black vote, 110–11; and Charles Sumner's Civil Rights Bill, 102–7, 130–31, 146; and Civil Rights Act of 1866, 60; and constitutional authority of federal government, 165n58; and equal rights, 31, 101–2; and Fifteenth Amendment, 62–65, 69–70; and Fourteenth Amendment, 60–61; and northern state elections, 51, 54–55; and patronage for blacks, 113–15; and public schools, 73, 96, 104, 107, 124; and Radical Republicans, 30–31, 52, 60–63, 125; and relationship with northern blacks, 4–5, 38, 42, 51–53, 101–2, 111–18, 125–28, 135–37, 143; and retreat from Reconstruction, 125; and social equality, 42–43; and southern Reconstruction, 116–17
Rhode Island, 40, 75, 94–95
Rochester Convention (1853), 3, 19
Rock, John, 17–20

San Francisco, 15, 29, 86–87, 144; and black vote, 110; and public school policy, 144; and urban railroads, 15
Schwalm, Leslie A., x–xi
Self, Robert O., x
Slaughterhouse cases, 123–24, 133–34
Social, Civic, and Statistical Association of the Colored People of Pennsylvania, 12–13, 29–30, 36, 54
Stanton, Elizabeth Cady, 68–69, 98

The State ex rel. Garnes v. McCann (Ohio), 120–24
State of Nevada ex rel. Stoutmeyer v. Duffy (Nevada), 121–23
State v. Gibson (Indiana), 124
Stevens, Thaddeus, 30, 50, 58; and black manhood suffrage, 52; and John Mercer Langston, 35
Stewart, William M., 101
Still, William: and black Civil War troops, 12; and class bias, 32; and generational tension, 32–33; and Republican Party, 126–28; and Social, Civic, and Statistical Association of the Colored People of Pennsylvania, 12–13
Stockton, California, 120, 144
suffrage, black female: and American Equal Rights Association, 67–68; and American Woman Suffrage Association, 98; black male opposition to, 66–67; black male support for, 67; and Fifteenth Amendment, 68, 98; and Fourteenth Amendment, 68, 98; and Frances Ellen Watkins Harper, 68–69, 98; and Harriet Purvis, 67; and National Woman Suffrage Association, 98; and Sojourner Truth, 68–69, 98; and white suffragists, 68–69. *See also* African American Women
suffrage, black male: arguments for, 42–47, 58–59; and black vote, 109–11; and Civil Rights Act of 1866, 60; and equal access to public schools, 88, 107–8; and Fifteenth Amendment, 64–65; and Fourteenth Amendment, 60; and impartial suffrage, 64–65; importance of in equal rights cause, 39, 43, 72–73; and National Equal Rights League, 43; and Pennsylvania State Equal Rights League, 29; and Republican Party, 48, 51–55; and state constitutions, 16, 44, 47–51, 109; tactics used on behalf of, 47–50, 55–66; and Ulysses S. Grant, 70.
suffrage, white female: and American Woman Suffrage Association, 98; and black manhood suffrage, 68; and Fifteenth Amendment, 69; and Fourteenth Amendment, 68; and National Woman Suffrage Association, 98; and Republican Party, 98
Sugrue, Thomas, x
Sumner, Charles, 52, 58–59, 102–5; and black manhood suffrage, 52, 59–60; and civil rights bill, 102–3; and equal rights, 102; and Liberal Republicans, 102; and national

black delegation, 56; and New Jersey Equal Rights League, 49
Syracuse Convention (1864), 2–3, 26–28, 43, 51, 71–72, 147; debates at, 23–25; delegates to, 1–2, 19–20; and equal access to public schools, 72; and launch of equal rights movement, 2–3; and National Equal Rights League, 22; organization of, 17–19; proceedings of, 19–25; themes articulated at, 20–22, 72. *See also* National Convention of Colored Men (1864)
Syracuse, New York, 1, 18

Tanner, Benjamin T., 101, 118, 137, 141
Truth, Sojourner, 67–69, 98

U.S. Supreme Court: and black suffrage, 148; and *Civil Rights Cases*, 146; and *Dred Scott v. Sanford*, 1, 10, 17; and *Plessy v. Ferguson*, 120, 150; and *Slaughterhouse* case, 123–24, 133–34, 142

Vashon, George B., 2, 9; and African Civilization Society, 25; and National Convention of Colored Men (1869), 63; and Pennsylvania State Equal Rights League, 27; and Syracuse Convention, 19, 25
Vermont, 40, 74

Wade-Davis Bill, 1, 60
Ward v. Floyd (California), 123, 143–44
Weekly Anglo-African: and all-black organizations, 36; and black Civil War soldiers, 11; and black manhood suffrage, 44; and Emancipation Proclamation, 12; and National Equal Rights League, 34; and Syracuse Convention, 19; and Union War effort, 14
White, Jacob C. Jr., 27, 64–65
Wisconsin, 50, 74
Wisconsin Equal Rights League, 50
Workman, Joseph, 91–94

```
E 185.2 .D38 2011
Davis, Hugh, 1941-
We will be satisfied with
 nothing less
```

OCT 0 4 2011